GOOD NEWS
for
ANIMALS?

GOOD NEWS
for
ANIMALS?

*Christian Approaches
to Animal Well-Being*

**Edited by
Charles Pinches
and
Jay B. McDaniel**

WIPF & STOCK · Eugene, Oregon

Wipf and Stock Publishers
199 W 8th Ave, Suite 3
Eugene, OR 97401

Good News for Animals
Christian Approaches to Animal Well-Being
Edited by Pinches, Charles and McDaniel, Jay B.
Copyright©1993 Orbis Books
ISBN 13: 978-1-59244-601-8
Publication date 3/21/2008
Previously published by Orbis Books, 1993

Contents

Introduction

Christianity brings good news to the world. At least it is supposed to do so. We, the editors, believe that it does. We speak as Christians who, with very different theological orientations, believe in the good news of God in Christ.

But does it bring good news to *animals*?

Asking this question may seem at best superfluous, at worst dangerous and offensive. As Theo Walker observes in his essay in this book, heartfelt sentiments about the welfare of animals can prove disastrous for certain humans. For example, we can become so zealous in our attempt to save African elephants that we ignore the collateral effects of our efforts, in this case, that some humans have been armed by governments against other humans – the poachers – and given shoot-to-kill orders. As Walker suggests, it is not just the killing of the humans that should be our concern, but also that a magazine like *National Geographic*, Walker's source, can report without flinching that poachers – not incidentally black men – are routinely killed in the fight to save elephants.

Walker's worry, of course, is that concern for animals may sometimes encourage us to forget our fundamental obligations to respect and cherish the lives and well-being of our fellow human beings. This point may be expanded theologically. For our concern about good news for animals may divert us from offering clearly the good news of God in Jesus to our fellow humans.

In our view, any response to such a concern must be to credit it, yet to maintain that – while this is a dangerous result of increased awareness and concern for the well-being of animals – it is not an unavoidable one. It is possible, surely, to be concerned both for humans and for animals. There is a place for both; this book is concerned to find a place for concern for the latter. We hope not at the expense of the former.

But the theological reply can go further. Paul, for instance, speaks plainly of the groaning of the whole of creation as it awaits full redemption through Jesus Christ (Romans 8:22). At the least, this implies that others besides humans are offered consolation and hope in the Gospel Christians preach. Indeed, while Christianity should caution us against an elevation of any love that displaces human neighbor love, it should also remind us that God is the creator not only of human souls but of human bodies, and of other bodies as well, notably those of animals. The opening chapters of Genesis tell us that animals are good in themselves, quite apart from their usefulness to us. And that, no less than us, they are to be fruitful and multiply. This suggests that we are to make space and to preserve habitats, so that they can do precisely that, so that they can flourish in their diversity and beauty.

In the first story of creation, so often recited by Christians and Jews, animals and humans are treated together; both created on the sixth day, they are together given seeds, fruits and green plants to eat, not one another (Genesis 1:30). It was only after the flood that meat eating was sanctioned by God, and here, so Andrew Linzey argues in this volume, the sanction was a concession to sin. Whether or not Linzey's claim is accurate, one thing is clear in the narrative: even after the flood, God continued to care for animals. The very first covenant in the Bible, God's covenant with Noah was a covenant with animals as well as with Noah and his descendants. "I establish my covenant with you ... and with every living creature that is with you, the birds, the cattle, and every beast of the earth" (Genesis 9:9-10).

A biblical Christianity which takes these texts seriously might indeed be good news for animals. Yet there is more in the Bible than the first chapters of Genesis, and Christianity, even when its biblical roots have been the strongest, has introduced ideas into the world that extend beyond the texts which gave it birth. So, while there is clear biblical warrant for concern for animals as well as for humans, we must be cautious not to assume that the question in the title of this book can be answered uniquivocally in the affirmative. It is not meant as a rhetorical question. One might press it, also, with an historical twist: Has Christianity been good news for animals? Or one might search for definitions: If it is supposed to be good news, good news of precisely what kind? And why that kind? Or: What, after all, *is* an animal according to Christian theology? How ought animals be regarded by us humans, both in themselves and in their relation to ourselves and to God?

These are the kinds of questions with which this anthology deals. While a spate of books and articles have been published recently on Christianity and ecology, very few have appeared on Christianity and animals. In contemporary theological circles, emphasis has been placed on Christian responsibilities to the earth and its life-support systems, but not on Christian responsibilities to protect, and enter into compassionate relations with, our closest nonhuman kin. The silence of contemporary Christian thinkers is surprising. After all, questions concerning animal rights and animal protection have been addressed by philosophers for several decades now. And the animal rights and animal protection movements have received much publicity from the media concerning their efforts to reduce animal suffering. Why have contemporary Christians been silent?

A complex historical investigation could unfold around this question. In the first section of essays which follow, directions for this investigation are opened up, and we hope they will be elsewhere pursued. However, it is not the principal concern either of these essays or of this book to investigate the possible historical causes of a general theological silence about animals. Rather, our commitment as editors is to end the silence. This is an anthology of essays by contemporary Christian theologians who are trying, some for the first time, to think deeply and seriously about animals.

You, the reader, may already be familiar with the conditions of animals in our world today. If you are not, we recommend that you begin with the essay called "State of the Animals" in Appendix A, dealing with myriad ways in which animals in our world are threatened. Written by Richard Clugston, Executive Director of the Center for Respect of Life and Environment, an affiliate of the Humane Society of the United States, this essay will give you a context for understanding the discussions in the body of the text.

Otherwise, we have divided this anthology of essays into four major sections, corresponding to four questions. The first question is: *What has been said about animals in the past?* The three essays in this section engage not only in investigation but also in vindication or critique—or both together—of the Western Christian legacy of reflection on animals.

The second question is: *What is being said about animals today?* Here the three essays each address the matter of with what eyes should Christians see animals, and so centers on the appropriate theological way to understand the relation between our human world and that of animals.

The third question is: *Should Christians eat animals?* While all the authors of the articles in this book are not vegetarians, the three contributors to this section are. Together they present the challenge of theological vegetarianism, although all in quite different ways.

The fourth and final question is: *How should Christians respond to current concerns about animals?* The four essays in this section have in common an assessment of the emerging yet ever more forceful movement in present Western societies which has come to be known as the "animal liberation" or the "animal rights" movement. Three of these authors, while supporting the political thrust of the movement, express some reservations about its main focus. The fourth author, the noted philosophical defender of animal rights, Tom Regan, responds directly to the essay by Charles Pinches, as well as offers his own brief description of the animal rights view as it might relate to Christian theology.

Besides the appendix containing Richard Clugston's "State of the Animals," we have included in Appendix B the text of "Liberating Life," a report written for the World Council of Churches by a special consultation it sponsored in Annecy, France, in 1988. In its own right this document is worth further study, for it is one of only a few public statements —and perhaps the strongest and most comprehensive—made by an established Christian body about animals. We include it also because Tom Regan and Charles Pinches refer to it frequently in their discussion and debate.

Many of the essays in the main sections of the book were first presented at a conference held at Duke Divinity School in Raleigh, North Carolina, October 4–6, 1990, then revised for this book. The conference was sponsored by the International Network for Religion and Animals (2913 Woodstock, Silver Spring, MD 20910), which is directed by Rev. Dr. Marc A. Wessels. We are grateful to Dr. Wessels and to his organization for helping make possible the conference at Duke.

Finally, a word about practical action. If you, the reader, find yourself wanting to know more about the actual ways in which animals are abused in Western industrial societies, we recommend that you peruse *Animal Liberation* (New York Review, 1975) by Peter Singer. Singer documents how animals are abused in animal agriculture and scientific testing. If you want to take practical action, beside the recommendations that appear in the two appendices of this book and the challenge to vegetarianism given in its second section, we recommend that you pick up the simple book *You Can Save the Animals: Fifty Things to Do Right Now* (St. Martin's Press, 175 5th Ave., New York, NY 10010) by Michael Fox, Vice-President of Farm Animals and Bioethics, the Humane Society of the United States. These, at least, are places to begin.

GOOD NEWS
for
ANIMALS?

Part I

WHAT HAS BEEN SAID
ABOUT ANIMALS
IN THE PAST?

The Western Christian Legacy

Aside from certain well-worn stories of St. Francis' or St. Jerome's kindness to animals, the Christian tradition has not supplied, especially for contemporary writers, much in the way of insights or vision regarding how animals ought to be regarded morally. Perhaps this is because, as many currently allege, Christianity at its core contains ideas and attitudes adverse to a moral reevaluation of human treatment of nonhuman animals. Or perhaps, an entirely different possibility, it is because Christianity has been misunderstood and therefore not mined for these insights when it could have been. Or perhaps, to strike a third note, it is because Christianity has either associated itself with or been understood in terms of certain ideas and attitudes which are adverse to this reevaluation; ideas from which it may possibly be extricated, although not without considerable effort.

The essays in this first part explore these possibilities. Each attempts to unearth in the past some root of present attitudes that needs either to be torn up or planted more firmly. Each author engages in morally critical historical analysis, and so opens the way to further reflection which might extend or redo Christian theological thinking of the past regarding animals.

1

Chapter 1

Caring for Animals

Biblical Stimulus for Ethical Reflection

George L. Frear, Jr.

All of us have experiences of animals. We can look into animal eyes and wonder. We can examine their physical forms and see their kinship with us, to varying degrees, of course. Even those of us who are most indifferent to animals, those who take a purely instrumental approach toward them, recognize that they are closer to us than any other earthly beings. Many of us have an intuition that animals have their own integrity, their own value independently of us. Determining the extent of animal value, however, and of the moral obligations that flow from it is not easy.

In the reflections that follow I shall, first, as an introduction, endeavor to show the limitations of two familiar approaches on the part of philosophical ethics to the question of the moral treatment of animals; second, as the main body of this study, examine what appears to be the biblical view of animals; and third, as a conclusion, attempt to derive from the Bible a stimulus toward the formation of our own moral convictions concerning animals. I stress in regard to this third point that I seek in the Bible a stimulus for us, not some overwhelming authority, some *Deus dixit* that silences our own reflection.

I

I turn, then, first to approaches from familiar categories of philosophical ethics. Much of the current philosophical discussion of the proper human

George L. Frear, Jr., is Professor of Religious Studies at St. Lawrence University in Canton, New York. His teaching concentrations are the Christian tradition, Native American religion, and religion and ethics.

treatment of animals mirrors recent philosophical ethics in general at least to this extent: in both, theoretical arguments typically seem to offer us a choice between utilitarianism and a deontological language of rights.[1] Of course, a mixed theory would also be possible.

The utilitarian approach centers upon the question of animal pain. Utilitarians who defend animals contend that animals suffer as genuinely as humans do. These utilitarians can lay before us images drawn from contemporary practice that trouble our consciences, images of animal pain in our methods of animal husbandry and slaughter, in animal experimentation, in zoo keeping, in hunting. This animal pain needs to be included, utilitarians hold, in our calculations of pain and benefit. Their basic contention is that humans inflict upon animals a vast amount of unnecessary and excessive suffering.

The utilitarian argument can lead to controversy concerning the extent to which animals process pain or experience anxiety or discomfort.[2] The question is complex, but I see no reason to deny the reality of some sort of animal pain. Nor would I deny its moral importance. Indeed, it is the merit of the utilitarian argument that it lays this problem before us. As far as it goes, the argument is irreplaceably important.

The limitation of the argument is that it does not go far enough in the direction of defending animal integrity. Confronted with the problem of pain, human ingenuity may try to find methods of breeding and training animals so as to create new species or adapt existing species to whatever is convenient for us. In my investigation I have come across the slogan, "Better to adapt the animals to the machine than the machine to the animals."[3] That slogan shows the whole problem of utilitarianism, a lack of respect for the independent value of animals, for their integrity.

The other major philosophical approach, the deontological argument for animal rights, maintains that individual animals have rights just as much as humans do. It immediately runs into the question, what does it take to claim rights? If it takes an ability to speak, do any animals really have rights?[4] If it requires some kind of biographical life and self-awareness, what animals qualify? All mammals? Some mammals? Anything other than mammals? It is striking that animal rights philosopher Tom Regan uses a practical definition of "Animals" as "mentally normal mammals of a year or more."[5] That is certainly not a definition of all animals. What about other animals, particularly those far different from normal, adult mammals?

A strange aspect of the deontological argument, furthermore, is that it is of necessity addressed only to humans. But a putative animal right to life is threatened not only by humans but by other animals. Ordinarily we expect that one who defends the rights of others defends them against all members of the community. That animal rights advocates do not so defend animals seems to be an implicit recognition on their part that animals do not really belong to the moral community, at least not in the same way humans do.

The deontological argument may persuasively make the case that certain "higher" animals deserve a commensurate treatment, but it does not and cannot make a case for respect for all animals in general. From neither utilitarianism nor deontology can one derive respect for overall animal life. Therefore, retaining from them the importance of concern for animal suffering and a recognition of the high abilities of certain animals, I turn elsewhere for a sense of respect for all animals as they are.

II

It may seem surprising that the elsewhere to which I turn is the Bible, since the Bible is not infrequently presented as the charter for the alleged purely instrumental approach to animals of Western culture. Whatever may be the case of later Western culture and Christians within it, however, the Bible itself, when read with impartial eyes, presents the bases for a moral treatment of our fellow animals, sharers with us in creation and redemption. In a brief article I can only offer the most general presentation.

For one thing, the Bible recognizes human kinship with animals. The terms "flesh" and "all flesh," for instance, often join human and animal together.[6] Even where we might think that the biblical author is only referring to humans, as when the prophet of the exile proclaims that "all flesh" will see the glory of the Lord[7] or when the Johannine prologue states that "Word became flesh,"[8] can we be sure that animals are not included at least in the margins of the author's consciousness? Clearly the author is thinking of the fragile living tissue we share with animals.

Sometimes English translations do not bring out the biblical sense of human and animal kinship. The Hebrew word *nephesh* denotes the "life" or "will" or "soul" of human and animal, but it receives varied translations. We must recognize it in such diverse passages as the psalmist's lament, "As a hart longs for flowing streams, so longs my *soul* for thee, O God,"[9] and the proverb that asserts, "A righteous man has regard for the *life* of his beast."[10] When *nephesh* is combined with the word for "life" we have a term meaning "breath of life" or "living being." In the Genesis accounts of creation this term is used first for the "living creatures" with which the waters swarm and which the earth brings forth. It then appears again when God blows into the newly formed human being the breath of life so that the human becomes a "living being." Later it returns as God brings to the human the newly made animals so that the human may give to every "living creature" its name.[11]

Of course, only humans according to the Bible are made in the image of God.[12] Animals can represent stupidity as when the psalmist tells us not to be like the horse or mule that needs bit and bridle,[13] and the late New Testament writings especially make passing illusions to lazy, or dirty, or irrational animals.[14] Still, this aspect of the biblical outlook only qualifies, it does not remove, the sense of kinship. Animals can even be used to shame humans as when the prophet Jeremiah proclaims, "Even the stork in the heavens knows her times; and the turtledove, swallow, and crane keep the time of their coming; but my people know not the ordinance of the Lord."[15] Similarly, Isaiah says, "The ox knows its owner, and the ass its master's crib, but Israel does not know, my people does not understand."[16]

The biblical story of the relation of humans and their animal kin is best told by considering, on the one hand, visions of creation and eschaton, and, on the other, the biblical approach to animals during the time in between. It is best to begin with the latter since we best understand the protological and eschatological visions in its light. In ongoing time biblical people are fundamentally pastoralists. Hunting and fishing are mentioned, the latter particularly in the New Testament, and there is no objection to them, but they play a minor role in comparison with the keeping of cattle.

Herders quite naturally distinguish between wild animals and domestic animals. Wild animals in the Bible represent freedom outside the realm of human management. Perhaps the most striking biblical passage concerning wild beasts is God's magnificent answer to suffering Job out of the whirl-wind. God summons Job to contemplate a creation beyond Job's mortal control. Chiefly God speaks of wild animals; God points to the freedom of the lion, the raven, the mountain goat, the hind, the wild ass, the oryx, the ostrich, the hawk, the eagle, and finally, touching on the mythological, Behemoth and Leviathan.[17] In the Psalms too wild animals are celebrated, they are under God's care, they praise God.[18] According to Jesus of Matthew and Luke, God's care over sparrows, ravens, and birds in general is an assurance of God's greater care over humans.[19] Jesus' *a fortiori* assurance of divine concern for humans, his main point, rests upon a *forte*, God's concern for the wild birds, a point we should not miss.

The affirmation of the free wild animal appears in the Bible despite the awareness of biblical people that wild animals are dangerous. How could shepherds not know that wild animals are dangerous?[20] It appears also despite full recognition that wild animals consume one another. The sage of the wisdom literature, the psalmist, and Jesus all declare with equanimity that such creatures as lions and ravens receive their food from God.[21]

Concerning domestic animals the biblical herding ethos involves simultaneously intimacy with animals and using and killing animals.

As far as intimacy is concerned, one of the striking biblical pictures is the use by the prophet Nathan of the story of human love for a lamb to reveal to King David his sin in killing Uriah and taking Bathsheba for himself.[22] From the New Testament come the images of the shepherd who leaves ninety-nine sheep in quest of the one that is lost and of a good shepherd who lays down his life for his sheep,[23] images that depend for their sense on the background of a shepherd's care for the domestic animal. And I have invoked only a few outstanding instances of a rich biblical pastoral imagery.

In keeping with this feeling for domestic animals are the provisions in the Torah of the Hebrew Bible, provisions that are in part found in the Decalogue, that require that laboring animals be given food and rest, relief from excessive burdens, respect for the separate species.[24] The New Testament, bereft of any direct provisions for human care of animals, shows Jesus justifying healing on the sabbath by referring to the quite natural fact that one will rescue a sheep or ox or donkey from a pit on the sabbath day.[25] This represents another *a fortiori* that depends on a *forte*. If what is involved in the sabbath rescue of the animal is only prudent husbandry, then the extension to the afflicted human, who of course can wait, does not follow. To return to the Torah, the thrice repeated injunction, "You shall not boil a kid in its mother's milk,"[26] represents a Hebraic reverence for animal motherhood that Orthodox Judaism has developed into the splendid practice of separating meat, the food that comes through death, from milk, the food that comes from the maternal nourishment of life.[27]

The other side of the herding ethos is to use animals for work, milk, wool, and, more important, to sacrifice and eat some of them. Within the Bible there is no objection to any of these things. The strong negative voices against sacrifice or against a false reliance on sacrifice never make the point that it is cruel to animals. Concerning the human use of animals when they are not killed, I only point out again the provisions for care of them. These operate as a restraint.

Sacrifice calls for additional comment. It tends to repel modern people. Yet we must remember that in its way it represents respect for animal life, reverence for animal blood. Animals are seen by sacrificers as a valuable gift to God. Their blood can make reparation; it can by purification restore the sinner, contribute to the ordination of a priest or the return of the nazarite to a profane status, help maintain the rhythms of the seasons.[28] Furthermore, there are two basic forms of sacrifice. While sometimes the animal was burned as a whole offering, at other times most of it was shared as a common meal. What we are familiar with under the term "peace offering" was a feast. Originally in biblical history all consumption of domestic animals took place as such a sacred meal.[29]

The Hebrew Bible countenances eating meat apart from sacrifice, and literal animal sacrifice disappears from the New Testament. But in both testaments, when the Bible envisions slaughter outside of sacrificial ritual, the vocabulary the texts use shows that they still move within the spirit of sacrifice, that is, within the spirit of a sacred and so a reverent killing. If our translations were stubbornly literal, we would read in Deuteronomy, when Israelites are permitted to kill away from the temple and so without ritual, "However, you may *sacrifice* and eat flesh within any of your towns . . ." Similarly in the Book of Acts, in Peter's vision of the unclean animals offered to him, the text literally says, "Rise, Peter, *sacrifice* and eat."[30] The verbs that mean "to sacrifice" took on a broader meaning, but it is safe to say, I think, that profane or matter-of-fact animal slaughter is not countenanced anywhere in biblical literature.

This general herding ethos with its reverence for wild animals, its affection for tamed ones, its use but its restraint in use provides the background for looking at biblical visions of the creation and of the end of history. The splendid priestly creation liturgy with which the book of Genesis opens displays a reverence for animal species and furthermore envisions a vegetarian world. God gives the vegetation, and only the vegetation, to humans and animals for food.[31] Similarly in the subsequent account of Adam and Eve in the Garden of Eden, the world appears to be vegetarian. Adam names the animals; there is no suggestion that he eats them or that they eat one another.[32] The much discussed "dominion" that the Creator gives to humankind,[33] then, involves no killing or eating. It must represent a kind of herding, if we can imagine herding birds and fish—and this is after all a vision, not a blueprint—but we have here a herding without its hard side.

Divine permission to kill and eat animals, and so "fear and dread" of humans on the part of animals, only enter the world after the flood when the world has become second best.[34] Therefore, it is not surprising that biblical visions of the end foresee a return to the peace of creation. The great example is the familiar "peaceable kingdom" passage in Isaiah where the prophet foretells that wolf will dwell with lamb, leopard will lie down with kid, cow and bear will feed together, and the human child will not be harmed by the poisonous snake.[35] From the New Testament, from the pen of the Apostle Paul who is sometimes described as indifferent to nature, comes something of a parallel. He describes the whole creation, not just humanity, as in birth pangs, stretching its neck toward liberation from its bondage to decay, eager for the glory that belongs to all the children of God.[36]

Biblical pictures of the end are admittedly not thoroughly unified. While some passages parallel those I have just mentioned, we also hear of the end as a banquet (a carnivorous one?), and there are predictions of the continuation of sacrifice and the banishing rather than the conversion of wild beasts.[37] Still, on balance the fundamental biblical picture is of joy and peace at the beginning and eternal and incorruptible joy and peace at the end.

Thus, the biblical ethos contains an incongruity. There is always caring for animals. Provisionally, the Bible countenances the use of animals, though with moderation, and the killing and eating of animals, but only with a sacrificial spirit. Ultimately, there is to be no harming and no killing.

III

The stimulus from the Bible for our ethical reflection I can deal with briefly. If one worships the same God the biblical authors worshiped, the same Creator and Redeemer,[38] then one must revere all God's creatures. Reverence leads to moderation. The foundation for this ethic is not a consideration for animal pain, although that is important, nor for the consciousness that some animals may have, although that too is important. The foundation is that animals are fellow creatures, close to us, not as close as other humans, but close nonetheless. So the Bible meets and supports what I think is our intuition, that animals are an independent value in their own right. Therefore, we must leave the wild animal free and we must use the domestic animal with care, even at some cost to ourselves.

The visions of beginning and end are particularly poignant. I do not believe we can accept them as describing a literal past or future. Since they are visions, clarity concerning them is difficult. Perhaps we can say that their meaning is that every individual animal is to be seen as ultimate, a fragment of eternity. A hymn popular today among many Christians opens with the words, "Morning has broken like the first morning, black bird has spoken like the first bird."[39] Perhaps that puts it as clearly as possible. Every day is the primal day and the final day. Every bird is the primal and ultimate bird. The same is true of every sheep, every cow, every guinea pig, even every insect. There is no way to simply live out that conviction. Vegetarianism is at most a witness to it, though I am thankful that now some Christians choose to be vegetarians.[40] In loyalty to biblical eschatology, we might renounce violence to other humans, but we cannot, even if we would, arrest the succession of days and of birds, the fleshiness of flesh. But we can see every use of animals as ambiguous, every killing as a costly sacrifice, the taking of an irreplaceable individual. It is fitting that a recent collection of articles on the use of animals in science bears the title *Animal Sacrifices*.[41]

The main moral stimulus of the Bible does not lie in the specifics of its various texts. This is particularly true when the Bible presents us not with a unified morality but with an approach that contains within it a strong tension. It bids us care for animals; it allows us to use them but only when we do so carefully. Its main stimulus lies in its proclamation when in individual or group worship, the Bible comes alive and moves us as whole beings with reason, will, and affection. I would hope that biblical proclamation today would more and more concentrate on the passages that celebrate and revere animal life. For animals are fellow creatures, with us from beginning to end, and we should meet them with care, respect, moderation, wistfulness, sorrow, gratitude, joy.

Notes

1. An excellent review of contemporary arguments concerning the use of animals in experimentation but with implications for their treatment in general is found in Jerrold Tannenbaum and Andrew N. Rowan, "Rethinking the Morality of Animal Research," *Hastings Center Report* 15, no. 5 (Oct. 1985): 32-43. The classic exposition of the utilitarian approach is Peter Singer, *Animal Liberation: A New Ethic for Our Treatment of Animals* (London: Jonathan Cape, 1976); the classic presentation of the animal rights approach is Tom Regan, *The Case for Animal Rights* (Berkeley: University of California Press, 1983).

2. See Marian Stamp Dawkins, *Animal Suffering: The Science of Animal Welfare* (London and New York: Chapman and Hall, 1980); also Tannenbaum and Rowan, "Rethinking the Morality of Animal Research," 38.

3. "Lieber die Tiere an das Gerat anpassen als das Gerat an die Tiere." Interview with Prof. Siegfried Scholtyssek in *Natur* 9 (Sept. 1982). Cited in Gunter Weinschenk, "Ethik und okonomik landwirtschaftlicher Tierhaltung," *Zeitschrift fur Evanqelische Ethik* 29, no. 2 (1985): 203.

4. See Nicholas Wolterstorff, "Why Animals Don't Speak," *Faith and Philosophy* 4, no. 4 (Oct. 1987): 463-85.

5. Regan, *The Case for Animal Rights*, 78. The Christian defender of animals, Jay B. McDaniel, in his *Of God and Pelicans* (Louisville, KY: Westminster/John Knox Press, 1989), 67, offers a much broader but still restricted view. He would accord rights to animals "who have discernible interests in living with some degree of satisfaction."

6. Gen. 6:17; 9:11, 15, 18; Ps. 136:25, etc.

7. Is. 40:5. See also Isa. 40:6 and 1 Pet. 1:24.

8. Jn. 1:14.

9. Ps. 42:1.

10. Prov. 12:10.

11. Gen. 1:20, 21, 24; 2:7, 19.

12. Gen. 1:26-27.

13. Ps. 32:9.

14. See 2 Pet. 2:22 which in part quotes Prov. 26:11. Other texts are Tit. 1:12; Jude 10; and its parallel 2 Pet. 2:12. Jude and 2 Peter use the classical notion of "irrational animals," although the contrasting definition of humanity as "rational animals" is not found in the Bible. See Rudolf Bultmann, *Theological Dictionary of the New Testament*, II, 873. The Titus text is a quotation from Epimenides, *de Draculis*. Rudiger Bartelmus suggests that there is a Hellenistic influence in the late New Testament. "Die Tierwelt in der Bibel: Exegetische Beobachtungen zu einem Teilaspekt der Diskussion um eine Theologie der Natur," *Biblische Notizen*, 37 (1987): 34.

15. Jer. 8:7.

16. Is. 1:3.

17. Job 38:1-41:34. I have referred to the oryx rather than the wild ox on the basis of Bill Clark, "The Biblical Oryx—A New Name for an Ancient Animal," *Biblical Archaeology Review* 10, no. 5 (Sept.-Oct. 1984): 66-70.

18. For celebration and God's care see Ps. 104; 36:6; 84:3; 136:25; 145:15-16; 147:9. For praise see Ps. 148:7, 10; 69:34; 96:11-12; 98:7; 103:22; 150:6.

19. Mt. 6:26; 19:29-30; Lk. 12:6-7, 24.

20. See Gen. 37:20, 33; Ex. 23:29; Dt. 7:22; 8:15; 32:10; Prov. 26:13; Ec. 10:8, 11; Is. 13:20-22; Jer. 50:39; Am. 3:4-5a; 5:19; Mal. 1:3; 2 Cor. 11:26, etc. See also 1 Cor. 15:32, although Paul is presumably speaking figuratively.

21. Job 38:39-41; 39:29-30; Ps. 104:21; 136:25; 147:9; Am. 3:41; Lk. 12:24; cf. Mt. 6:26.

22. 2 Sam. 11:1-12:7.

23. Mt. 18:12-14; Lk. 15:3-7; Jn. 10:1-18, 26-28.

24. Ex. 23:4-5; Dt. 22:1-4; Ex. 20:10; Dt. 5:14; Ex. 23:12; Dt. 22:10; 25:4; Lev. 19:19.

25. Mt. 12:11; Lk. 14:5.

26. Ex. 23:19; 34:26; Dt. 14:21.

27. On the interpretation of this text see Othmar Keel, *Das Bocklein in der Milch seiner Mutter und Verwandtes im Lichte eines altorientalischen Bildmotivs* (Freiburg: Universitatsverlag Freiburg; Gottingen: Venderhoeck und Ruprecht, 1980). See also Jacob Milgrom, "You Shall Not Boil a Kid in Its Mother's Milk: An Archaeological Myth Destroyed," *Bible Review* no. 3 (Fasil 1985): 48-51. On reverence for animal motherhood see also Ex. 22:30; Lev. 22:27, 28. Milgrom also interprets Dt. 22:6-7 as showing at least restraint in taking animals.

28. See two recent articles by Alfred Marx, "Sacrifice de Reparation et Rites de Levee de Sanction," *Zeitschrift fur die Altestamentliche Wissenschaft* 100/2 (1988): 183-98; and "Sacrifice pour les peches ou Rite de passage? Quelques Reflexions sur la fonction du Hatta't," *Revue Biblique,* 96/1 (1989): 27-48.

29. On the meaning of the "peace offering" see Gary A. Anderson, *Sacrifices and Offerings in Ancient Israel,* Harvard Semitic Monographs 41 (Atlanta: Scholars Press, 1987), 51. The statement that all consumption of domestic animals was originally a matter of sacrifice is found in Claus Westermann, *Elements of Old Testament Theology,* trans. Douglas W. Stott (Atlanta: John Knox Press, 1982), 201-02.

30. Dt. 12:15 and Acts 10:13. Similarly the word that literally means "to sacrifice" is used in Dt. 12:21 and Acts 11:7. It is also used in Lk. 15:23, 27, 30.

31. Gen. 1:24-25, 29-30.

32. Gen. 2:15-20.

33. Gen. 1:28.

34. Gen. 9:2-3.

35. Is. 11:6-9. Cf. Is. 65:25.

36. Rom. 8:19-22.

37. Parallels are Hos. 2:18 and Rev. 22:1-5; at least the latter seems vegetarian. There is a vegetarian aura to Jl. 3:18; Hos. 14:4-8; Am. 9:13-15. Banquet passages include Is. 25:6-9; Mt. 8:11; 22:1-14; Lk. 14:15-24; Rev. 19:9. Ezekiel (47:10) provides the model for Revelation, but he envisions fishing going on. For the continuation of sacrifice see Is. 66:18-23; Sech. 14:21. One would not expect to find this motif in the New Testament. Banishment of wild beasts is seen in Lev. 26:6; Is. 35:9; Ezek. 34:25. Some commentators see a return to the peace of creation in Mk. 1:13, but the passage is so brief that it is hard to give it much weight.

38. On this understanding of biblical authority see James A. Keller, "Accepting the Authority of the Bible: Is It Rationally Justified?" *Faith and Philosophy* 6, no. 4 (October 1989): 378-94.

39. The words are by Eleanor Farjeon. The hymn can be found as #8 in the 1982 Episcopalian hymnal, *The Hymnal* (New York: The Church Hymnal Corp., 1982).

40. The leading exponent among sophisticated theologians is probably Andrew Linzey. His most recent book is *Christianity and the Rights of Animals* (New York: Crossroad, 1987). See also his article, "The Place of Animals in Creation: A Christian View," in the book edited by him and Tom Regan, *Animal Sacrifices: Religious Perspective on the Use of Animals in Science* (Philadelphia: Temple University Press, 1986): 114-48.

41. Tom Regan, ed. (Philadelphia: Temple University Press, 1986).

Chapter 2

Men, Women, and Beasts

Relations to Animals in Western Culture

Rosemary Radford Ruether

Man the Hunter? The Paleoanthropological Evidence

Much of western anthropology, since its origins in the nineteenth century, has emphasized "man the hunter" and has seen in males hunting animals the primary roots of human culture. This concept has put a deep mark on exhibits in museums of anthropology and thus the public image of human nature and development. There is not space in this talk for a full review of the evidence for questioning this view, and a few remarks will have to suffice.

First, humans belong to the ape family. Early hominids split from their common ancestors with apes about a million years ago. Baboons and chimpanzees are primarily herbivores and insect eaters, who eat other animals occasionally, roughly about 5 percent of their diet. The human digestive tract remains that of its herbivore ancestors, and humans lack the canine teeth of baboons to strip meat from bones. While early hominids, like other apes, occasionally ate animals, for perhaps three million years these were generally not large, but small or weak, young animals, or the scavenged bodies of animals already dead.

It is interesting that this scavenging aspect of early hominid meat eating, and the killing of rodents or baby animals, have been entirely ignored in

Dr. Rosemary Radford Ruether is the Georgia Harkness Professor of Applied Theology at the Garrett-Evangelical Theological Seminary and The Graduate School of Northwestern University in Evanston, Illinois. She is the author or editor of twenty-three books and numerous articles on theology and social justice. Her most recent book, *Gaia and God: Eco-feminist Theology of Earth Healing*, is forthcoming from Harper San Francisco.

popular culture. Clearly it doesn't lend itself to the same ideology of male dominance and aggression as does that of man the hunter going up against mammoths with spears. Only when stone tools developed could humans strip meat effectively from bones. Later fire aided humans in the digestion of meat by allowing them to roast it.

Large-scale hunting awaited the development of more sophisticated hunting weapons, roughly about half a million years ago. But for most of the last 2 million years of human development, humans lived in small, fairly stable hunting-gathering communities. Although the ratio of animal food to plant food varied with the environment, the general pattern in the tropics, where humans first developed and predominated until about 100,000 years ago, was one in which female plant-gathering activity accounted for about 70 percent of the human diet.

Women were seen as owning and controlling the houses of the village, as well as the food supply they gathered and processed. Meat from male hunting was given high status, but in fact the males often returned empty-handed. A strong ethic of sharing controlled relations of all members of the village. Food was not saved or stored or regarded as private possessions of individual households. A rough equality of labor and power seems to have prevailed between men and women in most of these societies.

Ice Age art in the caves of Europe gives us a tantalizing glimpse of the relation of hunter-gatherers to the animal world during this period of 35,000-15,000 years ago. It was once thought that the vivid and dramatic pictures of bison and horses that adorn the walls of these caves were expressions of hunting magic, designed to put the animals in the control of humans to be killed. But then it was noticed that the animals depicted in the murals were not the ones predominantly hunted and eaten.

This suggests that the murals express much more of a mystic identification between humans and these animals rather than a strategy for killing them. Very few human figures are depicted, and those are largely stick figures. Perhaps this means that humans were not focusing on themselves as an exalted separate species, but rather absorbing themselves in communion with an animal world that seems much more wonderful than themselves.

The period after the Ice Age, from about 15,000 years ago, saw the transition from hunting-gathering to pastoral and agricultural ways of life. Hunters following herds of animals would cull out a few to kill and eat. Gradually they began to manage the whole herd, and to see themselves as owners of the animals. Likewise gathering bands harvesting wild grains began to replant some of the seeds they gathered. This transition to domestication of animals and plants changed the human relationship to animals, to land and to each other.

The hunter-gatherer gender division of labor seems to have carried over into males being the owners of the herds of animals. Where this is the predominant food supply, a patrilocal and patrilineal pattern often develops, with the male head of household trading herd animals for wives and seeing both women and animals as patrimonial wealth. Domestication of plants was probably developed by women. Where this predominates, women continue to be seen as owning the household and controlling the food supply in early agricultural villages. But this seemed to change as villages were linked together by more organized urban centers in the first city cultures.

About 8,000-3,000 B.C. male priestly and warrior elites develop and subjugate the population of surrounding villages. Tributary relations and slavery developed over conquered populations. Public works, such as irrigation systems, allowed these elites to control the water supply and to demand a part of the grain harvest, which became stored wealth in temple compounds. It is very likely that, in these early urban agricultural civilizations, meat eating began to reflect the new social and gender hierarchy. Although ordinary people might have a few domestic animals, the aristocracy set aside parks with herds of deer and other large animals, which they alone were allowed to hunt and eat.

Thus, I suggest, early urban states linked together four phenomena in close relation: organized warfare, domination of women, of conquered people and of animals. Ownership and control became the model of relationship to all of these "other" groups, which also accounts for the tendency to equate the three groups symbolically; i.e., to equate women and slaves with "beasts," and to equate conquered men with women. Perhaps yoking animals to the plow and driving them with whips also suggested that such plow animals were a type of slave, and slaves, who were similarly chained and driven to pull large stones for public works, were "beasts."

Hebrew and Greek Views of Animals

The Hebrews were patriarchal pastoralists who settled in and claimed the land of the early agricultural and urban civilization in Palestine in the last centuries of the second millennium B.C. They developed a concept of a patriarchal god who had covenanted with them and made them his elect people. He also imposed strict moral obligations on his people, having to do both with avoidance of the cults of the neighboring Canaanite people whose lands the Hebrews sought to conquer and settle, and with cultic and moral obligations that related the various categories of people among the Hebrews to each other.

These obligations included relations to animals. Hebrew law established a strict line between clean and unclean animals. Only the former were to be eaten. The exact basis for ruling out certain animals and marine life as unclean is uncertain, but some of the strictures against eating certain animals, such as pigs, or calves boiled in milk, probably had to do with their sacred status in the cults of neighboring peoples. Those animals that were to be eaten were to be butchered in such a way as to drain the blood. The warm blood of mammals was seen as the same as that of humans, and so this law had to do with avoiding drinking blood as the life force which humans and animals shared.

The Hebrew God was seen as the creator of the earth, who has made all parts of it very good and who exercises dominion over it. Humans were seen as separated from the rest of the animal world by being made in the image of this God. This meant that humans (in actuality, male heads of family) shared in this dominion of God over the animal and plant world. This concept of dominion probably did not mean that (male) humans were thought of as having wide powers over the whole of nature.

God was seen particularly as the controller of weather; bringing storms and droughts as the way of punishing his people for infidelity. Moreover, that dominion which they were to exercise over the world of domesticated animals and plants was as servants and delegates of God, and not as owners in their own right. This surely was understood in terms of (male) humans as good caretakers of the animals and plants of the earth, and not as exploiters or destroyers of them.

In the first chapter of Genesis humans are given all seedbearing plants and fruits for food. The animals, birds and reptiles are given the green plants for food. No animals are given as food for humans or for each other. This suggests that, in the original state of innocence, humans and even animals were vegetarians! Only after the corruption of humans in cities, and the flood by which God punished the wicked generation of early urban people, were clean animals and birds offered as sacrifices to God and given as food for humans.

This advent of animal sacrifice and meat eating is depicted as a distinct worsening both of human morals and of relations to animals. The inclination of the human heart is said to be "evil from its youth," and "the fear and dread of you shall rest on every animal of the earth and on every bird of the air, on everything that creeps on the ground, and on all the fish of the sea; into your hands they are delivered. Every moving thing that lives shall be food for you, and just as I gave you the green plants, I give you everything" (Gen. 8:21; 9:2-3).

Meat eating within limits is now justified, but as a distinct fall from original grace. Moreover, humans (Hebrews) still are to be good caretakers and not exploiters of domesticated animals. These animals are seen as sharing in the covenant between God and Israel and hence in the right to rest on the sabbath. Sons and daughters, male and female slaves and live-stock are all included in the mandate for sabbath rest (Ex. 20:10).

Moreover, every seven years, as a kind of atonement for the agricultural, animal-and-slave-holding way of life, Hebrews were mandated to return for one year to the gathering life, letting the fields lie fallow, not working the animals, and allowing humans and domesticated and wild animals to feed on what comes up from the fields on its own. This is also a time for the cancellation of debts, the release of (Hebrew) slaves who had fallen into servitude and for the return of land that had been alienated from poor farmers (Lev. 25).

Although the Hebrew (males) saw themselves as having been given a delegated dominion over the animals, they also saw themselves as kin of animals and of the earth. The name for human, Adam, means earth creature, the one who comes from the clay soil. Warm blood and sexual differentiation are characteristics humans share with mammals, and not with God. Like animals, humans are finite. A long healthy life, a just society in which enmity between humans and between humans and animals is overcome, where all God's creatures live in harmony with each other, this is the Hebrew vision of salvation.

By contrast, Greek culture moved to a more rigid notion of the superiority of the human to the animal, by virtue of his "rational" soul, and sought to establish an origin and destiny for this soul above the embodied world. This rigid separation of human and animal was not true in preclassical Greek culture, which preserved remnants of an earlier worldview where the Gods flowed between human and animal forms. Memories of a more matricentric world lingered in stories of powerful queens, amazons and Goddesses. Half-animal, half-human figures, such as satyrs and centaurs, preserved a wilder, animal-identified life.

But, in classical Greek culture, this view of the female and the animal as powerful, mysterious others shifts to a hierarchical worldview in which women, slaves and animals are lined up in descending order of inferiority under the ruling Greek male. The rational soul is seen as both the principle of rule over these inferiors and as the ultimate escape from the mortality of the body.

This is made explicit in Plato's creation story, the *Timaeus,* where the human souls are seen as partaking in the same substance as the world soul which the Creator infuses into the body of the cosmos as its principle of ordered motion. The remains of this soul substance are divided into pieces and placed in the stars to contemplate the eternal ideas. Only afterwards are these souls infused into bodies created for them by the planetary Gods and placed on earth.

This embodied state is seen as a temporary testing period in which the soul is to learn to control the passions that arise from the body. If it succeeds in doing this, it will be freed from the body at death and return to a happy existence in its native star. But if it succumbs to the passions of the body, it will be reincarnated into a woman or into some animal that resembles the "low state to which it has fallen." It must then work its way up through reincarnations until it becomes again a (ruling class Greek) male and can be freed from the cycle of reincarnation.

This hierarchy of ruling Greek male over female, slave and animal, as a relation of mind over body, is also made clear in Aristotle's treatises on politics and on the generation of animals. Here females are the prototype of that subhuman who lacks by nature the capacity for reason and self-rule and hence is a natural slave. Conquered people are then associated with this same slave condition that is the "natural" condition of the female. Animals and tools are identified as extensions of the relationship of the ruling male to those people and things which are instrumentalized as means of labor under his control and for his benefit.

Classical Christian Views of Animals

Classical Christianity inherited both the Hebrew view of (male) human dominion over the animals and the Greek view of the transcendence of the (male) rational mind or soul over the body, the woman and the animal. Over the first several centuries of its development, Christianity marginalized the Hebrew vision of salvation as a future time on earth of justice between humans and harmony with animals. Instead it focused its hopes on the escape of the soul from its encasement in the mortal body and its ascent above.

Scholastic theologians such as Thomas Aquinas reflected the Aristotelian tradition when they declared that animals have no rights of their own because they lack rational souls. Humans have unlimited rights to use animals for food or labor. The only reason for not abusing animals is not because causing the animal pain in itself is wrong, but because humans corrupt themselves and learn to be cruel to each other by being cruel to animals.

However, another minority view of animals is found in certain lines of the monastic tradition. Here the monk is seen as a kind of holy "wild man" who rejects civilization and its luxuries and returns to a gathering or subsistence economy in the wilderness. In reclaiming the paradisal life-style, the monk overcomes enmity with the animal world. Birds bring him bread, as he remains transfixed in prayer, and wolves befriend him. The tradition of Francis of Assisi, with his friendship with birds and wolves, lies in this monastic tradition of return to nature. Traditionally monks ate no meat, a practice which also had roots in the Pythagorean vegetarian tradition, which saw meat eating as exciting the "passions."

Changing Views of Animals in England, 1600-1850

Renaissance and Reformation England and western Europe inherited these scholastic views of animals as lacking all rights because of their lack of "souls." This instrumentalization of animals was carried to an extreme in the philosophy of Descartes, who insisted that animals feel no pain. Even though they may howl when butchered or dissected in laboratories, these are just reflexes. The animal is basically a complex machine, which lacks any interior animate principle, and so can be regarded as mere automaton that can be exploited, not only for food and labor, but now as subjects of scientific experiments.

This concept of the animal as lacking all rights was correlated with a more rigid subordination of women in the patriarchal nation state, as women lost some of the work and property rights they had enjoyed in feudal, landholding and guild societies. There was a new emphasis on the subordination of all women, as women, to men in the family, and their exclusion from public political rights. This was also the period of the revival of slavery, with the expansion of Europe into colonization of Africa and the Americas. The status of Africans and American Indians as fully human was widely denied. It was claimed that they were "semi-brutes," lacking equal humanity with Europeans.

Stuart England saw a new interest in natural science, and with it the effort to classify animals and plants scientifically. Medieval bestiaries, with their animal symbolism based on moral categories, were rejected in favor of Latin names and objective divisions into genera and species. This interest in classificatory knowledge was seen as an extension of (male) human control over nature. In Baconian thought, nature known and submitted to control by the male rational mind was nature "redeemed."

At the same time, traditions of "blood sports" continued among the upper and lower classes. Among lower classes bullbaiting and cockfighting were popular entertainment. The aristocracy kept to itself large parks, where their members alone were allowed to hunt and kill animals. Hunting, particularly riding to hounds, was closely linked with the military ethos of the nobleman, as it continues to be in England today.

At the same time there was a new rage among the aristocracy for pets, especially lap dogs. Dogs and horses owned by the nobility were assimilated into the aristocratic ethos by constructing animal pedigrees. Breeding "thoroughbred" and "purebred" animals whose bloodlines are traced through a line of noble "sires" established the animals owned by the nobility as aristocrats, strictly separated from the "curs" and "mongrels" owned by the lower class. Animal hierarchy was thus made to mirror human hierarchy. Animals were given official names. Favorites had their portraits painted, elegies written and tombs provided for them at their deaths.

The eighteenth and nineteenth centuries in England saw the rise of a distinct middle-class sensibility toward animals, pioneered by Puritans and Evangelicals, that separated itself from both aristocratic and popular blood sports. These Evangelicals campaigned especially against the cockfighting and bullbaiting of the lower classes, partly in aversion to the cruelty to the animals themselves, but also because such sports were seen as inciting the unruly "instincts" of the lower "orders" and thus as inimical to good order and social control.

Organizations such as the Society for the Prevention of Cruelty to Animals sought to outlaw such blood sports. Antivivisectionist societies arose to protest the dissection of live animals in laboratories. These middle-class reformers were remote from the rough-and-ready relation to animals of rural farm people, as well as the rural life of the aristocracy. Their relation to animals was primarily to pets. Some Evangelicals upheld the view that intelligent mammals had moral feelings like humans and their souls could be expected to survive death. John Wesley, founder of Methodism, was among those who contended that animal sentience indicates that animals have immortal souls.

This campaign against cruelty to animals was closely associated with parallel campaigns against cruelty to prisoners and for the abolition of slavery. The humane treatment of the poor in poorhouses, of the insane in mental hospitals and of the imprisoned, the quest to abolish cruel punishment of criminals by mutilation, flogging and torture, went hand in hand with the abolition of cruelty to animals. Recognition of the humanity of the slave or servant and the sentience of the animal were part of an ethic of humanitarianism, which was often combined with a certain paternalism toward those seen as under the care of the good master.

Toward an Ethic of Animal Rights

As James Serpell pointed out in his book *In the Company of Animals,* Western (English and American) views of animals are deeply dichotomous. On the one hand, we inherit the Scholastic-Cartesian view that animals have no rights and exist only for human use. The feelings of animals need not be considered, either in laboratory experiments or in factory-farming of animals for meat. Animals in these contexts are simply material objects to be used for human needs, for medical experiments that promote human health or for the meat *piece de resistance* of the meal, presumed to be necessary for the healthy diet.

On the other hand, another category of animals, particularly cats and dogs, but also other mammals, reptiles, birds and fish, are adopted into the human household. It is the assumed responsibility of the pet owner to give the pet the best of care, regular balanced diet and clean living conditions. The neglected pet can be seized by state authorities and the pet owner fined for cruelty or neglect. Certain animals, particularly cats and dogs, are given more than this. They are seen as kin and permanent children of the family. The affection lavished on these animals is closely associated with the ability of these animals to be responsive to human affection and to bond with humans.

The notion that animals feel no pain, or that it is not cruel to torture them in laboratories or subject them to a confined and terrorized existence in factory-farms, is directly contradicted by this quasi-kinship relation to the family pet. Modern societies mask this contradiction in several ways. Laboratory treatment of animals is shielded from the public gaze, and it is seen as part of the scientific ethic to be able to put aside such feelings for "science."

Likewise most meat-eating people have no direct experience with the conditions of the factory-farm or the slaughterhouse. Whole animals, with head and feet, no longer hang in butcher shops to confront us with the reality of the animal corpse. Instead the meat comes to us sanitized, in plastic-wrapped packages, which allows the meat eater to disassociate the meat from its reality as pieces of animal flesh. Only fish still retain their eyes and fins in the supermarket. But these are usually dismembered on the spot, so the shopper carries home only the portions stripped of head, skin and fins. In short, we carefully keep ourselves from looking into the eye of the animal we are to eat.

Animal rights activists basically seek to make this contradiction visible, audible and emotionally present. They portray the sufferings of the animal caged in the factory-farm, the terrorized animal in the slaughterhouse, and the maimed, dazed animal in the laboratory, and make us identify our kinship feelings for the pet animal with these hidden victims of exploitation. They seek to evoke the same moral and emotional feelings of revulsion for this treatment of farm and laboratory animals as we would feel if such treatment were meted out to the beloved family dog or cat. Although they appeal to the libertarian tradition of legal "rights" for human persons, as extended to animals that share a common sentience with humans, their emotional, motivational power lies in this relation of humans to pets.

This evocation of human bonding with pets, on behalf of suffering animals in laboratories, factory-farms and slaughterhouses is, I believe, quite proper. Human relationship with family pets should not be trivialized, but should be taken seriously. It is the major opportunity that most people in industrialized societies have to experience a cross-species relationship between humans and animals. The pet dog or cat is, in many ways, a colonized animal, often overbred in an unhealthy fashion, reduced to forced leisure and assimilated into a totally human environment, mostly denied relationships with other animals of their own species. Yet, it is the one place humans interact with beings of other species and experience personhood in nonhuman forms. However unnatural this relation is, it is a major experiential resource to arouse us to concern about animal suffering.

Yet the question can well be asked whether it is enough. Can the language of personal rights and the appeal to a common sentience carry us into a broad enough concern with what modern industrial society is doing to the nonhuman world? I would suggest that its appeal is valid, but limited. It can arouse us to concern for certain categories of animals, the kind of sentient mammals with which humans can feel bonding and kinship. It has little power when the issue becomes the preservation of vanishing species of fish, reptile or insect. This is not a criticism, so much as an indication that our relationship with the nonhuman world is so fragmented and disconnected that we need to use different ethical and motivational appeals in different contexts.

I would like to conclude by discussing a series of such ethical and motivational appeals, and their limits, and asking whether there is a more comprehensive principle that can deepen and connect them.

1. One appeal is to the rights of animals in captivity to be free from pain and to have a certain modicum of a happy life. This appeal draws on our recognition of animal sentience and personhood. If forced to confront the horrible living conditions of such animals, many people will respond at least to the sort of reforms that will spare such animals pain. They might suggest that animals should be sedated before slaughter or in laboratory experiments. Perhaps some may go so far as to buy meat only from farms where animals are allowed a more traditional "freedom" in the barnyard before slaughter. Some would support a great reduction of animals used for "unnecessary" experiments; i.e., cosmetic testing or nonvital research. But most remain convinced that animals can be justifiably used for "vital" research. Few are willing to stop eating meat in the name of animal rights.

2. Eating low on the food chain is another ethical appeal which seeks to greatly reduce meat eating, but primarily in the name of interhuman welfare, rather than animal rights. In this appeal the meat diet is shown to be a "food swindle" that is a major cause of world hunger. A hundred pounds of grain and fish protein is used to produce one pound of meat. By greatly reducing the raising of animals for meat and using this grain and fish protein directly to feed humans, many more could be fed.

In addition, the clearing of forests for cattle raising is seen as dangerously unecological, destroying ancient forests needed to prevent desertification and soil erosion and promoting climatic changes, such as global warming, that could be catastrophic to the whole planet. A dramatic reduction in meat eating along either of these two lines would obviously mean that the population of domestic animals itself would be greatly reduced, but, like human population reduction, this could be accomplished by cutting back reproduction. Land could then be restored to wilderness conditions where animals could roam freely in natural ecosystems.

3. Preserving biotic diversity and curbing the extinction of species is a third appeal. Expanding human and domesticated animal populations are shown to be destroying more and more of the habitats of free animals and plants. This represents perhaps as many as a million species threatened with extinction by the year 2000. The call to preserve biotic diversity, including large numbers of tropical insects unknown to most of us, rests primarily on appeal to human self-interest. These many species might provide future medicines and foods.

There is also an appeal to the welfare of the planet as a whole. The great diversity of species contributes to the health of the planetary community. There is also a concern for scientific knowledge. We must not tear out hundreds of thousands of pages of evolutionary development before we have learned to know these species. Through this knowledge we can learn better how to preserve the health of the whole planet. Here it is the species in relationship to other species in communities that has "rights," rather than the individual animal or plant.

Each of these appeals assumes a certain capacity and "right" of the human species to "manage" the planet, both in its own enlightened self-interest and on behalf of the welfare of all the other beings. Human "dominion" over the earth and its "creatures" is assumed. Is this assumption appropriate? This concept is often decried in the ecological movement. The "deep ecologists" particularly have called for a renunciation of human dominion over nature. Paul Shepard, in his book *Nature and Madness* (1982), has called for a return to the hunter-gatherer society, restoring large areas of wilderness.

As some ecofeminists have pointed out, the deep ecology perspective has a hidden machismo. Its view of the wilderness exalts the idea of "man the hunter" as the epitome of male mystic communion with "nature." Since there could be no return to the unmanaged wilderness, in which humans compete with animals as one species among others, without an enormous reduction of the human population from its present 5.6 billion back to perhaps 1 million or so, one wonders what kind of mass destruction of humans is expected to accomplish this goal?

John Cobb, in his book *Matters of Life and Death*, calls for a recognition that humans indeed do have dominion over the earth. Only humans are capable of transcending their narrow self-interest and taking the perspective of beings other than themselves. Therefore only humans can finally care for the earth as a whole. What is needed is not renunciation of dominion, but a further development of it to a true "stewardship" of the planet, for the welfare of all its members as one planetary community.

While I partly agree with this approach, I think that people of the biblical traditions have to ask more seriously, who gave humans "dominion"? Is the "God" of human dominion the God of earth? Has this God not been created on behalf of the dominion, not of all humans, but a male elite? Is he women's God? the God of Indians? the God of animals? We need to recognize more seriously the latecomer status of humans to the planet, arising in the last 100,000 years of a 450,000 million-year earth history, not to mention an 18 billion-year history of the cosmos.

Looked at from this perspective, it is absurd to say that the God of earth's creation gave humans dominion over this planet, much less over the cosmos, unless one believes that this 4.5 billion (or 18 billion)-year history of evolution was intentionally guided only for our very recent emergence as a species, with its achievement of a cancerous growth that is threatening the biotic life of this whole planet.

Perhaps it is more appropriate to say that dominion is a usurpation given to (male) humans neither by animals nor by God. The God who gave (western male) humans dominion arose at a recent and particular context in human history. It is not by divine right. Dominant males need to begin by recognizing its shaky foundations and by seeking to consult with women and native people, and with animals and plants, to find that wisdom by which we all can learn to reshape our relation to the earth from destructive domination to one that can sustain living beings that have come into existence before and alongside us. Perhaps, in that way, what arose in usurpation over other humans and nonhumans can eventually become a genuine life-giving covenant with each other.

Chapter 3

Beast-Machines and the Technocratic Reduction of Life

A Creation-Centered Perspective

William C. French

In Eden we were given the authority to name the animals. However, much of our shared history with the animal species since has been marred through misnaming. Animals are very easy to name falsely because they are unable to protest the names we give them. Kant misnamed them, for example, when he described them as merely nonrational, natural beings, "things."[1] Apes were described in medieval *Bestiaries* sometimes as representations of the devil and sometimes as *naturae degenerantis homo*, humanity degenerated via carnal temptation and sin.[2] Wolves have traditionally been named "bestial," "cruel," and "wicked." In anti-Semitic medieval Europe, when a Jew was executed, a dog or an ape was on occasion strung up on the gallows as well. In this way a two-way naming occurred which justified the execution through the visual association with subhuman wickedness.[3]

While such misnaming seems archaic to us today, one dominant tradition of animal misnaming continues to plague our popular thinking about animal life. This tradition — naming animals as machines or automata — has its roots in Cartesian philosophy with its affirmation of a strict dualism between the sphere of mental experience and the sphere of bodily movement and sensation. This notion of beast-machines gained plausibility and influence from the general scientific authority of the picture of the world as a vast machine popularized by Galileo, Francis Bacon, and the "godlike" Newton. While

William C. French is an Associate Professor in the theology department at Loyola University of Chicago. His work on environmental issues has appeared in such forums as *Second Opinion*, the *New Theology Review*, the *Journal of Religion, Commonweal*, the *Christian Century*, and the *Chicago Tribune*.

the Darwinian and Einsteinian revolutions have transformed twentieth-century science—both in biology and in physics—oddly for much of this century, the beast-machine tradition survived in behavioral psychology's preference for mechanistic accounts of animal behavior and movement. The quest to achieve scientific legitimacy for the discipline of psychology drove many to restrict their claims to observable data about animal behavior and to eschew claiming the presence of invisible mental states—feelings, purposes, or desires—in animals. In their rightful concern to avoid anthropomorphizing animals, leading schools of behavioral psychology developed an uncritical preference for mechanistic descriptions of animal behavior.

By continuing to shape our popular understanding of the animal species, mechanistic categories work forcefully to sustain entrenched moral evaluations of animals as lacking any intrinsic value, significance, or rights. Happily the bias for mechanistic descriptions has begun to be challenged in the last four decades by the emerging authority of ethology, the science of studying animals within their home habitat and in interaction with members of their species and members of other species. More complex behaviors are seen in the field than in the constrained environments of controlled experiments and laboratory cages. Likewise, the emergence of widespread ecological concerns has generated a new sensitivity to our interdependency within the environment, and this has posed a powerful challenge to the traditional western view that humanity holds a moral monopoly on intrinsic worth and rights.

In what follows I first examine the main elements of the Cartesian beast-machine notion. Second, I focus upon the way scientism and behaviorism carried mechanistic philosophy into the twentieth century as the preferred way of naming nonhuman living beings. Third, I examine the challenge the new sciences of ethology and ecology are posing to the mechanistic description of animal life. Fourth, I focus upon the return of the Aristotelian notions of telos and purpose in current accounts of animal activity given in the emerging science of ethology. In a concluding section, I look at Francis of Assisi's and Thomas Aquinas's understandings of animal life. Francis's stress on our kinship with animals and Thomas's direct use of Aristotelian notions of animals' purposivity in action offer important resources for generating greater sensitivity to the value of animal life than has been typical in Catholic thought for some time. While many have rightly noted the inadequacy of Thomas's views of animals as instruments of service to human welfare and diet, still medieval Catholicism's stress upon the doctrine of creation can be helpfully retrieved, I believe, to provide important insights for Christian reflection upon our common life with animals and our obligations to them.

The Beast-Machine Tradition

The rise of modern science in the sixteenth and seventeenth centuries exchanged a picture of nature as fundamentally organic and alive, with teloi and purpose, to one of nature as a machine, a realm of inert substance moved by extrinsic forces, a realm open to human manipulation and use. Slowly the plausibility of Aristotelian science diminished under the combined impact of new commercial and urban values, new technological advances in engineering and metallurgy, and advances in mathematics, physics, and physiology. Emerging technological capabilities promoted new capabilities of scientific experimentation, and these in turn reinforced advances in technology and engineering.[4]

Developed by French intellectuals Mersenne, Gassendi, and René Descartes (1596–1650) in the early part of the seventeenth century, the new mechanical philosophy used the dominant metaphor of the machine as a means for understanding the cosmos, society, and the self. In 1637 Descartes published his *Discourse on Method* in which he outlined his mechanistic understanding of space, matter, and the realm of extension. The systematic metaphysical dualism which he drew separating mind sharply from matter, *res cognitans* from *res extensa*, reason from body, led him to develop his famous notion of the "animal machine." He believed two different principles of causation generate the motions and actions of human beings: (a) a purely mechanical, corporeal force arising from "animal spirits" and the disposition of our bodily organs and, (b) the incorporeal mind, "a thinking substance," the immortal soul. Animals, lacking any mind, reason, or true speech, according to Descartes, are thus essentially bodies driven by strictly mechanical impulses.

In explaining how blood flows from the heart, he states that the "laws of Mechanics" are identical to "those of Nature."[5] He uses the analogy of "different *automata* or moving machines" to account for the movement of "animal spirits." Regarding the bones, muscles, veins, and other physiological components of bodies, he states that they may be "regarded as a machine which, having been made by the hands of God" is far better arranged and more complex than any developed by humanity. He argues that if complex machines were to be built which possess the "organs and outward form" of an animal, we would be unable to discern the difference. However, he states that no machine could duplicate the complexity of human language and activity. "[T]his does not merely show that the brutes have less reason than men, but that they have none at all . . ." While some animals betray passions through sounds and movements, this does not show that they have reason. Rather it shows that "it is nature which acts in them according to the dispositions of their organs, just as a clock . . . " The human rational soul, however, is not "in any way derived from the power of matter" but expressly created by God. While the worst error is to deny the existence of God, the next worst is to "imagine that the soul of the brute is of the same nature as our own . . . " It is the soul's independence of the body that means that it is immortal and that humans, but not animals, after death have something to "fear or to hope for . . ."[6]

His investigations into the "motions of animals" showed him, he tells, that "they could all originate from the corporeal and mechanical principle." "I henceforward regarded it as certain and established that we cannot at all prove the presence of a thinking soul in animals." Yet he continues, stating: "I do not think it is thereby proved that there is not, since the human mind does not reach into their hearts." In following what is "most probable," he holds that "it seems likely that they have sensation like us" for they have "eyes, ears, tongues, and other sense-organs like ours." However he breaks with those who would deduce from this that animals also have thoughts.[7]

An influential interpretation of Descartes' views has ascribed to him the "monstrous" belief that "animals are without feeling or awareness of any kind." Yet he explicitly accepts that animals have sensations though not thoughts.[8] He acknowledges similarities between human and animal physiology, but he breaks with those who ascribe thoughts to animals, for if they "thought as we do, they would have an immortal soul like us."[9] In denying thought to animals, he does not deny that they have "life" or bodily "sensation." "Thus my opinion," he argues, "is not so much cruel to animals as indulgent to men . . . since it absolves them from the suspicion of crime when they eat or kill animals."[10]

Even if Descartes' views are less monstrous than many believe, nonetheless many of his philosophical disciples believed that he did hold such views and they used his authority to justify such beliefs. Port-Royal-des-Champs, the Jansenist stronghold, does seem to have accepted that Descartes meant to deny that animals can experience pain or suffering. As Fontaine later described some of the new scientific attitudes vis-à-vis animal experimentation:

> They administered beatings to dogs with perfect indifference, and made fun of those who pitied the creatures as if they had felt pain. They said that the animals were clocks; that the cries they emitted when struck were only the noise of a little spring which had been touched, but that the whole body was without feeling. They nailed poor animals up on boards by their four paws to vivisect them and see circulation of the blood which was a great subject of conversation.[11]

The popularity of the notion of the "beast-machine" stemmed both from scientific and theological sources. After Descartes' death, many scientists embraced the notion because it silenced qualms about vivisection and animal experimentation. Many theologians likewise employed the idea of the beast-machine to secure the doctrine of the uniqueness of humanity's gift of an immortal soul. Though many ascribe to Descartes the origin of the idea of animal insensibility, of animals as "unfeeling automata," it appears more likely that the priest-scientist Nicholas Malebranche (1638-1715) was initially responsible for developing the beast-machine concept so as to emphasize the nonconsciousness and insensibility of animals.[12]

The new mechanical philosophy gained wide influence both because it provided an integrated account of the cosmic and social order and because it provided a justification for the quest for power and control over nature and nonhuman life forms. As Descartes emphasizes, we can, with the new practical knowledge, "employ them (heavenly and earthly forces and bodies) in all those uses to which they are adapted, and thus render ourselves the masters and possessors of nature."[13]

Indeed the machine metaphor proved so influential that in 1747 Julien Offray de La Mettrie (1709–1751) employed it in his book, *l'Homme machine (Man a Machine)*, to argue that the whole problem of mind should, like the body, be rethought as a problem of physics. Humans are mechanical beings, he argued, both physiologically as well as psychologically. Our mental life is dependent upon bodily processes. The book created a fire storm of debate and was roundly condemned from many quarters. The outcry illustrates well how general society, while quite ready to accept mechanistic accounts of nature and animal life, balked at the implication that humanity too is fundamentally a part of that machine world.[14] In short, mechanism proved popular as long as it promoted the enthronement of humanity over nature. At those points when mechanism began to turn to dethrone humanity, general society broke from allegiance to mechanism. This same ideological dynamic has colored the popular reception of behavioral psychological accounts in this century.

Behaviorism and the Reductive Description of Animals and the Natural World

The prestige that the natural sciences attained via their use of empirical testing, their statistical rigor, and the ability to verify their results did not go unnoticed by philosophers or psychologists in the early decades of this century. In philosophy the movement known as logical positivism emerged first among the Vienna Circle of philosophers strongly influenced by the early work of Ludwig Wittgenstein and in Britain and later America under the combined impact of Bertrand Russell and Wittgenstein. In short, this movement sought to reject metaphysics as a meaningless enterprise, meaningless because its statements of fact can neither be verified nor falsified.

An allied positivist movement developed as well in psychology, and its general dominance in the field of animal study for the first half of this century promoted a general account, seemingly a rigorously scientific one, of animals as instinctual, reactive organism-machines.[15] This movement, behavioral psychology, was initiated in Pavlov's experiments on the conditioned salivary reflex in dogs, and developed theoretically and rather imperialistically by American psychologists John B. Watson and later B. F. Skinner. It rejected the introspective psychological methods of William James and Sigmund Freud and restricted itself only to the observable, that is, to overt behavior. Central to behaviorism thus was what Mackenzie has termed "the repudiation of unobservable entities and processes — particularly the mind and consciousness . . ."[16] This was necessary, they believed, because appeal to claims about entities and processes that cannot be observed simply defy verification or falsification and thus offer no grounding for scientific certainty. Descriptive rigor thus appeared to require the repudiation of any appeals to the mentality, consciousness, or emotions of either humans or animals. While behaviorism never achieved clear dominance over other psychological, psychoanalytic, or traditional religious and philosophical accounts of human experience, its principles, during the first half of this century, became elevated to near dogma status regarding the nature of animals.[17] The justified concern to avoid anthropomorphism in the description of animals ironically served to sanction a model of description of animal behavior that constituted an unwitting retrieval of the Cartesian notion of the beast-machine. The proper concern to avoid anthropomorphism was not matched by any sensitivity to the category mistake of imputing mechanistic causality to animal behavior.

The behaviorists attempted to transform psychology into a science of behavior by translating all teleological explanations of human and animal behavior as purposive, as self-directed toward a goal, into nonteleological explanations of behavior as movement, mere reaction to stimulus from the environment. While the mechanistic terminology tapped into the prestige of the natural sciences, the price paid has been a methodological commitment to reject any notion of genuine purpose, intention, or will and thus systematically to translate examples of human and animal self-directed action into mere reactive behavior shorn of any notion of purpose or orientation toward a goal.[18]

As happened earlier with *L'Homme machine*, many rejected such a radical redescription of human behavior because it appeared to fly in the face of our everyday experience as subjects and agents and our ordinary language descriptions of human action as purposive, intentional, and goal directed. Again parallel to the earlier reception of the beast-machine notion, far fewer were familiar enough with the complex action and sociality of the various animal species in their natural habitat to challenge the emergent hegemony of the behaviorists' account of animals as mere reactors. In this way behaviorism attained a level of popular credibility and influence regarding its analysis of animals that it never attained in its analysis of human beings.

Critique of the Conceptual Mechanization of Living Beings

Whereas our ordinary language about human and animal action helpfully preserves notions of self-direction and purposive behavior and distinguishes them from cases where one doesn't "decide" but "is driven," behaviorism translates such complex descriptive accounts of action into a seemingly "theoretically neutral data language."[19] Behaviorism assumes that "data language" provides a privileged descriptive account of some unit or example of observed behavior, but it nonetheless develops its description by attending selectively to reality via the lens of prior conceptual commitments. As Charles Taylor explains:

> For in the ordinary sense of the term I can observe . . . that my dog wants the meat in my hand . . . We might say that the dog wants the meat from his behaviour. But this doesn't mean I infer it from his movements. I know he wants the meat because he is not only drooling, but snapping at it, or begging me for it. In other words, his behaviour in the sense of *action* is that of a dog wanting food. And this *action* is observable . . . this confusion of action with movement can often be used to lend credence to behaviourism. It is true that we learn about people through their behaviour. This becomes even more true if we include speech in "behaviour." But it does not follow that we learn about them through their movements or through their autonomic reactions, or through the chemical processes which their bodies undergo. For the behaviour we mainly learn from is action, and it is only *qua* action that it is revelatory, just as speech tells us little or nothing as a stream of sound, but much as meaningful language.[20]

Description always entails selection, classification, and interpretation. Accurate description of a self-directed activity such as a "wink" requires an explicit acknowledgment of its purposive character as communication. To describe a "wink" as a "blink," thereby by failing to include its goal-directed character and its meaning for the agent performing the act, simply fails to describe adequately such an event.[21] Such a procedure may masquerade as empirical, but it is in fact unscientific, for it neglects a significant range of data due to methodological distortion and ideological commitment.

There are various schools of behavioral psychology, but they generally share certain models for interpreting and describing animal behavior. Many adhere to a central "stimulus-response" model (S-R) which avoids any notion of animals as genuinely "directing" their behavior and hence "acting." Rather stimulus from the environment is said to trigger a certain pattern of response or reaction. "Receptor impulses" are received and physiological needs or "drive-states" determine the behavioral response.[22] Animals are thus not construed as agents or subjects, but rather as "reactors" which are instinctually "driven." Similarly, drive theories were developed. They exclude the possibility of an animal directing its own behavior by a prior methodological commitment to portraying the animal as a passive instrument compelled to respond to external stimuli by physiological drive mechanisms and instincts.[23]

A central area of behavioral investigation has been in the area of learning theory, in which animals in a closed environment are trained via the use of rewards or punishments to run a maze or peck or pull a lever. The term "learning" is generally avoided because of its implication that the animal develops an increasing awareness or knowledge of its environment or reinforcement schedule. Rather the animal is said to be "conditioned" to react when certain stimuli are presented. The metaphor of "conditioning" neatly suggests that purposive activity is restricted to the human technician who initiates the stimulus. The animal directly and with no cognition or calculation just reacts, much as in the case of starting a machine or in tapping one's knee with a rubber hammer.[24]

The behaviorist pointedly avoids having to label such response a purposive act, which would entail understanding the animal as a self-directing subject or agent. To accept that the animal's response is best conceptualized under rules governing action rather than mechanistic rules governing movement would require conceiving of animal conditioning as a process whereby the animal comes *to know* certain features of its environment and to calculate what responses will best serve its needs and wants. In short, it would require understanding animals (at least the higher ones) as agents with awareness, purposes, needs, wants, and interests. For Taylor this is precisely how we must understand animals. As he states: "[W]e commonly do speak of animals as emitting actions, and even as desiring, and it is hard to see what is wrong with this procedure."[25] Against the behaviorist belief that animals move, but don't *act*, he rightly holds:

> We seem to have good physiognomic grounds for distinguishing between, e.g., a dog's salivating or the flexion of his forelimb under cortical stimulation, on the one hand, and his chasing a cat or seeking food, on the other. We seem to have equally good grounds for attributing desire, frustration, pain, fear, and so on, to at least some higher animals. In short, we have at least grounds for classing them as agents in this sense . . .[26]

While they are not "full agents," lacking the capacity humans enjoy of "self-avowal," animals have "intermediate agency," and must be understood as not merely reacting, but genuinely acting on purposes.[27] Mary Midgley supports Taylor's contentions. As she argues:

> There is nothing anthropomorphic in speaking of the motivation of animals. It is anthropomorphic to call the lion the King of Beasts, but not to talk of him as moved, now by fear, now by curiosity, now by territorial anger. These are not the names of hypothetical inner states, but of major patterns in anyone's life, the signs of which are regular and visible. Anyone who has to deal with lions learns to read such signs, and survives by doing so. Both with animals and with men, we respond to the feelings and intentions we read in an action, not only to the action itself.[28]

Where behaviorists have attempted to account for animal behavior in discrimination tests or in cases of maze learning as "conditioning" to a certain set of stimuli, the ordinary descriptive notion of "learning" is a more adequate account. The S-R view infers from behavioral change during a particular training program that the animal has acquired "a tendency to emit a certain response or set of responses in certain conditions."[29] But the ordinary teleological type of explanation highlights rightly that animals don't "emit behavior," rather they "act" to acquire food or sex or to avoid predators or pain.

Bernard Rollin has pointed out forcefully the dilemma facing behaviorists regarding the rationale for many of their own experiments on animals. On the one hand if they argue that animals lack significant consciousness and the capacity to suffer, they may feel that this gives them a free hand in experiment design and execution, but it also suggests that using animals for experiments designed to learn about the physiology and psychology of pain makes little sense. On the other hand, if they insist that animals are similar enough to humans to generate important data about pain and other physiological and emotional reactions, they are accepting that in fact these experiments do indeed induce severe pain and stress in sentient beings. Rollin rightly argues that the whole point of using animals in medical, industrial, and psychological experiments is because experimenters believe that there are strong continuities between human and animal life.[30]

Animals as Thinking, Purposive, and Communicative: The Emerging Portrait from Ethology

If animals are not mere things or machines, what then are they? Emerging in the last forty years, yet building upon the important field research of the nineteenth- and early twentieth-century naturalists, the new science of ethology has sought to investigate this question freed from some of the physical laboratory and conceptual constraints of behavioral psychology. Pioneering work by Niko Tinbergen and Konrad Lorenz employing the method of direct observation of animal behavior in the open environment of their natural habitat has provided an alternative to behaviorism, yet one which remains fully committed to empirical testing and observation. Whereas the design in behaviorist experiments such as maze learning tightly circumscribes the range of animal behaviors to a narrow choice by closing in the environment, ethologists seek to observe animals as they freely act within their home habitat. Where the artificial, closed environment of the behaviorist studies tends to eliminate the possibility of complex action, sociality, communication, or displays of insight and thus is methodologically biased by eliciting only a narrow range of possible behavior or activity, ethologists rightly insist that accurate animal studies require an open environment (namely, their local habitat) so as not to eliminate any possible sorts of complex behavior or communication that may occur when the animals enjoy their freedom.[31]

The second defining mark of ethology is that it lacks behaviorism's absolute commitment to nonteleological forms of the explanation of animal behavior. Lorenz emphasizes significant differences between the "goals of physical and biological research" and the methods appropriate to each.[32] He rejects behaviorist's "explanatory monism" which includes a full-blown causal account of a complex living organism arbitrarily built upon generalizations drawn from an isolated part of that complexity.[33] For Lorenz, explanation must be as rich and multivalent as the natures of the complex living creatures studied.

As Donald Griffin argues, careful ethological studies demonstrate that awareness, purposes, and thought should be ascribed at least to the "higher" animals. As he puts it: "The study of specialized communicative behavior between animals is more promising than learning experiments because it seems to have evolved to serve a purpose quite similar to what we want to use it for—namely, conveying to another animal the content of the communicator's thoughts and feelings."[34]

With its critique of the behaviorist description of animal life, ethology thus challenges the validity of the assumptions undergirding the traditional ethical devaluation of animals as mere "things" or "instinctual machines." The early studies of Wolfgang Kohler and Robert Yerkes in ape cognition; the recent work of Alan and Beatrice Gardner, Roger S. Fouts, and David Premack in ape communication; studies by John C. Lilly, L. M. Herman, C. K. Taylor and G. S. Saayman, K. Pryor, et al., of the dolphin; Karl von Frisch's remarkable discovery of the communicative nature of the honeybee's "dance," and the classic studies of animal display behavior by Konrad Lorenz and Niko Tinbergen are shattering our traditional accounts of the animal species as nonrational, non-language-using, nonpurposive, instinctbound reactors.[35]

The debate between behaviorist and ethological accounts of animal activity well illustrates how "facts" are theory dependent, that is, how theoretic models, basic metaphors and concepts guide the isolation, selection, and thus the interpretation of scientific data. This debate is one campaign in the broader conflict between rival metaphysical accounts of nature: nature construed via a technocratic, mechanistic, nonteleological hermeneutic and nature interpreted via an ecological, teleological view, at once more ancient and more modern.[36]

Any challenge to the traditional descriptive accounts of animals as non-rational, nonpurposive, non-language-using or non-"interest bearing" entails a challenge to the tradition of ethical anthropocentrism which has authorized this tradition of description. In short, ethology is challenging the legitimacy of drawing Kant's dualism between humans respected as "persons" and thus "ends-in-themselves" and relegating all nonhumans to the classification of mere "things" meant to be used for the service of humans. Instead of a strict dualism between humanity and other animal species, ethologists are highlighting the continuities between human life and some remarkable forms of animal life. Ethical notions traditionally restricted to defend human life and value must in justice be extended across the species line to recognize and protect the inherent value of at the least dolphin, apes, and other high-functioning species. Given the historical entrenchment of ethical anthropocentrism, this partial broadening of the "moral community" to include some nonhumans is no slight achievement.

However, I believe the implications run much farther. Animals are part of the world of nature. If they have inherent value, then the nonhuman natural world taken as a whole contains such value. Animal studies are important as simple reminders that humanity itself is part of the natural world. If parts of nonhuman nature have intrinsic value, then nature taken as a whole surely does, for the parts make up and help perfect the whole.

By recognizing at least some animals as purposive actors, ethology suggests that such animals do have significant "interests" in their own welfare and that we must recognize in them certain corresponding rights such as the right not to be needlessly abused.[37] At the very least, the ethological data shifts the burden of proof upon those who continue to endorse the traditional view that animals lack purposive action, insight, true "interests," and hence inherent value and rights.[38]

Thinking Eco-Theologically

In reaction to the emerging authority of the mechanistic world picture, dominant schools of liberal theology in great measure came to see history as the sphere of freedom and subjectivity while assessing nature as the sphere of objects and determinism. God's personal encounter with humanity can be seen as occurring within history. Existentialist and personalist thought in this century encouraged theologians to be sensitive to the categories of personal meaning, freedom, decision, and historical action, but to pay little attention to natural history or to humanity's interaction with nature. As Gordon Kaufman has suggested, the modern theological "disregard for nature" arose in part from the traditional dominance of anthropomorphic models and metaphors which ground Christian understandings of God. Understandably Christian reflection has tended to concentrate upon the divine-human encounter, where both are characterized by capacities of personality, freedom, agency, and love. Nature, especially when construed via mechanistic categories, easily comes to be viewed as peripheral to the central drama of salvation history.[39] The general acceptance of the construal of nature as machinelike suggested to most theologians that it could appropriately be ceded over to the disciplinary purview of science with little theological loss.

However, increasingly we are realizing that affirmations of God as graciously acting in history lack intelligibility unless we recognize that human history is enfolded within, and sustained by, the broader natural, evolutionary history of the biosphere which altogether is borne up by divine power and grace and which experiences divine judgment. The emerging threats of environmental degradation, however, are making it clear to some that theology must critically correlate itself to the understanding of the world which is emerging in the ecological sciences. Many feel now that there are compelling reasons to bridge the gap that has for so long stood between religious reflection and scientific reasoning. Good theology requires careful attention to scientific discussion as well as to the implications of the energy and tempo of technological development.

Religious communities should note that as contemporary science overthrows the mechanistic worldview the picture emerging—one of energy fields, relationality, interconnectedness, life, telos—holds certain affinities with earlier scientific accounts. For example, ethology's reintroduction of teleological explanations of animal action accords closely with some key descriptions in the Aristotelian tradition.[40] The convergence between the contemporary ethological, biological, and medical perspectives and the Aristotelian tradition of teleological explanation has been emphasized recently by Leon Kass. As he puts it: "[L]iving things display a *directedness*, an inner 'striving' toward a goal," "*a directed and inwardly determined activity to an end for a purpose.*" Animals, he holds, must be understood via a model of "internal teleology" which rightly catches the purposiveness and function of their activity.[41]

The emerging picture of nature as biosphere, as a sphere enlivened by telos and purpose, holds distinct affinities also with interpretations of creation found in some medieval Christian traditions. In what follows I will briefly focus on the views of Francis of Assisi (c. 1182-1226) and Thomas Aquinas (1225-1274) to show their relevance for informing current Christian thinking about our relation to animals and nature in general.

Even those critics who view Christianity as invidiously anthropocentric have cited Francis as a remarkable and positive exception. The Catholic Church itself has begun to recognize Francis's importance by the recent papal recognition of Francis as the patron saint of ecology. Where Francis develops a powerful vision of creation rooted in a strong sense of humanity's intimate kinship with animals, trees, the sun, the wind, and many living and nonliving natural elements, Thomas explicitly draws upon Aristotelian biological categories to describe the similarities and differences between humanity and the other animal species. Both thinkers present an understanding of humanity as a participant within the broader community of creation, and this general portrait offers the basis for generating a strong prophetic challenge to the modern technocratic vision of nature as a mere resource bank and field of things.

Francis drew upon the tradition of biblical nature allegory, troubadour poetry, and his own experiences of the graced nature of all creation, to develop an original and compelling vision of nature and our relationship to it. His vision focused on: 1) God's love for all creatures, 2) our close kinship with animals and nature, and 3) the natural world understood as a community of creation with a harmony and balance achieved through the participation of varied interdependent species and elements. Francis's most famous writing, "The Canticle of Brother Sun" (what *The Mirror of Perfection* calls his "Praise of the Creatures of the Lord"), boldly displays the directness of his mystical vision via his personification of natural elements like "Sir Brother Sun," "Sister Moon and the stars," "Brother Wind," "Sister Water," and "Brother Fire." As he states: "Praised be You, my Lord, through our Sister Mother Earth, who sustains and governs us, and who produces varied fruits with colored flowers and herbs."[42]

Many hagiographical reports attest to his strong "I-Thou" sense, his deep feeling of fellowship regarding animals and birds. Following a common saintly tradition, he is reputed to have preached a sermon to the birds: "My little sisters the birds, much are ye beholden to God your Creator, and always and in every place ye ought to praise Him for that He hath given you a double and triple vesture." After reminding the birds that God had given them freedom, preserved them from the Flood in the Ark, given them air to fly on, food and drink, mountains and valleys as "refuge," and trees as homes, he states: "wherefore your Creator loveth you much, since He hath dealt so bounteously with you; and therefore beware, little sisters mine, of the sin of ingratitude . . . "[43] Likewise *The Little Flowers* recounts the famous occasion when Francis converted a fierce wolf at Gubbio to peacefulness by hailing it: "Come hither, friar wolf; I command thee in the name of Christ that thou do hurt neither to me nor to any man." The wolf, once a terror in the region, accepts peace with the townspeople in exchange for their pledge to set out food every day for him. By this miracle the people were freed from their fear, came to love the wolf, and wept at his death of old age two years later.[44] These tales follow an important hagiographical tradition. The saint heals the rupture between humanity and the beasts and has the power to foster, even if only briefly, a return to the peaceable kingdom before the fall.

The boldness of Francis's sense of kinship with animals and nature is complemented by his view of the natural world as a vast community, sustained by God's love, and a web of interdependence linking living species and natural elements of creation. As Roger Sorrell argues, the most impressive aspects of Francis's vision lie in his "assumptions about the worth of creation, and the complex relationships of interdependence and mutual service among creatures." Francis's "Sermon to the Birds," Sorrell holds, demonstrates "graphically that humanity should concern itself with the welfare of creatures as a part of the Christian mission. . . . [H]e proclaimed the indissoluble kinship and community between humans and their fellow creatures under God."[45]

While St. Francis's love of animals and all of creation is widely regarded today as an exemplary model of Christian ecological sensitivity, Thomas Aquinas's views are not typically so well regarded. Many have rejected Thomas's system both because of its strict ethical anthropocentrism and its alleged allegiance to a static, outmoded metaphysics. It is not surprising that anthologies pick out the texts where Thomas suggests that animals, because they lack reason, exist for the sake of the human and are properly used as means. As "instruments" to the end of human interest, they lack "mastery" of their acts and thus are "naturally subject to slavery."[46] Many focus on Thomas's citation of Aristotle's *Politics* as his authority that "it is not unlawful if man use plants for the good of animals, and animals for the good of man."[47] His affirmation of the use of nonrational life by rational life grounds his notion that it is not wrong for humans to use, kill, or eat animals. While he holds that cruelty to animals is wrong, his rationale is that such cruel acts can lead to cruelty to humans, or can damage humans in some other way.[48]

By accepting the naming of animals in this way, Thomas helped establish a tradition of misnaming which has plagued Catholic moral theology until only recently. In the manualist tradition it became a standard practice to emphasize, as does the Jesuit natural-law philosopher Joseph Rickaby, that "brute beasts, not having understanding and therefore not being persons, cannot have any rights."[49] Such views became so established in the Catholic hierarchy that Pope Pius IX refused permission to allow a chapter of the Society for the Prevention of Cruelty to Animals to be founded in Rome. The fear, it seems, was that such an establishment might somehow draw moral concern away from issues of human well-being.[50] This is a part of the Thomist legacy that should not be retrieved.

There is, however, another set of namings Thomas employs to describe animals which is theologically insightful and ecologically sensitive. Thomas's analysis of animals as instruments properly subject to slavery arises from his penchant for the hierarchical model where lower forms serve as the means to the ends of higher ones. Yet Thomas also employs another model of reasoning to generate descriptions, one which describes a being via an examination of its multiple relations with other created beings, with its species, with the common good of creation as a whole, and with God, the cause and final end of all. In an era where much theological ink is spilt in defining humans vis-à-vis our relations to texts, traditions, modes of interpretation, and history, Thomas's project stands out as a deeply ecological one in that our relations (and God's relations) to the rest of the natural cosmos are central within it. The Great Chain of Being is a multivalent metaphor. The same metaphysical model Thomas uses to stress hierarchical gradations of value linked to the scale of being also, at other points, leads Thomas to highlight continuities and linkages throughout a conjoined cosmos pulsing with life and sustained by God's energy and love. While his stress on hierarchy generates a narrowing of direct moral concern restricted to human value and well-being, his stress upon all creatures' participation in the broader community of creation generates an expansive vision of all beings as related to one another and to God. If his strict anthropocentric moral theory is not helpful today, perhaps his expansive view of the community of being might be, for it provides a powerful alternate language which channels our attention more carefully to our relationships with other living species.

For Thomas, animals are a path to God, for God created them and sustains them in being. As Thomas puts it: "[W]e know and name God from creatures." Elsewhere he states: "Creatures of themselves do not withdraw us from God, but lead us to Him."[51] While holding that only rational beings are created in the "image of God," he does describe animals (all creatures) as created in the "likeness" of God, bearing marks of their Creator. "[I]n all creatures there is found the trace of the Trinity ..."[52] These are both simple and remarkable claims. All created things desire God who is their cause. "God is in all things ... as an agent is present to that upon which it acts."[53] God contains all existing beings within the mystery of the divine mind. "God loves all existing things ... the love of God infuses and creates goodness [in things]."[54] The beasts are under God's providence, even if rational creatures are so in a special way.

Following Aristotelian biology, Thomas classifies animals as nonrational and thus lacking the capacity for eternal life. While humans act from free choice, animals, he states, act "by natural instinct."[55] Thus they are not masters of their action. Animals who live on the land, he holds, are generally "more perfect than birds or fishes" though he notes (not unlike some contemporary sociobiologists) that "some imperfect animals, such as bees and ants, are more intelligent in certain ways." Scripture implies that land animals are "living souls with bodies subject to them."[56] Humans are of the same *genus* as other animals, but differ in species. Animals have a sensitive soul, while humans have an intellectual soul which includes all of the powers of the sensitive soul of animals and the nutritive (or vegetative) souls of plant life.[57] Still animals enjoy a "natural estimative" power as well as the power of memory, and these together guide animal perceptions and action toward objects that are useful to them and promote them to flee predators.[58] While a stone falls not through the power of any judgment, and a human acts through the power of a deliberative, and hence, free judgment, animals act from "natural judgment" as when "the sheep, seeing the wolf, judges it a thing to be shunned." He cites Augustine as an authority for the view that the part of the soul which is informed by images, "namely, the imagination — is *common to us and beasts*."[59] Animals, he states, "take delight" in their ordering to food and sex.[60]

The ecological structure of Thomas's reasoning comes out most forcefully in his insistence that beings must be understood in their multiple relationships to each other, to creation as a whole, and to God. "[A] corporeal creature can be considered as made either for the sake of its proper act, or for other creatures, or for the whole universe, or for the glory of God."[61] Elsewhere he states: "[E]very creature exists for its own proper act and perfection, and the less noble for the nobler ..." "[E]ach and every creature exists for the perfection of the entire universe. Furthermore, the entire universe, with all its parts, is ordained towards God as its end."[62]

Species diversity, he states, is required of a maximally rich universe which alone is capable of adequately representing the overflowing range of divine goodness. "[T]he whole universe together participates the divine goodness more perfectly, and represents it better than any given single creature whatever." For this reason God allows some evil to exist, for the "life of a lion" would not be preserved "unless the ass were killed."[63] Likewise, in a point of considerable contemporary significance, Thomas affirms that the good of the order of creation is higher than the good of humanity alone, for creation includes humanity and much besides. The highest good "among created things, is the good of the order of the whole universe, since . . . each part is found to be for the sake of its whole. Thus, among created things, what God cares for most is the order of the universe."[64] Policies which promote species extinction and ecosystem degradation are therefore, from a theological perspective, idolatrous and sinful.

Conclusion

Too many who have never seriously examined Christianity dismiss it as ecologically bankrupt. Sadly many who know little of Catholicism cite certain unfortunate parts of a long and varied tradition to dismiss it as holding no helpful resources for promoting responsible care of animals or the ecosystem. Yet the reemergence of the categories of telos and purpose in ethology, biology, and physics suggest that some elements of medieval Catholic thinking may prove helpful as we ponder our moral responsibilities owed to animals and creation in general.

Francis's magnificent sense of intimate kinship with animals and elements of nature is nicely complemented by Thomas's vision of humanity as participants in a vast community of being. Francis's powerful insistence upon naming animals and nature via personalistic language focuses our attention upon our connectedness to them. His way of naming nature and animals as "brother" and "sister" thus heightens awareness of our responsibility to restrict sharply some of our current consumptive and productive practices which are degrading creation, weakening its stability, and endangering its species.

Similarly Thomas's stress upon the priority of the common good over private good—mere individual interest—can sensitize Christians to our obligations to animals and the rest of nature. Thomas typically develops his notion of the common good as the well-being of a particular human community or a state. In his "Treatise on Law," Thomas develops the common good as an ethical-political principle. However, Thomas's notion of human government is modeled upon reflection about God's government over creation. He speaks of a common good higher than that of a human community or state, namely, the "good of the order of the universe." At various points Thomas thus develops the common-good notion as a cosmological-ecological principle which emphasizes that the good of a human community is situated within an even broader community, the community of all of creation. This expansive interpretation of the ecological community focuses well the need for an expansive understanding of ethics that is committed not just to defending human life and interests, but to defending all life, all creation. Disturbing ecological "signs of the times" suggest the need for an ecologically expanded understanding of the traditional concept of the common good. This expansion of moral attention and loyalty is critical for an era in which we are beginning to recognize the increasing range of humanity's power to extinguish various animal species and to degrade the planetary ecosystem.

New powers bring new responsibilities, and these require new styles of thinking. As new fears sensitize us to new duties, we come to examine our religious traditions with new eyes. Francis and Thomas Aquinas provide interpretations of animal life and creation which stand in marked contrast to both the beast-machine tradition and the modern technocratic vision of nature as a realm of things or mere resources to be shaped and used. Francis and Thomas well exhibit how core elements in medieval Catholicism can be marshalled today to provide a prophetic challenge to those who continue to construe animals as things lacking in intrinsic value, valuable only in their service to humans, and cut off from God's love, grace, and care. Those who dismiss Francis's views as naive and tainted by "nature-mysticism," and Thomas's as tied to outmoded, static "classicist" metaphysics would do well to reconsider the resources they offer us for helping the Christian churches both to take the doctrine of creation more seriously and to think more critically about the duties we owe to animal life and to nature in general.

Notes

1. Immanuel Kant, *Foundations of the Metaphysics of Morals*, trans. Lewis White Beck (Indianapolis: Bobbs-Merrill, 1949), p. 46.

2. H. W. Janson, *Apes and Ape Lore in the Middle Ages and the Renaissance* (London: University of London, The Warburg Institute, 1952), pp. 13-37, 79-81, 107-133.

3. Ramona and Desmond Morris, *Men and Apes* (London: Hutchinson, 1966), p. 31.

4. Carolyn Merchant, *The Death of Nature: Women, Ecology and the Scientific Revolution* (San Francisco: Harper and Row, 1983), p. 217-18. See also E. J. Dijksterhuis, *The Mechanization of the World Picture*, trans. C. Dikshoorn (Oxford: Clarendon Press, 1961).

5. René Descartes, *Discourse on Method* in *The Philosophical Works of Descartes*, trans. Elizabeth S. Haldane and G. R. T. Ross (Cambridge: Cambridge University Press, 1968), vol. 1, p. 115.

6. Ibid., pp. 116-118.

7. René Descartes, "Letter to Henry More" (5 February 1649), in *Descartes: Philosophical Letters*, trans. and ed. Anthony Kenny (Oxford: Clarendon Press, 1970), pp. 243-244.

8. See N. Kemp Smith, *New Studies in the Philosophy of Descartes* (London: Macmillan, 1952), pp. 136 and 140. See also John Cottingham's fine article "A Brute to the Brutes?: Descartes' Treatment of Animals," *Philosophy* 53 (October 1978): 551-559. He argues that Descartes denies animals have thought, language, and self-consciousness, but not consciousness and feelings (i.e., physical sensations — pain, pleasure, joy).

9. Descartes, "Letter to the Marquess of Newcastle," in *Philosophical Letters*, p. 208.

10. Descartes, "Letter to Henry More," p. 245. For a helpful collection of these texts see Andrew Linzey and Tom Regan, eds., *Animals and Christianity: A Book of Readings* (New York: Crossroad, 1988), pp. 45-52.

11. Fontaine, *Memories pour servir a l'histoire de Port-Royal* (1738), II, 470, quoted in Leonora Cohen Rosenfield, *From Beast-Machine to Man-Machine: Animal Soul in French Letters From Descartes to La Mettrie*, preface by Paul Hazard (New York: Octagon Books, 1968), p. 54.

12. See Hester Hastings, *Man and Beast in French Thought in the Eighteenth Century* (Baltimore: Johns Hopkins Press, 1936), p. 21. See also Desmond Connell, *The Vision in God: Malebranche's Scholastic Sources* (Louvain: Éditions Nauwelaerts, 1967), pp. 1048.

13. Descartes, "Discourse on Method," in Haldane and Ross, eds., *Philosophical Works of Descartes*, p. 119.

14. Aram Vartanian, *La Mettrie's L'Homme Machine: A Study in the Origins of an Idea* (Princeton: Princeton University Press, 1960), pp. 13-39, 95-113.

15. On the intimate connection between logical positivism and behaviorism, see the study by Brian D. Mackenzie, *Behaviourism and the Limits of Scientific Method* (Atlantic Highlands, N.J.: Humanities Press, 1977), pp. 28-43, 104-08. See also B. F. Skinner, *About Behaviorism* (New York: Knopf, 1974), p. 16. But see Laurence D. Smith, *Behaviorism and Logical Positivism: A Reassessment of the Alliance* (Stanford: Stanford University Press, 1986), who suggests that the behaviorist theorists were only indirectly influenced by the philosophical analyses of the positivists, even though from their own commitments about physiology and the nature of science they developed a set of views closely convergent with positivist doctrine.

16. Mackenzie, *Behaviourism*, p. 54.

17. See Stephen R. L. Clark, *The Nature of the Beast: Are Animals Moral?* (Oxford: Oxford University Press, 1982), p. 14.

18. See Bernard E. Rollin's excellent treatment of the reasons for the success of the model of behavioral psychology in his recent book, *The Unheeded Cry: Animal Consciousness, Animal Pain and Science* (Oxford: Oxford University Press, 1990), pp. 100-106.

19. Charles Taylor, *The Explanation of Behaviour* (London and Henley: Routledge and Kegan Paul; New York: Humanities Press, 1964; paperback reprint, 1980), p. 75.

20. Ibid., p. 90.

21. Clifford Geertz, "Thick Description: Toward an Interpretive Theory of Culture," in his *The Interpretation of Cultures: Selected Essays* (New York: Basic Books, 1973), p. 6.

22. Taylor, *Explanation of Behaviour*, pp. 111-115.

23. See R. S. Peters, *The Concept of Motivation* (London: Routledge and Kegan Paul; New York: Humanities Press, 1960; reprint edition, 1974), pp. 1-51, 95-129.

24. See Hans Jonas, *The Phenomenon of Life* (Chicago and London: University of Chicago Press, 1966), pp. 108-127, where he criticizes behaviorists' accounts of animal activity.

25. Taylor, *Explanation of Behaviour*, p. 64.

26. Ibid., pp. 66-67.

27. Ibid., p. 67.

28. Mary Midgley, *Beast and Man: The Roots of Human Nature* (Ithaca, N.Y.: Cornell University Press, 1978), 106.

29. Ibid., p. 163.

30. Rollin, *Unheeded Cry*, pp. 116-117.

31. Taylor, *Explanation of Behaviour*, p. 199. See also Konrad Z. Lorenz, *The Foundations of Ethology: The Principal Ideas and Discoveries in Animal Behaviour*, trans. Konrad Z. Lorenz and Robert Warren Kickert (New York: Simon and Schuster, 1981, Touchstone Book, 1982), pp. 40-53.

32. Lorenz, *Foundations of Ethology*, p. 18.

33. Ibid., p. 67.

34. Donald R. Griffin, *Animal Thinking* (Cambridge, Mass.: Harvard University Press, 1984), p. 163.

35. The literature in this field is extensive. For general introductions to the relatively young discipline of ethology, see Lorenz, *Foundations of Ethology*; Niko Tinbergen, *The Study of Instinct* (Oxford: Oxford University Press, 1951); Robert A. Hinde, *Ethology: Its Nature and Relations with Other Sciences* (New York: Oxford University Press, 1982). On ape intelligence, see Wolfgang Köhler, *The Mentality of Apes*, trans. Ella Winter, 2nd ed. (New York: Liveright Publishing Co., 1927, paperback edition, 1976) and Eugene Linden, *Apes, Men and Language* (New York: Penguin Books, updated edition 1981).

36. See R. G. Collingwood, *The Idea of Nature* (London: Oxford University Press, 1960, reprint edition 1981), pp. 14-15.

37. For a magisterial argument in favor of animal rights see Tom Regan, *The Case for Animal Rights* (Berkeley: University of California Press, 1983). For other similar arguments for animal rights based upon animals' capacities for having "interests," see Joel Feinberg, "The Rights of Animals and Unborn Generations," in *Philosophy and Environmental Crisis*, ed. William T. Blackstone (Athens, Ga.: University of Georgia Press, 1974), pp. 43-68. This is reprinted in Joel Feinberg, *Rights, Justice and the Bounds of Liberty* (Princeton, N.J.: Princeton University Press, 1980), pp. 159-184. See also Alan Gewirth, *Reason and Morality* (Chicago and London: University of Chicago Press, 1978), pp. 120-123, 144-145.

38. For one such sustained argument see R. G. Frey, *Interests and Rights: The Case Against Animals* (Oxford: Clarendon Press, 1980).

39. Gordon D. Kaufman, "A Problem for Theology: The Concept of Nature," *Harvard Theological Review* 65 (July 1972): 337-366.

40. Martha Craven Nussbaum, *Aristotle's De motu animalium* (Princeton, N.J.: Princeton University Press, 1978, paperback edition, 1985), p. 38. See Nussbaum's excellent interpretive essay "Aristotle on Teleological Explanation," pp. 59-106, especially on p. 86, where she paraphrases Aristotle: "The way the food-getting mechanism functions in a lion is via that lion's beliefs and desires."

41. Leon R. Kass, M.D., *Toward a More Natural Science* (New York: Free Press, 1985), pp. 256-257.

42. Regis J. Armstrong, O.F.M. CAP, and Ignatius C. Brady, O.F.M., eds., *Fran-*

cis and Clare: The Complete Works (New York: Paulist Press, 1982), pp. 38-39. *The Little Flowers of St. Francis; The Mirror of Perfection; St. Bonaventure's Life of St. Francis*, intro. Fr. Hugh McKay (London: Dent; New York: Dutton, Everyman's Library, 1910, reprint edition, 1973), p. 274, 289-295.

43. *The Little Flowers of St. Francis*, pp. 29-30.

44. Ibid., 39-41.

45. Roger D. Sorrell, *St. Francis of Assisi and Nature: Tradition and Innovation in Western Christian Attitudes toward the Environment* (New York: Oxford University Press, 1988), pp. 137, 141.

46. Saint Thomas Aquinas, *Summa Contra Gentiles*, trans. Vernon J. Bourke, 4 vols. (Notre Dame, Ind.: University of Notre Dame, 1975), Book 3, Part 2, chapter 112, 4:115-16. See also Thomas Aquinas, *Summa Theologiae*, 1a, q. 86, art. 1-2, in St. Thomas Aquinas, *Summa Theologiae*, trans. Fathers of the English Dominican Province, 5 vols. (New York: Benziger Brothers 1948; reprint ed., Westminster, Md.: Christian Classics, 1981), 1:486-487. See H. Paul Santmire, *The Travail of Nature* (Philadelphia: Fortress Press, 1985), pp. 84-95 for a helpful examination of Thomas's deep subordination of nature to humanity.

47. Thomas Aquinas, *Summa Theologiae*, 2a, 2ae, q. 64, art. 1 in Christian Classics ed., 3:1460.

48. See Saint Thomas Aquinas, *Summa Contra Gentiles*, Book 3, Part 2, ch. 112, para. 13, 4:119 and Thomas Aquinas, *Summa Theologiae*, 2a, 2ae, q. 64, art. 1, ad. 3 in Christian Classics ed., 3:1460.

49. Joseph Rickaby, S.J., *Moral Philosophy: Ethics, Deontology and Natural Law* (London: Longmans, Green and Co., 1929), p. 248. See also Henry Davis, S.J., *Moral and Pastoral Theology*, 4 vols. (New York: Sheed and Ward, 1935), 2:228. See James Gaffney, "Animals and Ethics: A Catholic Blind Spot," *America* 163 (October 27, 1990): 297-299.

50. *Life of Frances Power Coobe by Herself*, 2 vols. (Boston: Houghton, Mifflin and Co., 1894), 2:489.

51. Thomas Aquinas, *Summa Theologiae*, 1a, q. 13, art. 1, ad. 2; and q. 65, art. 1, ad. 3 in Christian Classics ed., 1:60 and 1:325.

52. Ibid., 1a, q. 45, art. 7, in Christian Classics ed., 1:238.

53. Ibid., 1a , q. 6, art. 1, ad. 2, and q. 8, art. 1 in Christian Classics ed., 1:28 and 1:34.

54. Ibid., q. 18, art. 4, ad. 1 and q. 20, art. 2 in Christian Classics ed., 1:102 and 1:115.

55. Ibid., 1a, q. 19, art. 10 in Christian Classics ed., 1:111.

56. Ibid., 1a, q. 72, art. 1, ad. 1 in Christian Classics ed., 1:351-352.

57. Ibid., 1a, q. 75, art. 3, ad. 1 and q. 76, art. 1 in Christian Classics ed., 1:365 and 1:370-372.

58. Ibid., 1a, q. 78, art. 4 in Christian Classics ed., 1:395.

59. Ibid., 1a, q. 83, art. 1 and q. 84, art. 2, ad. 1 in Christian Classics ed., 1:418 and 1:423. See also q. 86, art. 4, ad. 3, 1:443.

60. Ibid., q. 91, art. 3, ad. 3 in Christian Classics ed., 1:464.

61. Ibid., 1a, q. 70, art. 2 in Christian Classics ed., 1:347.

62. Ibid., 1a, q. 65, art. 2 in Christian Classics ed., 1:326.

63. Ibid., 1a, q. 47, art. 1 and q. 48, art. 2, ad. 3 in Christian Classics ed., 1:246 and 1:250.

64. Saint Thomas Aquinas, *Summa Contra Gentiles*, Book 3, Part 1, ch. 64, para. 10, in Bourke, ed., 3:213.

Part II

WHAT IS BEING SAID
ABOUT ANIMALS TODAY?

*Constructive Efforts to Include Animals
in Christian Vision*

Christians have been taught by their tradition to speak a distinctive idiom. Any issue they address must to some degree be understood in their own language, which includes terms such as "Trinity," "church" and "creation." Christian theologians have frequently emphasized the need to ask who *humans* are, and to expect that their theological answer as expressed in the distinctive Christian idiom will differ from other answers. In turn, it seems appropriate to urge them to ask who *animals* are for Christians, and to expect distinctly theological answers which may differ significantly from other answers expressed in different terms.

The essays in Part II attempt to understand animals in the light of certain central Christian notions such as the three mentioned. In no case is the theological identification of animals morally neutral, for evidently how one thinks about what or who animals are bears directly on how she should treat them.

45

Chapter 4

Animals in Christian Perspective

Strangers, Friends, or Kin?

L. Shannon Jung

Few things more vividly expose the consumerist values of our culture than its treatment of animals. It is, furthermore, very difficult to detect a difference between those dominant cultural values and behaviors and ones that Christians affirm. This paper examines the too-long dormant issue of Christian treatment of animals from one particular limited viewpoint.[1]

My purpose is to retrieve values implicit in the Christian tradition in order to enunciate new directions for the treatment of animals in our culture. My basic thesis is that the disembodied spiritualism of the culture has obscured our basic relationship with animals. By way of remediation, I argue that a recognition of our embodied kinship with animals is illumined by and consistent with the Christian moral tradition.

The essay begins by making the case that spiritualism is so pervasive in our culture that we are tempted to forget our political and material nature as human beings. It is disembodied, depoliticized spiritualism — not anthropocentrism — that is the villain of this piece. (There may of course be plenty of room for both!)

The second section of the paper will deal with the question that is implied in the title of this paper. That is, what is the relationship of human beings and animals? Does the relationship come closest to being that of strangers, of friends, or of kin? My view is that it is more productive to speak of the *relationship* of humans with animals than to speak of animal

L. Shannon Jung teaches Christian environmental ethics and is Director of the Center for Theology and Land at the University of Dubuque and Wartburg Theological Seminaries, Dubuque, Iowa.

47

rights. The resources of the Christian faith can help clarify our relation to animals; so the third step of the argument will contrast an ethics of animal rights with a Christian communitarian ethic.

By moving toward the construction of a vision of who animals are, the essay offers a clearer vision of who we human animals are. Asking the question of who or what animals are to us will also bring into better focus aspects of ourselves that we've forgotten or obscured. Those beings or things with whom we have or enter relationships reveal things about ourselves which only they can.[2]

Disregard for Animals — A Dominant Value

Ruth Harrison's *Animal Machines* (1964) describes how eggs are mass-produced through an intermediary means — chickens.[3] In 1989 the Humane Farming Association's newsletter, *Watchdog*, published an almost identical description.[4] Let me quote only five or six sentences:

> After they have been in the grow-house for about four weeks, the chicks are debeaked. Debeaking is a painful procedure whereby much of the chick's sensitive upper beak is seared off with a hot blade . . . [At restocking time] hens are packed into the wire battery cages . . . A cage with the floor space the size of the front page of a typical newspaper will hold from six to eight hens . . . [and] are commonly stacked four tiers high . . . each level of birds (except the top level) is splattered by the excrement falling from those above.[5]

That this goes on, and has gone on for quite some time, signals a substantial lack of regard for animals in the United States. My hypothesis in this section is that such disregard has been consistent with the values of the dominant culture.

The most devastating of those cultural roots is *spiritualism: the separation of mind from body and body from mind in the human species.* Rather than seeing these aspects of ourselves as interpenetrating in holistic ways, spiritualism separates and dichotomizes them. It ascribes superiority to the mental or spiritual part of us, and downgrades the physical or natural.[6] The language of "souls" emphasizes this separation and was seldom used in anything but a spiritualist sense.

What I am pointing to is a disembodied spiritualism, *not* a holistic spirituality. This separation of the superior mind from the inferior body has resulted in a distorted view of human nature. Furthermore, perceiving ourselves in this way usually involves reducing all nonhuman beings to their physical or material aspects — materialism. Thus animals and plants and all inanimate entities are simply things, objects.

Dualistic spiritualism is especially pernicious because it seems so trivial, so much only a philosophical issue. Therein lies its subtlety and destructiveness. Two cultural forces — patriarchy and hierarchialism — grow out of this dualism. I intend in this essay to show why a reconnection of the body-mind relationship is significant to the issue of the treatment of animals.

Associated with this body-mind dichotomy are other dualisms which are destructive of human and animal well-being. They have been used as forces of oppression. Women and animals have been associated with the inferior pole of the dualism because they were culturally defined as closer to nature, closer to the physical, "creaturely" (!) aspect of our being.[7] Men were associated with the superior pole because they were assumed to have transcended their creaturely selves. They represented the rational, cultural, technological-scientific, and spiritual aspects of our being. Notice the resulting dualisms:

$$\begin{array}{lllll}
\text{mind} & = \text{spirit} & = \text{men} & = \text{human} & = \text{culture} \\
\text{body} & = \text{nature} & = \text{women} & = \text{animal} & = \text{material}
\end{array}$$

These dualisms contain hierarchical ascriptions of superiority and inferiority. Those ascriptions do not flow logically from differences in characteristics. However, what we see in these dualisms are ascriptions of ontological superiority and inferiority. What quality establishes ontological superiority? What characteristics are ascribed superiority? The two most likely candidates are: (1) a being's ability to consciously and rationally change its environment, and (2) the ability to be self-reflective. The consequences of that ordering come to a head in its depreciation of animals but also, I think, in what it implies about humankind.

Ascriptions of ontological superiority support and generate ascriptions of moral superiority. This issues in a "logic of domination," as Karen J. Warren names it so well.[8] This logic can be expressed as the premise: For any X and Y, if X is morally superior to Y, then X is morally justified in subordinating Y. In the list of dualisms just mentioned, the top pole can be symbolized as "X," the bottom pole of the dualism as "Y." If this premise holds true, then it follows that X is morally justified in subordinating Y. Notice here that the determinative premise rests on the prior establishing of differences as morally superior or inferior.

Spiritualism, patriarchy, and hierarchial thinking reinforce one another and are only separable for heuristic purposes. The church has not escaped the influence of these cultural forces, of course, although none of the three is compatible with traditional Christian values.

When translated into the realm of theology, what I have described here is a disembodied spirituality, one that simply does not and cannot take the material, natural world as seriously as it does "the realm of the spirit" (basically synonymous with mind or soul).[9] Thus, and for many other reasons as well, United States theology has become overbalanced toward the individual and has fostered the general depoliticization of the culture.

In order to avoid making the same mistake of depoliticization, it should be noted that there are corporate interests which have every reason to suppress any question of the culture's treatment of animals. There is a great deal of money riding on the continued strength of spiritualism. The accelerating concentration of the meat industry into three giant corporations and their generation of constituency support groups (the Beef Producers and Pork Producers Associations, USDA)[10] are not only economic forces, they are political as well.

The cultural forces mentioned do not operate in a vacuum. There are institutional groups and social values which buttress them and transport these values into homes, restaurants, city halls, and Congress. The present mistreatment of animals is underwritten by a vast economic and political network. While they should be understood as symptomatic and reinforcing, rather than foundational, consumerist values are the end result of this network. Those values are the product of our acquiescence in the system we United States citizens enjoy and are misshapen by.

Commenting on George Bush's view that the Iraqi invasion of Kuwait constituted nothing less than "a threat to the American way of life" columnist Russel Baker wrote that Bush apparently means "our ability to buy the carry-out fried chicken in the drive-by lane at the fast-food shop, as well as our power to sit one-commuter-per-car for forty-five minutes every day on the way home from work."[11] The seductive power of microwave ovens, processed food, and instant *private* transportation has blunted our political and moral sensitivity. We have come to enjoy the comfortable, but not good, life. We of the middle class seem to enjoy just enough of the privileges of money and power that we do not seriously question the political and economic costs of our ease.

Even in this petroleum- and gadget-worshiping culture, however, we could not have become so blind without the power of regnant spiritualism. If there were not the separation — in the academy, in churches, in the media — between people's mind/spirit and their bodily/material existence, we would not be led around by our consumer preferences. The dominant definition of ourselves as mental and rational, cut off from material desire and wisdom, results in a denigration of the physical and natural. We believe that we are not what we eat; we are not the results of our material choices. The material world is underestimated, treated lightly.

Our material choices do not really or centrally inform our mental images of ourselves. Thus we can eat chickens who have been debeaked, brutalized, and treated like anything but one of God's creatures. Thus we drink coffee without counting the cost to the Salvadoran *campesino*. Chicken and coffee are simply reduced to consumer preferences and disposable income. We believe that there are no political, environmental, or personal costs involved. We believe that because we ignore those consequences that they do not affect us. What is the cost of our self-narcotization, our addiction? If we ignore this part of our ourselves, what other parts as well? If animals are reduced to consumer commodities, what might that imply about ourselves?

What Are Animals to Humans?

At this point we are prepared to consider the relationship of animals to human beings. In the previous section I made some claims about the actual values that inform the culture's (and too often we Christians') treatment of animals. Now I turn to the question of what our relationships with animals are.

This section will consider three ways that animals and human beings are related—as strangers, as friends, and as kin. While I believe the kinship relationship most accurately describes what is the case, there are elements of truth in each of the other two as well. My overall contention will be that conceiving of the relation principally as one of strangers participates in the spiritualism of mind over matter, mental over physical, human animal over other animals. Conceiving of the relation as principally one of friends falsely suggests that there is no difference between animals and ourselves, that there is *no* distinctiveness to the human spirit. Conceiving the relation as principally one of kinship is attractive because it recognizes that both the physical and mental aspects of our selves are interrelated, integrated into an inseparable whole.

Our anthropocentrism tempts us to see animals, falsely, as either objects or as pets. Seeing animals either as objects or as pets entails a misconception because it does not recognize the independent standing of animals. The relation is conceived wholly from a human point of view, on human terms.[12] Conceiving the relation as kinship offers the hope of crediting the truths offered by the other two relationships and of avoiding anthropocentrism as well as the spiritualism to which I have referred.

Animals Are Essentially Strangers to Human Beings

According to one view prevalent in the culture most animals are and remain strangers; they are, simply, commodities to be used. In that instance the relationship of being strangers means "those who do not have any relation to us at all." As such, this view is simply false. Obviously we eat animals; they sustain our lives.

There is, however, a less pernicious interpretation of this relationship. We could consider the primary feature of strangers to be "those who are not essentially like us." Interpreted in that way, the view that animals are strangers to human beings rests on a spiritualism that obscures any more intimate relationship.

The culture, through special interests, has invested a considerable amount in maintaining a distance between human beings and animals. (We will later look at an exception to this—the relation between humans and "their pets.") The present situation includes corporate domination of the means of defining animals. That control could not continue without strong cultural definitions reinforcing it, as the previous section of this paper indicated.

Spiritualism obscures the many similarities which human and animal species share. In addition to the multiple ways in which our physiological functions are identical, most animals have group cultures, live in families, and exhibit varying degrees of intelligence. Here I mean to point to a multiplicity of similarities here rather than to single traits. Spiritualism, by contrast, emphasizes only mental capacities to differentiate humankind from other animal species.

It is instructive that Western Christianity has emphasized the stewardship of creation as the benchmark norm of environmental responsibility. This norm tends to highlight differences between humankind and the rest of the created order. Humankind is called to subdue, dominate, work, and care for creation, and is accountable to God, in whose image they are made. Their shared creaturehood with animals has not been emphasized. By contrast Eastern Orthodoxy has located the essential difference among beings as lying between the uncreated and the created order. There humankind's creatureliness/createdness comes far more clearly into focus.

My assessment is that, while the relationship of stranger is the one most people would use to describe their interaction with and feelings about animals, it is the least accurate and morally the most troublesome. Nevertheless, there is descriptive strength in the stranger relationship. Animals *are* different from human beings; it is true that animal species have their own integrity which is irreducible to that of humankind.

The weakness of the stranger relationship which renders it untenable is its claim that animals are *essentially* different from humankind. The conception of stranger obscures a sameness with human beings and encourages the continuation of spiritualism, an essential ingredient in the logic of domination. It is this lie that permits us to reduce animals to their economic functions *for us* and to treat them — often in the name of stewardship — as things.

Animals Are Essentially Friends to Human Beings

Household pets constitute an exception to my judgment that we see animals as essentially strangers. Many people see their pets as companions or friends, not as strangers. They have great affection for their dog, cat, or ferret, which the animal reciprocates. Sometimes we project traits onto the animals, which obscure their independent nature as well as the characteristics we share with them. We personalize pets much as we personalize an object such as a doll or car or favorite baseball glove. The relationship is one-sidedly defined by the man or woman, boy or girl. We do not take cognizance of the integrity of the dog or cat in its own being. We don't take the independent being of the pet seriously enough to call the relationship one of friendship.

Friendship implies a relationship of equality, to some extent or kind — at least to the extent of involving reciprocity. Sallie McFague, in her *Models of God*, gives a concise understanding of friendship as "a bonding of two by free choice in a reciprocal relationship."[13] McFague does not consider the question of whether animals can be friends to people, but her definition would seem to all but foreclose that possibility, at least to the full extent of her definition.

There are *elements of friendship* that might apply to human relationships with particular animals: companionship, affection, and a form of nonvoluntary reciprocity. Indeed, I still treasure relationships with cats and dogs that were family pets. Perhaps we could speak of animal friends, since certain animals do seem able to reciprocate our affection and companionship. Basically, however, human friendships are different primarily because they develop "by free choice." Even the affection of pets is not really a matter of free choice. Perhaps that element of free choice is less important than we have assumed. If we do recognize our own physicality, our lives seem less "freely chosen" than consented to.

The descriptive inaccuracy of calling animals friends should not, I think, imply that human beings shouldn't be friends *to* animals. People can impute to animals an equal or almost equal status, in the same way God imputes to humankind an equality or near equality of friendship, for example, in the table fellowship of Jesus that McFague cites.[14] Imputed status is not exactly the same as equality, as nearly as I can tell.

It is important to avoid romanticizing the treatment of animals, and considering animals as friends does romanticize them. Nonetheless animals do exhibit friendly characteristics. The strength of conceiving the relationship as one of friendship is that it signals the interrelation of species and it suggests that animals do have gifts for people.[15]

Animals Are Essentially Kin to Humankind

My thinking has led me to assess the relationship of kinship very positively, both descriptively and normatively, in part because it completes the insights of the other two.

Consider the following five salient features of kinship:

1. We share with kin an essential similarity in physical makeup.
2. We do not *choose* our relatives; instead we *find* that we are kin.
3. We cannot change kin relationships; whether we ignore or embrace them, they remain kin.
4. We can find out much about ourselves by investigating those with whom we are kin.
5. We are, however similar, different from any of our relatives; we have our own integrity and independence.

As I shall suggest, these five features will prove valuable in articulating some moral limits.

Animals and human beings share many of the same physiological functions. They are basically members of the same biological family: warm-blooded mammals. Some animals have a longer, some a shorter gestation period; some are larger, some smaller; some are more group-oriented, some less; some mate for life, some don't. Since our physical makeup influences our entire being — feelings, thoughts, values, beliefs — the similarity of physiology we share with animals should not be underestimated. It suggests a possible similarity of feelings and values. Indeed, we just don't know to what extent animals are capable of thinking and believing. Our spiritualism and drive to see human beings as distinctive has been self-reinforcing; it has screened out areas of research which questioned humanocentric axioms.

A second way that we are kin is that we are both thrown into the world. We do not choose our families or anything about our families. Rather we simply discover that we are relatives. Unfortunately our blindness to the degree of our determination by other forces has resulted in unbelievable destruction. This is nowhere more evident than in our treatment of land and other species.

However much we might want to change our families at times, we cannot. We can hate them or love them, but they remain our families. Similarly animals and humans are stuck with their families, even their extended families. For humankind this implies a recognition of their family ties with animals. Of course there is a difference: Human beings do seem to have the capacity to act responsibly, some of the time; we do think that human beings can choose to act to change their environment in morally positive ways while animals cannot. If we assume this to be true, then human beings (who cannot change their families) can change the way they relate to their families. Those families include animals, whose relation is far more than a passive sharing of physiology.

Family therapy and generational analysis are very popular these days. We accept the view that we can find out much about ourselves by investigating those with whom we are kin. Perhaps we have arrogantly assumed that we could only learn from other human beings; this is another effect of the thoroughgoing spiritualism of the culture and theology. If we look, we can learn from animals that we are physical, natural, and bodily determined. We may learn to enjoy, to celebrate our bodily selves, our health, our physicality with animals. Or even to recognize our feelings as *morally significant and educative.* (I think of what seems like the almost natural curiosity, sympathy, and compassion of human children for animals.) We may even learn to trust our selves.

Finally, we are different from our relatives. Both individual human beings and animals share the majority of their traits with others, but each individual and species has its own integrity and relative independence. We each have our own niche in the biotic pyramid but are not totally defined, as individuals, by that niche or function. We have distinctive cultures and ways of being the creatures we are. We each have value both in the functions we play in the ecosphere and also beyond those functions. This value derives, for the Christian, from the source of all value, who in creating the world assigned each species its own goodness and value. Each being and species continues to have its own beauty, a shadow of the divine beauty.

My assessment of the kinship relationship is obviously positive. Yet I see one or two possible weaknesses. First we can overstate the degree of kinship similarity. Insofar as we know, the fact that men and women are subject to God and morally accountable to each other and the rest of creation is a characteristic not shared by animals. There are differences, as the stranger relationship made evident. A second potential weakness derives from a romantic view of the kinship relationship. That image suggests that all are equal in a family, that relations are never conflictual or hostile, and that everyone loves everyone else. However, characterization of kinship here is intended to deflate this romantic notion. By contrast my experience is that kinship stimulates our capacity for sin and altruism, vice *and* virtue. Kin depend on each other; that means their relationship can be life-enhancing or frustrating. We are stuck with each other, for better or worse. How much better or how much worse is at least partly in human hands.

The Question of Right Relations with Animals

We are now confronted with the question of right relations between human beings and animals: How can we articulate those relations normatively? One of the most important norms bearing on the question of treatment is that it be appropriate to the nature of the relationship.

Clearly part of my motivation in describing the relationship has been the question of right relations. Rather than reiterate positions articulated by other essays in this book (see especially those by Frears and Comstock), I will build on the perspective offered here. Specifically, in the space remaining to me, I will address the question: If we understand the relationship between humankind and animals to be that of kinship, what ethics best expresses the way we should treat animals?

As one way of beginning to think about that question, let us examine two systems of ethics briefly. One is the prominent "animal rights" school; the other is a considerably more loosely defined Christian communitarian ethic.

Animal Rights

The approach to right relations which invokes animal rights is, at best, inappropriate. It operates on the basic perspective of seeing animals as strangers, and short-circuits its own manifest intent to encourage humane treatment for animals. It basically undermines relationality. Further, the Enlightenment legacy which stands behind the language of rights also contributed to the spiritualism which often has the effect of reducing beings to only one of their dimensions.

This is evident in the criteria of "shared sentience" which animal rights theorists use to argue against the mistreatment of animals on the basis that animals and humans share an ability to feel pain. At first, that foundation of "shared sentience" seems to suggest that we are not strangers, after all. However, in locating this as the significant feature animals share with us, the larger message seems to be that we *are* essentially strangers — except in this respect. The effort to *extend rights* to animals, associated with the implied reduction of similarity to sentience, reinforces the notion that animals are strangers (essentially unlike us; therefore, the need to "extend" rights). A shorthand encapsulation of my point can be achieved if you ask yourself: Do we talk about extending rights to friends and relatives? Or to those who are unlike us in significant ways?

Karen Warren and Jim Cheney have helped me place my discomfort with rights language. Their claim is that rights grow out of relationships. Thus, the language of rights is a shorthand that too often loses the relational context out of which it grew. So, Karen Warren:

> Jim Cheney would claim that our fundamental relationships to one another as moral agents are not as moral agents to rights holders, and that whatever rights a person properly may be said to have are relationally defined rights, not rights possessed by atomistic individuals conceived as Robinson Crusoes who do not exist essentially in relation to others. On this view, even rights talk itself is properly conceived as growing out of a relational ethic, not vice versa.[16]

The language of rights grows out of liberal social philosophy which maintains that society rests on a social contract. This underestimates the way in which we humans are relational to the core of our being. Besides that, it vastly exaggerates human freedom and choice. Worse yet, social contract theory is both spiritualistic and humanocentric. It fails to take animals into account at all in its rendering of the relationships from which rights are derived.

In defense of rights language, it does seem necessary in those situations in which basic human regard for the other has been grievously violated. Rights tend to get expressed in law, and there is a genuine place in law to establish minimum standards of right conduct among equals. The realization of rights also depends on being capable of claiming those rights.

Unfortunately, animals cannot claim rights. Like other aspects of the environment upon which we depend for life, and which depends on us for its life, animals and we live in a symbiotic kinship relationship. We are interdependent, just as the members of a family are. And just as the litigation appropriate to rights language would undercut the bonds of kinship, so the language of rights obscures and undermines the deeper and more fragile familial relationship we humans (and animals) require to survive and flourish.

Elizabeth Wolgast, in *The Grammar of Justice*, demonstrates how the language of rights emerges from an atomistic view of society.[17] Rights are asserted *over against* the other; claiming them requires an individual assertion, a separation *from* the other. This individualistic perspective is precisely the problem in our consumerist culture which fails to take seriously the very physical bonds that unite us. Wolgast considers the case of child abuse, a case analogous to the mistreatment of animals. "The difficulty," she writes, "is with the strategy of putting rights in the hands of dependent children, rights they must exercise if they can against *those on whom they depend*."[18] The rights model is that of two independent and equal peers entering a voluntary contractual agreement. The model is not helpful in dealing with child abuse or animal abuse.[19]

Rights language has a useful and legitimate place. This is not that place. Rights always rest on and grow out of relationships. Their invocation in the case of the treatment of animals does not do justice to our kinship with animals; it reinforces spiritualistic separation of the mental from the physical; and it winds up undercutting precisely the relationality of kinship. When this narrow theory is applied to the environment, it is particularly disastrous in its consequences.

A Christian Communitarian Ethic

Rights language cannot capture the Christian vision of living in response to the grace of God. The relationship out of which rights language develops suggests that we humans *deserve* consideration from God for what we are or do. Rather, Christians affirm that our value comes as a gift from God; any graciousness we might have is the result of God's creating goodness. Thus rights language can be seen, at best, as the political minimum owed by some *persons* to *other persons* in voluntary contractual relationships — the very lowest secular common denominator of gracious love.

A Christian communitarian ethic is built precisely on relationality which takes the health and well-being of the whole to be primary to the health and well-being of its component parts. It is the whole biotic community that is primary. Obviously traditional Christian commitments — creation, incarnation, blessing, the presence of God throughout the cosmos — have undergirded this essay throughout. Let me, however, be explicit in enunciating Christian moral benchmarks.

My wager is that the major resistance to adopting a kinship model of the animal-human relationship is the centuries-old learning that the physical just cannot be the bearer of the spiritual. We don't trust our feelings, even though we do reflect on them. *If we could accept our physical kinship with all other beings — plants, animals, human, then we could perceive that what unites us outweighs what divides us.* The need to differentiate ourselves as ontologically superior rather than interdependent arises out of some hubris, some sense that we really are not at home in this world. It rises out of an insecurity, an anxiety about the trustworthiness, the goodness of life. For Christians, this bespeaks a lack of faith in God's grace and providence. *In order to overcome this spiritualistic separation of body from mind (which some have called "angelism"), a communitarian ethic needs to return to the doctrine of creation.* Such a return would indicate our physical and mental similarity with the rest of the good created order. It would establish on biblical and traditional theological grounds the source of all things in God and God's continuing creation and care for all of the created order. A very helpful emphasis in regard to the question of right relations is God's continuing presence throughout the world—of animals as of humankind. This bespeaks God's delight in the animal world and the place which all elements of the world have in working together—the divine ecology. It is also God who blesses the animal cosmos and will redeem it along with humankind. We as human beings have the eco-niche of being able to relate to the world in the way God relates to it—at least our relating *should* imitate God's insofar as possible.

Two other images become prominent in this ethic. One is *the notion of covenant; the model of covenant most relevant here is the Noachic.* (See also the McDaniel essay in this volume.) The covenant that God made with Noah (Genesis 9:8-17) is also made "with every living creature that is with you, the birds, the cattle, and every beast of the earth." It is significant that God chooses to enter into relationship with humankind *and* with animals *totally on God's own initiative.* Nothing is asked in return. This is no contractual relationship with certain rights and responsibilities specified and consequences enumerated.

The covenant is helpfully understood in continuity with creation and redemption. God creates out of God's good pleasure, out of the desire to enter into relationship. Similarly covenant is in continuity with redemption where God chooses to save all beings out of a love for us all which remains finally mysterious. The terms of the Noahic covenant reveal that it is a promise of caring relationship between God, persons, and all living creatures. It is also very concrete and material; Christian theologians understand the necessity of being concrete and material when speaking of creation. If we were to "despiritualize" covenant and redemption, what might that mean? It would imply at least that the physicality of the incarnation be taken seriously as well as the whole material world; it would also render "salvation" an immediate and not only future concern.

Just as covenant is not only in continuity with the kinship model but also indicates the source of that kinship, so the second image reinforces the kinship between animals and humankind: the parenthood of God.

Incorporating the kinship view of the human-animal relationship in the wider communitarian framework, we begin to glimpse an image of this planet as our home. Our animate brothers and sisters—animals and plants—enjoy life in interaction with our place. They support life in our neighborhoods, and we support their life as well—or fail to. Through their functioning—giving milk or eggs, inhaling carbon dioxide and exhaling oxygen—our lives are enabled. The kinship relationship suggests a reciprocity rather than a competition. To this Christian faith adds the capstone: God is Parent to this family. This home is one where God governs through the healthy interaction of Her children. Apparently God will not intervene when the children begin to abuse their home and, indeed, their family to their own and its own ill health.

What this image reveals is that competition is not the basic social dynamic of the environment. It is part of spiritualist hierarchialism to introduce bifurcation or dichotomy as the basic frame for rational thought and competition as the basic social dynamic into our reflection on the environment. If this is our home, then measuring costs and benefits is not the basic moral logic. Rather, it is a concern for the health of all the creatures belonging to a given place, from the creatures in the soil and water to the humans and other creatures of the land surface to the birds of the air.

Of course Christians affirm that God is Redeemer as well as Creator. The redemption is progressive and involves the interdependence of family working together to restore broken relations. We are thus enabled to see animals as our brothers and sisters rather than as commodities. That involves our own being liberated from seeing ourselves as consumers and machines. We cannot respect ourselves in fullness without respect for animals; we cannot know our full physical selves without animals.[20] Indeed, completed redemption will involve a great community of creatures who participate together in God's household. The recognition that we are family carries us one step in that direction.[21]

Notes

1. I recognize myself as what Jay McDaniel characterizes as a "land ethicist." That implies certain values: (1) a tendency to be oriented toward systems, rather than toward individual flora or fauna; (2) the extension of moral considerability to all beings in the biosphere; and (3) to have thought more about the health of the whole (the common good) than about the suffering of an individual or even species. See Jay McDaniel, "Land Ethics, Animal Rights, and Process Theology," *Process Studies* 17:2 (Summer 1988), pp. 88-94.

2. Underlying this exploration of relationships are the questions: What are animals to God? What is the relationship of God and animals? Here I clearly tip my Calvinist hand, and my adoration of St. Jonathan Edwards, but affirm as well the influence of my Roman Catholic wife and colleague, Patricia Beattie Jung.

Elements of the Roman Christian tradition which I find suggestive for environmental ethics are: a strong sacramental tradition; the blessing of animals and farms; and an elimination of the Protestant gulch between nature and grace.

3. Ruth Harrison, *Animal Machines* (London: Ballantine Books, 1964).

4. The Humane Farming Association, "Scrambled Priorities," *Watchdog*, Spring 1989, pp. 3-5.

5. Ibid., p. 4.

6. Let it be clear that the position taken here is that the physical is mental, natural, and spiritual, and that the mental is similarly inseparable. On this interpretation see my "Ethics, Agriculture, and the Material Universe," in *The Annual of the Society of Christian Ethics 1986* (Washington, D.C.: Georgetown University Press, 1987), pp. 219-250.

7. On this point see my "Feminism and Spatiality: The Recovery of a Hidden Dimension," *Journal of Feminist Studies in Religion* 4:1 (Spring 1988), pp. 55-71.

8. Karen J. Warren, "The Power and the Promise of Ecological Feminism," *Environmental Ethics* 12:2 (Summer 1990), pp. 125-146.

9. I have railed at length about this in "The Recovery of the Land: Agribusiness and Creation-Centered Stewardship," in Rowland A. Sherrill, ed., *Religion and the Life of the Nation: American Recoveries* (Urbana, Ill.: University of Illinois Press, 1990), pp. 109-127.

10. A. V. Krebs, *Heading Toward the Last Roundup: The Big Three's Prime Cut* (Des Moines: PrairieFire Rural Action, 1990). Cost is $6.50 from 550 11th Street, Des Moines, IA 50309.

11. Russell Baker, "We All Are Hostages to Oil Supply," *Des Moines Register,* August 24, 1990.

12. Charles Pinches made this very helpful observation.

13. Sallie McFague, *Models of God: Theology for an Ecological, Nuclear Age* (Philadelphia: Fortress Press, 1987), p. 162.

14. Ibid., pp. 175-178. This image of God as Friend is one of many nuances in McFague's thought and book. I find it helpful, among others.

15. At one point McFague writes that "the model of friend does not have a physical base, a base that provided the mother and lover models their power as well as their problematic features" (p. 159). It would be worthwhile exploring the claim that friendship does not have a physical base. I find some animals to be companionate when we are together and that physical presence carries significant value. I wonder as well whether the presence of God does not carry theological significance of a physical kind.

16. Warren, "The Power and the Promise," p. 141. See also Jim Cheney, "Eco-Feminism and Deep Ecology," *Environmental Ethics* 9:2 (Summer 1987), pp. 115-145.

17. Elizabeth H. Wolgast, *The Grammar of Justice* (Ithaca, N.Y.: Cornell University Press, 1987), especially Chapter 2.

18. Ibid., p. 37.

19. In some ways animals are dependent, nonvoluntary younger brothers and sisters to humans. In other ways they can be our wise parents.

20. I had hoped to develop this thought more completely. One line of that development would pick up on Emmanuel Levinas's analysis of the other person who is at once (and always) both "beggar" and "teacher" in relation to us. As beggar the other is subject to our acceptance and openness; we have the power to ignore the other or treat the other as kin. As teacher we are subject to the other; we have much to learn from the other about ourselves. That depends on the other's accepting us openly. I believe a similar sort of analysis can be mounted in regard to animals. In an earlier piece I made the point that, if Levinas's analysis is correct,

then one cannot have regard for the other without regard for the self. The reverse is also true. See my "Autonomy as Justice: Spatiality and the Revelation of Otherness," *The Journal of Religious Ethics* 14:1 (Spring 1986), pp. 157-183. Autonomy and justice may be co-implied.

Another line would explore the spatiality of both animals and humans. By developing a formulation of the embodied nature of human life, certain aspects of life come more into view: feelings, particularity, relatedness, limitation. Some of them also apply to animals. Because we are spatial beings, as are animals, we cannot escape the conclusion that we are coinhabitants whose very nature rests on relationality. This description, it could be argued, serves as an empirical underlining that points to God's intention that we all live in community.

21. Drawing out the moral implications of this vision of who animals are in relation to humankind is an important task that cannot be undertaken here. The *general* direction that moral guidelines would take can be inferred easily: humane treatment of animals; respect for the integrity of the physical being and cultural system of animals; little or no intervention in the cultures of wild animals; reduction or elimination of pets except as their own culture and well-being can be served; eating lower on the food chain (at least); and all else that respecting our home implies. The particular policy directives and decisions regarding each species (the bovine growth hormone debate, legislation regarding veal calves, etc.) have to be worked out within this framework.

The health of the land, crops, and wild species of flora are clearly interconnected with this moral vision and its ramifications. As the life-support system of both animals and humankind, plants provide the heating, cooling, feeding, air purification, and shelter-providing components of our home. Policies supporting their sustainability also sustain the whole family.

Chapter 5

A Trinitarian Theology of the "Chief End" of "All Flesh"

Stanley Hauerwas
and
John Berkman

This article[1] seeks to engage the issue of the relation between "the world of humans" and "the world of animals" in the most thoroughly theological manner possible. This task is admittedly both ambitious and fraught with difficulty, because there is painfully little precedent for this endeavor in most traditions of theological discourse. In approaching this subject, the main enemy is what we call the "theological mercenary," one who uses theology merely to confirm what many of us have already decided on other grounds. Our task, therefore, is to try to show what difference it might make when one strives to discuss the relation between humans and animals in a way that seeks to do justice to the integrity of theological discourse.

The article proceeds in four parts. The first section addresses four hazards in the path of this project, four possible detours which might prevent the reader from taking seriously this challenge to theologically rethink how Christians relate to other animals. The second section presents a Trinitarian interpretation of creation, showing why such an account is crucial for rightly seeing and living in relation to our fellow creatures. The third section makes suggestions about what is involved in living in the way of the Trinity. The fourth and final section posits vegetarianism as an eschatological act, and shows analogies between following the call of Jesus in not doing violence to other humans and not doing violence to the other animals.

Stanley Hauerwas is Professor of Theological Ethics at the Divinity School, Duke University. His most recent publication is *After Christendom* (Abingdon Press).
John Berkman is completing his Ph.D. in theology and ethics at Duke. His dissertation is on contemporary Roman Catholic moral theology.

I

The very phrase "the integrity of theological discourse" in the opening paragraph can be misleading, for it might indicate that this essay is simply trying to show how a belief system separated from concrete practices might influence how we think about the relationship between humans and other animals.[2] While there are, no doubt, valuable things to be learned from such a procedure, such an understanding of the discipline of theology is severely inadequate, for our practices in all their diversity — including our sinful ones — exercise coercive power over us with regard to our ability to think about these matters. This is the first hazard that needs to be flagged.

For instance, this paper is written by one person who eats animals and one who does not. That may sound like an irrelevant biographical detail, but we are convinced of its deep significance. For our practices, more than our arguments, reveal and shape what is truly important to us.

Hauerwas has argued this same point in the past with regard to pacifism,[3] that our theological commitments are distorted insofar as our lives are not shaped nonviolently. Thus, Christian pacifism is not the result of our holding certain beliefs, nor is pacifism even so much what it might mean to know these beliefs truthfully. Rather, living as a pacifist is in a sense *the very condition for even knowing what we believe about pacifism*. Likewise, if Christians are to engage seriously with this issue, vegetarianism may well be a prerequisite.[4]

Acknowledging this first point, that our practices with regard to other animals shapes our beliefs about them, it is clear that the very consumption of animals by Christians has shaped and continues to shape how Christians have thought about them. Here lies a second hazard which threatens to derail our project — our latent anthropocentrism. Returning to the analogy with war, in the same way that our engagement in war encourages a form of patriotism or ethnocentrism which leads us to depersonalize the enemy by turning them into the "Other," that is, a "Gook" or "Hun" or "Madman," our eating of animals undoubtedly encourages a form of anthropocentrism. We find theological warrant for neither this patriotism nor this anthropocentrism.

It is very revealing that the most determinative attack on anthropocentrism in modern theology does not address theologically the issue of the relationship between humans and other animals. Given James Gustafson's general perspective in *Ethics from a Theocentric Perspective*, that is, that we are all ultimately doomed, one can conclude that neither human nor animal life has any special status vis-à-vis God.[5] To be sure, Gustafson's position is much more complex than is indicated here, but it is interesting that this supposedly quite extreme theocentric position ironically maintains a most basic form of anthropocentrism: in failing to address theologically the issue of the relation between animals and humans, it continues to assume that humankind has a special status vis-à-vis other animals.

Of course, this is but a way of developing the point with which the article began, that theology oftentimes ends up underwriting classifications that are not intrinsic to its own discourse.[6] Avoiding implicit anthropocentric assumptions is no easy task, as the authors found whenever they met to discuss what would go in this paper. For example, one issue that came up was whether we have a stake in the survival of particular species that might go out of existence if we stop eating and experimenting on animals.[7] One of us raised the question as to whether we should even have a stake in retaining the very notion of "species." Aristotle meant one thing by "species," medieval theologians meant quite another, and modern biologists mean still something else again. What reasons, if any, does Christian theology have for preferring one of these ways of classification over the others?

Put more radically, it is not clear that Christians have a stake in *any* kind of classification of ourselves vis-à-vis other creatures. That is not to say that there is anything wrong with such classifications in and of themselves, but it may also be the case that they represent interests that may be antithetical to the practices of Christians.[8] For example, such classifications might underwrite an anthropocentrism antithetical to the Christian conviction that God, not humanity, is the end of all creation. So one must investigate who is making these classifications and the reasons for which they are made.

Classification systems aside, we are suspicious of almost all purported theological justifications for distinguishing humans from other animals. Of course we as humans generally think of ourselves as "animals with a difference." Yet the account produced to elicit that difference makes all the difference in the world!

To put it most simply, this paper shall argue that the only significant theological difference between humans and animals lies in a unique *purpose* given to humans by God. Herein lies what it means for God to create humans in God's image. This *unique purpose* which God gives humans with regard to animals lies in our job of telling animals who they are. We do this by the very way we relate to other animals. We think there is an analogous relation between the fact that animals need humans to tell them their story and the fact that we who are Gentiles need Jews to tell us our story.

This account of what "image of God" means—that it involves solely a *unique purpose* which humans are given by God—is admittedly a minority viewpoint. The dominant view with regard to what constitutes the image of God is that it is some unique human capacity or ability, such as human rational ability. The presumption of this dominant view has been forcefully challenged by Millard Schumaker.[9] Schumaker argues that it owes far more to Cartesian presuppositions than to Christian theology.[10] Schumaker's attack on this presumption is surely accurate, as there is simply no good theological reason for claiming that what it means to be human is to possess some unique capacity which distinguishes humankind from that which is nonhuman.

The second part of this paper will develop this "purposive" understanding of image of God in a Trinitarian context. Indeed, it will try to show that the only reason for giving special attention to humankind is because Jesus is the second person of the Trinity, because salvation for all comes through one made human. In the same way that animals are privileged through One who became human, so we Gentiles are privileged through One who became a Jew. For Christians, the image of God cannot be understood apart from the image of Christ.

A prime reason why Christians have such difficulty with the question of what it means to live in the image of God lies in a failure to live our lives in the faith, hope and love of the Trinity. This is particularly true with regard to our inability to live our lives with a Trinitarian view of our history and of time, and thus of our inability to live in the light of our ultimate end, and to see animals in light of their ultimate end.

The emphasis on the Trinity in this paper should be understood as in opposition to much of contemporary theology which countenances an implicit Deism. By *implicit Deism,* we have in mind the view in which God is basically understood as first cause, which results in a faulty view that understands creation solely in terms of the accounts of Genesis 1 and 2. This error is further exacerbated by reading the Genesis 1 and 2 accounts as being the creation of a world which is more or less the same as the world in which we presently dwell. Ironically, it is only from within a Trinitarian context that the anthropocentrism so characteristic of our lives can be challenged. For this reason, we will devote the second part of our paper to putting in a Trinitarian context both the doctrine of creation and the concept of the image of God.

We are well aware of the ways in which our call for a serious theological consideration of these issues can be quite tiresome. Confronted by the horrors of our cruelty toward animals, we are tempted to use any arguments we can to stop it. This temptation is made even more enticing by the fact that our society gives theological language almost no status for operating in the realm of public discourse. At most, theological language is allowed credence for guiding people's so-called private lives, and more often than not it is thought to be pure mystification. Thus, we find ourselves sorely tempted to use a language that has greater currency in the marketplace of public discourse when addressing issues of public concern. At present, be the issue one of the homeless or homeowners, of minorities or majorities, of humans or animals, the language with by far the widest appeal is that of rights. Though this is not the appropriate context to critique the notion of rights in any fullscale manner, there are compelling reasons to avoid this language which require brief mention.

Our hunch is that the language of rights finds mass appeal in a society where individuals can no longer sustain their civic order on the basis of shared ends and purposes. The very notion of inalienable rights is the product of individuals who no longer trust their lives to the hands of those they live with, and who thus seek to protect themselves through having "trumps" against the actions of their neighbors. There are, of course, other accounts of rights besides this rather individualistic one,[11] but this account is still quite prevalent. Moreover, we also understand the appeal of universal, inalienable rights, as they seem so humane and enlightened when compared with particularistic and retrograde moral traditions, such as those itself associated with Judaism and Christianity!

Ironically, though, this use of the language of rights embodies the very anthropocentrism that is antithetical to the goals of those who participate in the movement known as "Animal Rights." For the language of rights, when understood as inalienable rather than as correlative of social duties, presupposes that those who are candidates for these inalienable rights are agents with the kind of rationality that is generally ascribed only to humans, and thus this view of rights is inextricably bound up with the Cartesian perspective we criticized earlier. Thus, on this view of rights, animals only have rights as a reflection of human interest. This very notion of rights presupposes a world at war with itself, which is exactly antithetical to Christian convictions about God's good end for creation.[12]

The situation is not significantly different if we understand rights on a contractarian view of human society. Humans come together and agree that they have certain rights that cannot be overridden. This conception of rights also seems to preclude the possibility of the participation of animals in the social contract, except as a reflection of the interests of particular humans. As any rights theorist knows, having an interest is very different from having a right.

From this all-too-brief discussion, we conclude that to ascribe rights to an animal may in the short run be a strategy for its survival, but in the long run this language will simply maintain the current understandings of and practices in relation to other animals that continually bring about their destruction. Our reasoning is as follows.

First, we have already noted our suspicions about whether we live in a society that is able to sustain — either conceptually or practically — the language of rights. Our society at present shows its inability to sustain the language of rights by the way it overrides so-called rights whenever it has a compelling interest. If this is the situation with human rights, how successful will it be to appeal to animal rights? To give animals rights is to radically broaden the traditional uses of the term *rights* into an almost all-encompassing term. If our society is unable to sustain the concept of human rights, what chance is there that it will be able to sustain this radical redefinition of rights? From a purely pragmatic viewpoint, rather than having to struggle against a society that is for the most part unwilling to see the language of rights used in the way animal rights activists would like, animal rights people would be better off coming up with a new concept. Our suspicion is that many animal-rights activists, like many human-rights activists, don't really know what they are advocating when calling for rights, besides saying there are certain things we really, really don't want to be seen done to humans or animals, and the way we prevent these horrible things is to say humans or animals have a right to protection from these horrible things.

We think that Christians have far richer resources by which to address the question of how we should relate to other animals. Any appeal to rights pales in relation to the peace and love of Christ to which the Christian is called. Thus, while we do not wish to argue for animal rights, neither do we wish to argue for human rights. Andrew Linzey is quite correct when he argues against those who favor human rights but not animal rights and claims that "the most consistent position is that . . . of Christians who *consistently* refrain from all such [rights] language."[13] However, Linzey then errs when he assumes that "It is *inevitable*, however, that 'rights' language *should* have an appeal to Christians."[14] The appeal of the language of rights to the Christian community only becomes inevitable when the community can no longer articulate and sustain its own particular Christian convictions about human relations with other animals. Contra Linzey, there simply are no good *theological* reasons why rights language should appeal to Christians. It will be the task of the second part of the paper to develop this alternative theological account.

The final hazard—one relating to our earlier remark about the power our sinful practices exert over us—is our fear of criticizing our most impressive institutions. This is particularly the case when we realize that what we think of as our most humane institutions—the medical profession, those dedicated to the development of food for the hungry—have routinized this cruelty toward animals. However, we take these horrible truths to be, as much as anything else, reminders that good and humane people are capable of doing terrible things, as we Gentiles well know from our actions in the Holocaust.

II

We have outlined only briefly what we take to be some of the major obstacles to even raising questions about the relationship between humans and other animals. The first section has challenged the presumption that the issue should be posed in terms of questions such as "How should we treat animals?" or "Do animals have rights?" Instead, the place to begin is with God's creation of the world.

Of course, the notion of creation is not self-explanatory. In much of the literature devoted to questions concerning how Christians conceive of the environment and animals, the term *creation* too easily becomes synonymous with "nature" and why nature is important. On such an account, the affirmation of creation becomes simply an affirmation of a kind of nature romanticism.

Though we stand in awe of our so-called natural world, we certainly do not intend to stand for this kind of romanticism.[15] We discussed earlier how the language of inalienable rights presupposes a world at war with itself, a view which is antithetical to the Christian understanding of creation.[16] However, our opponents may rightfully argue that the natural world is also at war with itself. We are acutely aware that animals still eat animals, even under the best of conditions. We cannot avoid the fact that hawks eat rabbits, lions eat gazelles and cats eat mice. If necessary, we human animals eat all of them.

The tragedy of the natural world being at war with itself inevitably leads to "survival of the fittest" conclusions, unless we realize that the words *nature* and *creation* are not referring to the same world. Those who believe that nature and creation are synonymous often buy into an implicit Deism. This quasi-Deist view (which sometimes also goes under the name Theism) believes that God functions primarily as "the first cause of it all" and thus presumes that nature is coextensive with what Christians mean by creation.

This implicit Deism fails on two counts. First, it fails to recognize that the world created in the Genesis accounts is radically different from our present natural world, and thus ignores the significance of the Fall for an account of our present tragedy. Even more significantly, this implicit Deism is oblivious to the fact that Christian convictions about creation correlate to christological and eschatological (i.e., Trinitarian) convictions. On our Trinitarian view, nature must be understood as "creation in bondage."

The Westminster Catechism begins by asking us "What is the chief end of man?" This question—a question concerning the ultimate end for life— is the one with which Christians must begin, if we are to understand ourselves and other animals. So, minus the sexism and anthropocentrism of the original question, let us begin by discussing the chief end for all God's creation.

We have criticized the view that understands nature and creation as coextensive and its attendant survivalist ethic. This survivalist ethic is frequently underwritten by theologians, not only on the issue of human relations with animals, but also in debates concerning nuclear weapons.[17] It is particularly important that the position being argued for in this section be distinguished from this survivalist ethic, because Christians simply do not have an overriding stake in the survival of the earth or our own survival. As God's creatures, our chief end is not to survive, but to be capable of serving one another, and in doing so serve as signs of the kingdom of God. In comparison to this service, survival is a secondary commitment.

Thus, we must not allow the Christian doctrine of creation to function as an apology for a survivalist ethic. In the end, this ethic requires us to sacrifice not only many fellow human beings to guarantee human survival, but also any other animal that may possibly help guarantee human survival.

We oppose this survivalist ethic because we believe that the Christian affirmation that we are God's creatures means that neither our lives nor the lives of other animals are at our disposal. This Christian affirmation requires a very different attitude toward the world.

These kinds of reflections are intended to help make clear that the doctrine of creation is by no means self-explanatory. The survivalist ethic just discussed is what one gets when one is without a theologically disciplined account of creation. When the exponent of this survivalist ethic understands God fundamentally as first cause, creation begins to be thought of as the way Christians, and perhaps other religious people, explain the fact that the world had to have a beginning. On this view, creation comes to look like an explanation rather than a confession.

In Christian theology, the last thing creation does is to serve as an explanation. Rather, creation is a christological and an eschatological affirmation that derives from the Christian confession that the God who has discovered us in Jesus of Nazareth, the God who intends for us to share in God's peaceable kingdom, is a saving God from the beginning. Christians do not believe that the notion of God as creator is conceptually self-sufficient, to which one then has the option—if one so chooses—of specifying further the nature of God in terms of Jesus of Nazareth. Rather, creation is part of a narrative of fulfillment. From our conviction that God redeems all of creation we learn that God, having created all things, wills that all things enjoy their status as God's creatures.

As for how Scripture is thus to be read, this means that a Christian understanding of creation cannot be guided first and foremost by Genesis 1 and 2. These passages must be read in the light of our redemption in Christ and our end in the kingdom of God, to which we are guided by the Holy Spirit. More specifically, we cannot understand creation solely in terms of Genesis 1:31—"Behold, it was very good"—but must read this passage in conjunction with Romans 8:19-21 and Isaiah 11, that the original creation must be understood in relation to the present bondage of creation and of the dawning eschatology of the new creation.

In light of the scriptural witness that humans and other animals share in the ultimate end, which is God's peaceable kingdom, we thus believe that each and every creature is created to manifest God's glory. Animals do not manifest God's glory insofar as their lives are measured in terms of human interests, but in terms of their end to manifest God's glory. As part of God's created order, humans live well as God's creatures when we see that animals exist not to serve us, but rather for God's good pleasure. We live well as creatures of God when we learn to see animals in like manner to how God sees animals.

To understand creation in this way decisively challenges many traditional theological efforts to make a sharp distinction between our status as humans and that of other animals. Too often the story of God's creation of humans in God's image has been read falsely as licensing humankind to dominate the animal world. Thus the language of dominion in Genesis 1:28 is used to justify human manipulation of the rest of God's creation for humanity's own ends, thereby underwriting the presumption that all the world is created for the flourishing of humankind.

However, as Schumaker makes clear, that sense of dominion cannot be justified theologically. At most, the concept of dominion can mean that God has chosen humanity to be an image of God's rule in the world. That God appoints humans rulers is not on account of any special trait intrinsic to human beings, but is rather simply on account of God's sovereign will — that humans are to act as God's deputies amidst God's good creation. In other words, the deputy status humans are given is not because we are rational and other animals are not, but simply because we are chosen for this task.[18]

Thus, following Schumaker, we must reconceive the image of God in terms of specific purposes that God assigns to humans, rather than to any metaphysical or morphological difference between humans and other animals. Specifically, we need to discover what it means for a human to be an image of God's *rule* in the world.

At this point, we realize that our understanding of how we are to rule over animals is directly connected with how we understand God to be ruling over us. If we are to throw off the view that dominion means domination over the other animals, we must turn to a Trinitarian understanding of what it means for us to be in the image of God.

The "image of God" of Genesis 1 cannot be read for Christians apart from what it means for us to be the "image of Christ." Ultimately, true likeness to God is not found in the image of God found in Genesis 1, nor even in our present striving to live in the image of Christ, but will only come at the end of time, when we shall see God face-to-face. Moltmann puts this point very well: "The restoration for new creation of the likeness to God comes about in the fellowship of believers with Christ: since [Christ] is the messianic *imago Dei*, believers become *imago Christi*, and through this enter upon the path which will make them *gloria Dei* on earth."[19]

Thus, our lives are to display this functional understanding of the image of God. In Genesis 1, the image of God is part of the vision of a peaceable creation, both between human and animal and between animal and animal, a peace where it is not necessary to sacrifice one for the other. Similarly, for us to live as the image of Christ means to live according to the call of the kingdom of God. In Gethsemane — in taking up the way of the Cross — Christ shows us clearly that the way of the kingdom of God is not the way of violence. Finally, the ultimate end of all our strivings, the peaceable kingdom of God, is where we shall finally live in true shalom with all creatures of God.

III

To see our place in the world in such a manner is to think of our lives in community with all flesh. The temptation of this line of thinking is to then think that what it means to be God's creature is to see ourselves in continuity with nature and the animals. The difficulty with putting the matter in this way is that it privileges the notion of nature and animals, on the assumption that we know how to distinguish between nature and animals on grounds separate from our knowledge of God. We are not denying that such classifications are possible, as they obviously exist all around us, and we constantly use them. Our challenge is to root out the origins of such classifications, to know why they are being produced and who is producing them.

We are aware that the claim that creation is a christological and eschatological affirmation will appear odd and probably unnecessary for consideration of the place of animals. However, we believe that it is extremely important, as can be illustrated by the very phrase "the place of animals." The new notion that we have a standpoint that requires us to determine a place for the animals already denotes a sense of power on the part of human agents, and a sense of separation between ourselves and our fellow creatures, that we think problematic.

To say that creation is an eschatological notion is to say that the universe is part of the drama that is not its own making. That is, creation is part of a story that we learn through being initiated into a community that has learned to live appropriately to that story. Since one cannot understand creation apart from initiation into such a story, we do not believe that creation is something that all people can affirm. Rather, it is a confession made by people called to be church in a world that does not know it is in fact creature.

Therefore, there can be no separation of creation from its ecclesial presumptions. The church's confession of God as creator is also a confession of God in Jesus Christ and the Holy Spirit; therefore, confession of the Trinity is necessary if Christians are to affirm that God is creator of all. Jesus is not simply the restorer of a lost creation known separately from Jesus himself, but rather in Jesus we discover the very nature of the created order. In short, in Christ we know that creation was not an act in and for itself, but for a purpose. That is what is meant by saying that God's creation of the world is an eschatological confession insofar as the original creation is aimed at a new creation, the creation of a community that glorifies God.

Thus, we believe the church is faithful when it lives out the fact that nature has a sacred element, not because we wish to uphold or preserve nature for its own sake, but because nature is creation in travail, and as such has its own end to glorify God, rather than to serve humans. Thus, we must strive to understand human and animal life in terms of our common end as life in the peaceable kingdom, the kingdom of God. In addition, we will strive to read Jesus' parables of the Kingdom as indications that our everyday actions can be signs of the kingdom — that our everyday acts may be signs of the power of Christ who will bring about the coming of the kingdom.

IV

If we have been right so far about the Trinitarian context of creation and of the church's participation in that, we think this puts the practical issues of Christians' relationship to the other animals in a different framework. In this respect, we think that there is a significant similarity between the issues of pacifism and vegetarianism. Just as we believe that Christians are not called to be nonviolent because nonviolence is a strategy to free the world from war, but because as Christians we cannot conceive of living other than nonviolently in a world of war, so it may also be true that Christians in a world of meat eaters are called to live nonviolently. Thus, the perspective we have presented that leads us toward vegetarianism cannot be the perspective of anyone, but rather it is the perspective that a peculiar people called church must embody in their relationship to other animals, given that Christians live in God's space and time. So Christian vegetarianism might be understood as a witness to the world that God's creation is not meant to be at war with itself. Such a witness does not entail romantic conceptions of nature or our fallen creation, but rather is an eschatological act, signifying that our lives are not captured by the old order.

Perhaps another way to put this is that those in the Christian community who would eat animals bear the burden of proof. This can be understood in much the same way that just-war reflection works in the Christian community. Just-war theory presupposes that nonviolence is the fundamental stance of Christians. This is because Christian just-war theory is most appropriately understood as a theory of exceptions, exceptions for allowing Christians to engage in limited forms of violence in order to protect the neighbor.[20] Analogously, we believe that Christians need to develop similar criteria of just meat eating, if it is not to be forbidden entirely.[21]

If any form of meat eating can be justified, we believe this must be understood as animals making a sacrifice for us that we might live, analogously to the way soldiers are seen to be making a sacrifice of their lives for their nation-state, empire or tribe. This is but a reminder that as Christians we cannot understand the story of our lives apart from the importance of sacrifice, because we believe God sacrificed his Son Jesus that we might live.

We are aware that the language of sacrifice is dangerous language, and we have no desire to underwrite the way this language of sacrifice has so often been used in the past and no doubt will continue to be used to justify all kinds of murderous deeds. However, Christians cannot give up the language of sacrifice if we are to be the kind of people that Jesus has made possible. After all, it is the great good news that in our eucharistic celebrations God has called us to walk in the way of the sacrifice of Jesus — the Way of the Cross and the Way of Resurrection Life — so that the world might know that we are meant to live at peace with God, with one another, and with the other animals. In this time between the times, the good news for the other animals is that Christians do not need to ask animals to be part of a sacrifice that has no purpose in God's kingdom.[22]

Notes

1. This article was originally presented at the conference "Good News for Animals? Contemporary Christian Approaches to Animal Well-Being" in Durham, N.C., on Oct. 5, 1990.

2. In writing this essay we have struggled with the very issue of how to describe the relationship between humans and animals. We soon found ourselves resisting phrases such as "our relationship with animals," because we found that this implicitly underwrites a cozy distance between humans and animals. We continue to struggle with the lack of a language to articulate better these relationships.

3. See Stanley Hauerwas, *The Peaceable Kingdom* (Notre Dame, Ind.: University of Notre Dame Press, 1983).

4. Can one seriously discuss these questions with someone who is in the midst of eating a hamburger? We take this to be a serious question.

5. See James Gustafson, *Ethics from a Theocentric Perspective* 2 vols. (Chicago: University of Chicago, 1981-84). Although Gustafson follows Midgely in arguing for an increased appreciation of the continuity between humans and other animals, there is no appeal to any traditional theological categories for understanding this relation. (See Gustafson vol. 1, *Theology and Ethics,* pp. 281-293).

6. As to the question of what constitutes theological discourse, no universal agreement is expected, but it would be a big improvement if we could get this to be an important issue!

7. If we do have a stake in their survival, it would be along the lines of an argument by James Rimbach, who argues that Noah takes all the kinds of animals into the Ark, even those that are unclean (which he says means unfit for human consumption) "to keep their kind alive upon the face of the earth" (Gen. 8:17). See James Rimbach, "All Creation Groans: Theology/Ecology in St. Paul," in Granberg-Michaelson, ed., *Ecology and Life* (Waco, Tex.: Word, 1988), pp. 161-177. We thank Oliver O'Donovan for bringing to our attention the question of whether Christians should have a stake in the survival of particular species.

8. For a powerful example of the way particular Enlightenment theories of biology and their attendant classifications have been used for wicked ends, see Cornel West, "A Genealogy of Modern Racism," *Prophesy Deliverance: An Afro-American Revolutionary Christianity* (New York: Westminster Press, 1982). West strongly argues that Enlightenment biologists, anthropologists and naturalists were primarily responsible for producing a new and peculiarly modern form of racism, where "racial differences are often grounded in nature, that is, ontology and later biology" (p. 64).

9. Millard Schumaker, *Appreciating Our Good Earth: Toward a Pertinent Theology of Nature* (Kingston, 1980).

10. Though some might accuse Aquinas and other medievals of holding a similar view with their discussion of "rational souls," we think that much more determinative for Aquinas's view is his definition that a human is "an animal that laughs." We do not think this is the kind of peculiar capacity that moderns have in mind when trying to distinguish humans from other animals.

11. See, for example, Robert Nozick, *Anarchy, State and Utopia* (New York: Basic Books, 1972).

12. This claim may be confusing to those who think of "creation" as synonymous with "nature," for it often appears that nature too is at war with itself. In the second part of the paper we will argue that "creation" must be understood as something both radically different and more widely encompassing than "nature."

13. Andrew Linzey, *Christianity and the Rights of Animals* (New York: Crossroad, 1987), p. 72.

14. Ibid.

15. As we will try to show, it is profoundly important that creation does not become just another way of praising the importance of "Mother Earth." Much has been written already about how we need to learn more from Native American attitudes about the earth, the sky, and the water. We admire much of what native peoples affirm about the nature of their world and how they should live in it, but we are not sure how, if at all, these insights are to be related to what should inform Christians on this matter.

16. For a massive critique of theories which assume an ontology of violence, see John Milbank, *Theology and Social Theory: Beyond Secular Reason* (Oxford: Blackwell, 1991).

17. For a defense of a "survivalist ethic" on the issue of nuclear weapons, see *In Defence of Creation: The Nuclear Crisis and a Just Peace,* The United Methodist Council of Bishops, Graded Press, 1986.

18. This functional understanding of the *imago Dei* is given a historical base by Schumaker. Schumaker argues, following Mendenhall, that the Genesis story is to be read as patterned after treaties of Mesopotamian feudal empires. According to such a reading, "Eden is to be considered as like a vassal state in the empire of the Great King, God: Adam is to be seen as ... a governor appointed by God to manage Eden." (Schumaker, *Appreciating Our Good Earth,* p. 12). Schumaker goes on to argue that this idea in itself is very difficult for us to accept, because we are suspicious of any kind of monarch or hierarchy, so that we cannot distinguish between the dominion of a monarch and the domination of a tyrant, or more basically, the leadership of anyone we have not elected. Christians too believe this when they forget that what they long for is the Kingdom of God, a kingdom of love and peace rather than one of tyranny and oppression.

19. Jürgen Moltmann, *God in Creation* (New York: Harper and Row, 1985), p. 226.

20. On this issue, we might ask how the possibility of human starvation might make a difference for how we understand our relation with other animals.

21. We also think it important to mention the significance of saying "grace" before meals, and the element of thanking God for the sacrifice animals make so we might eat them. We think this is one necessary, though certainly not sufficient, condition of our eating meat.

22. Thanks to Len Baglow, Gary Comstock and Brent Laytham for helpful criticism.

Chapter 6

A God Who Loves Animals and a Church That Does the Same

Jay B. McDaniel

Many Christians find themselves enriched by a sense of kinship with animals and the Earth, and yet unable to experience Christianity, at least in its institutional and doctrinal expressions, as supportive of such kinship. It is as if they live in two worlds: an "animal and Earth connected world" that is spiritually linked with fellow creatures and with the Earth, and a "Christian world" that highlights human-divine relations at the expense of animals and the Earth. Whereas the animal-and-Earth side of them seeks intimacy with the web of life and its nodes, the Christian side of them neglects or even discourages such intimacy.

Caught in a spiritual schizophrenia, these Christians develop a dissatisfaction with the Christianity they know. They come to realize, as scholarly studies have shown, that the dominant attitudes toward the Earth of Western Christian theology have been ambiguous at best, and that the dominant attitudes toward animals have been worse.[1] They come to recognize that the New Testament is bereft of any direct provisions for the human care of animals or the Earth.[2] They come to suspect that this lacuna in sensitivity may have something to do with a subordinationist mind-set that characterizes the very origins of Christianity: a "patriarchal" mind-set that subjugates women to men and, by a similar logic, the Earth and animals to humans (cf. Ruether 1975, 1983; Daly 1990).

For many, the dissatisfaction leads to an abandonment of Christianity. Some seek solace in other religions that seem more sensitive to the Earth and animals. They turn to Buddhism and Jainism, for example, with their

Jay B. McDaniel is Professor of Religion at Hendrix College, Conway, Arkansas. He is the author of *Of God and Pelicans* and *Earth, Sky, Gods, and Mortals*. He is editor of *Liberating Life* and *After Patriarchy*.

moral care for domesticated animals; or to Native American and other primal traditions, with their primal awe of wild animals. Others abandon everything associated with "religion" and devote themselves to the causes of environmentalism and animal rights. Both groups relinquish the Christianity they once embraced. Struck by Christian anthropocentrism, they see the alleged "good news" of Christianity as bad news for the Earth and animals.

Still others choose to remain in the Christian tradition, albeit with ambivalence. They stay for different reasons. Many appreciate the Christian faith's emphasis on compassion for humans, on community between humans, and on the special needs of the human oppressed. They may also have discovered that unique form of wholeness which Christians call "salvation," and which emerges when a person is deeply grasped by the overwhelming, unmerited love of God. But even if they are grasped by this love, "salvation" is not enough for them. There is another form of wholeness that they have partially tasted at various points in their lives and that they seek to taste further. This other form of wholeness might be called "community with creation." In their case it lies in being intimately connected with the rest of creation, with the Earth and with our closest kin, the animals. The Christianity they know simply does not meet this need. They seek a creation-inclusive Christianity.

The good news for them is that creation-inclusive theologies are now emerging in abundance. I use "creation inclusive" as shorthand for a host of late-twentieth-century theologies that describe themselves in different ways: theocentric, ecological, environmental, life-centered, ecofeminist, process, creation centered and otherwise. Today there are many types of creation-inclusive theologies that exist in healthy tension. Some are Protestant and some are Catholic; some are First World and some are Third World; some are evangelical and some are liberal; some are feminist and some are Orthodox; some are sacramental and some are mystical. Regardless of their orientations, they emphasize respect for life and environment as an integral feature of Christian life, and many try to understand Christianity in a more cosmic context, one that sees Christianity itself as a movement within the Earth's ongoing history. These theologians are not unlike the priestly authors of the creation story, who sought to understand the history of Israel in light of the creation of the cosmos. Nor are they unlike Irenaeus, the later Augustine, Francis, and Aquinas, all of whom sought to understand the history of Christianity in a context more cosmological and less anthropocentric than modern Western Christianity.

This essay deals with that dimension of a creation-inclusive Christianity which is sensitive to animals. I focus on animals because, in the development of many creation-inclusive theologies to date, animals have often been ignored. Like some environmentalists, many creation-inclusive theologians have been neglectful of concerns for animal protection.[3] Even as these theologians rightly lament industrial civilization's unparalleled assault on the Earth's life-support systems, they often fail to realize that the costs of global warming, of our chemical poisoning of land and water, and of the destruction of rain forests are greatest for wild animals. This is to talk about life-support systems but neglect the nonhuman lives those systems support. And even as they rightly critique the Western approach to creation as mere "commodity" and "resource," they too often remain silent on the plight of the billions of "commodities" who are reared and slaughtered for food, cruelly tested for cosmetics and household products, brutalized in rodeos and bullfights, casually dispatched in science classrooms, and slaughtered for fashion. This is to emphasize the web of life but neglect the nodes in the web. Such creation-inclusive theologies are too abstract, too aesthetic, too preoccupied with the big picture. They neglect the moral claim of the individual animal with his or her numinous eyes. What is needed is an ecologically sensitive Christianity that respects eyes as well as rainforests.

An ecologically sensitive Christianity that respects eyes might be called a "life centered" version of creation-inclusive theology. At least this is the phrase that I have used in another context (McDaniel 1989). I use the term life centered to name an alternative to that human centeredness which has characterized so much modern Christian thinking. As I think of it, life centeredness is not an alternative to theocentrism; rather it is a specific way of being theocentric. To be centered in life is not to worship life at the expense of God, but rather to be interested in the well-being of life along with God. My proposal, to be amplified later in this essay, is that the very God in whom Christians trust is interested in the well-being of each and every life. A God of this sort is life centered. We are faithful to this God by being similarly centered.

The very emergence of a life-centered Christianity in our time depends on an honest recognition of just how far many of us in urban, industrial Christian churches are from community with animals. Only as we acknowledge that distance can we repent, or turn around, and begin to find that community with the Earth and animals toward which, as I will argue subsequently, the covenantal God beckons. Thus I begin the essay, in the first section called "Howling Wolves," with an anecdote that illustrates my own recognition both of the need to commune with animals and of contemporary Western Christianity's alienation from animals. In so doing I hope you, the reader, will compare your own experience of the Christian faith to mine, discerning for yourself whether the faith as you have experienced it is open to communion with animals.

The subsequent two sections of the essay might be collectively called "Divine Dreams." In these sections I develop two ideas which I believe those of us in Christian communities might internalize in the context of local congregations if we are to overcome our alienation from animals and thus become more life centered. The first is the idea of a God who enters into covenant, and thus into community, with animals, and who dreams that we might do the same. The second is that of a Christian community, a church, that lives in fidelity to the divine dream.

Howling Wolves

Prior to that cool summer's evening in 1989, I had not often howled with wolves. There were about a hundred of us, invited as friends of a nonprofit environmental organization to enjoy a musical concert deep within rural Arkansas. Our ranks included biologists and sociologists, business people and social workers, housewives and househusbands, government workers and musicians, teachers and farmers. All of us were interested and involved in environmental concerns. We were sitting in the presence of the master howler, jazz musician Paul Winter, and his invitation to "have a good howl" had a strange appeal. After all, we were not in a concert hall in the middle of a city, where animals are rarely seen much less heard. Rather we were at a rustic conference center in the foothills of the Ozark Mountains, guests to countless plants and animals, wolves included, who surrounded us in the dark.[4] The moon was full, and the lights in the auditorium had been dimmed. We could barely make out one another's silhouettes in the moonlight. Winter was inviting us to enter into community with our lupine cousins.

Some of us were already acquainted with Paul Winter through his records. We knew that he was artist in residence at the Cathedral of St. John the Divine in New York and that he had created a kind of "earth jazz" that combines the music of whales, eagles, wolves, insects, rivers, and oceans with ethnic, folk, and classical melodies. A few of us in the audience had even heard the particular piece in the middle of which — during a period of silence — Winter wanted us to howl.[5] We had heard "Wolf Eyes," a haunting record which starts with a recording of a lone wolf howling and then answers the wolf's call with an extended soprano saxophone melody, surrounded by piano and strings. From liner notes on one of his albums, we even knew the background of "Wolf Eyes." We knew that Winter had himself gone to a research center in California's Sierra Nevada Mountains in 1975, played his saxophone to captive wolves, and discovered that they howled back answers.

Still, even those of us who had heard "Wolf Eyes" had only *listened* to it. Unlike the wolves in the Sierra Nevada Mountains, we had never howled back. This was not the kind of thing we did in public, in private, or, as I will note shortly, in church. Winter wanted us to *become* wolves in our imagination, communally and as a religious rite. Thus, on that summer's night in 1989, with Winter's gentle urging, we howled. For three or four minutes, we "became wolves" in our imaginations and joined the ranks of the people all over the world, and even at the United Nations, who have "had a good howl" at a Paul Winter concert.

Of course, in the first few seconds of our own three-minute experience with howling, many of us were embarrassed. We were not sure we wanted to become "animals." Most of us hoped the person sitting next to us could not actually hear us howl. But after a few seconds, as occurs in singing a good hymn in church, the self-consciousness ceased, and the joy of howling took over. The howling became a kind of chant that emerged from our mouths and throats naturally. It was freeing to howl, almost like singing *Amazing Grace* in Protestant worship service. Howling for us became an ecological version of a Gregorian chant, a wolf mantra.

Postconcert Reflections

Our postconcert reflections helped us understand what had happened. As we talked about it afterwards, we recognized that several things had been going on as we howled. On the one hand, howling had enabled us to affirm our solidarity with *wolves*, who once ranged over most of North America, but who, since European settlement, have been systematically exterminated until the early 1970s. On the other hand, we realized that the howling also enabled us to affirm something else, what one person called "a collective archetype: The Animal." This was not the animal that Western civilization had taught us to suppress, the animal that is "mere brute." Rather it was the animal that our distant human ancestors, the paleolithic peoples, seem to have respected for tens of thousands of years; and perhaps that the contemporary heirs of oral, nature-centered traditions respect still today. It was the animal that is part of our archetypal subconscious; that is mysterious and beautiful and awesome in its presence; and that links us to the rest of life. For a brief moment, we urban dwellers "civilized" by Western civilization had a living totem.

What struck so many of us was how "spiritually important" it had been to affirm the animal. We recognized that urban dwellers such as ourselves, generally cut off from wilderness and wild animals, have a deep spiritual need to feel connected with animals and the Earth. Winter's music had enabled us to feel that connection. We further realized how empty our lives are without those connections, and how inadequate those religions are that fail to encourage such connections.

A biologist among us put it this way. She said that howling enabled us to recognize and even celebrate our kinship with animals, and that the experience had meant so much to us because, save with our relationships to companion animals, we are rarely able to do this in urban, industrial societies. "After all," she said, "the wolves *are* our evolutionary cousins. Our roots and theirs go back to a common origin in the oceans, and to the first terrestrial mammals that evolved from them. What's more, we have parallel paths of evolution. Our ancestors on both sides evolved as highly social creatures capable of remarkable forms of coordination and cooperation. It is no accident that dogs, heirs of the wolves, can be our 'best friends.' Howling has been our way of recognizing long-lost cousins."

This remark stimulated an exchange with a sociologist. He pointed out that the origins we share with wolves must be weighed against cultural influences, and that the latter are deeply influential in our psyches and in our spiritualities. He remarked that we were separated from wolves by a long series of cultural phases which we, and not the wolves, had undergone: an age of gathering and hunting, an age of agriculture, an age of classical civilizations, and, most recently, an age of science and technology. For good and ill, he said, these ages are our legacy. They are "who we are" as cultural beings. "As we arrived at the concert tonight," he said, "we brought along memories wolves can never understand."

"But we also brought our bodies," said the biologist. Her point was that our bodies are forms of memory in their own right, and that, bodily speaking, we have much more in common with animals than we recognize. "Our bodies, too," she continued, "are part of the legacy we inherit, and they carry within the accumulated wisdom of the very origins of life and of the universe." At birth and throughout our lives, she continued, our bodies give us knowledge that was learned long before we were born, knowledge we share with wolves and other animals. "Just as we inherit ways of feeling from our cultures," she said, "we also inherit ways of feeling from our bodies." We asked for examples and she was quick to list some: "the urge to eat, to play, to explore, to procreate, to mate, to take care of our young, to express approval and disapproval, to vocalize."

Moreover, she added, bodies are vessels of *tradition*. "We normally think of traditions as advanced by creeds, codes, cults, and stories," she said, "but they can also be advanced by plasma and genes." No less than cultural artifacts, she said, our bodies tell a story and participate in a story, that of the history of creation. In so doing they, no less than art and literature, transmit information and wisdom from one generation to the next. "Our wolf mantra," she said, "was a celebration of a common tradition, a shared past, a mutual story."

I realized as she talked that the "story" of which she was speaking was "the new story of creation" told by Thomas Berry, Catholic theologian and author of *Dream of the Earth*. Here was no biologist captivated by the mechanistic perspective that assumes evolution is only the blind activity of matter in motion. Here was a biologist who thought the whole process had an inward dimension in which we and animals share.

Enter Christianity

A few of us at the concert were Christian. We stayed after the postconcert reflections to have further discussions. The entire experience, the howling and the postconcert discussion, gave us pause for reflection. We wondered if Christianity was one of those religions that could encourage a sense of kinship with animals and the Earth.

On the one hand, we acknowledged that the experience of howling was as spiritually meaningful for us as it was for any of the non-Christians in our midst. We, no less than others at the concert, had been healed through a recovery of connections with animals. Some of us felt that divine grace was present in the healing. On the other hand, we could not easily assimilate this kind of bonding with Christianity as we knew it. We associated Christianity with the Bible and sermons and the church, with interhuman relations and community, with God and forgiveness. But we could not feel Christianity as a religion that encouraged howling with wolves, sensitivity to the animal archetype, or a deep sense of kinship with animals.

One among us, a Southern Baptist, put the issue this way. "Why do so many of us in North American Christianity lack the capacity to howl, to experience solidarity with the animal world? Why do our worship services occur inside rather than outside, with the voices of creation — except our own — blocked out? And given that they do occur inside, why do we never hear recordings of wolves and oceans and insects? And why do we not howl, or chirp, or whinny in choral response? Why do we laugh, or snicker, at the very thought of it? What has happened that we are so out of touch with our paleolithic roots, our evolutionary heritage, our primal roots?"

"You would think," he continued, "that an incarnational faith — a faith that celebrates the word becoming flesh — would find itself at home in the 'tradition of the body' and in the world of enfleshed creatures. But it does not. At least not in my church. It is not that we are unable to enjoy the sounds of the Earth and animals. But even when we do so, we do so through the lens of a dualistic theology that we have imbibed from our churches: a theology in which human beings are seen as one kind of reality, and the Earth and animals quite another. When we listen to the Earth and animals through this dualistic theological filter, we do not really hear the sounds of creation in their numinous quality. We hear the sounds of the Earth as if these sounds were only background for human activity, as if the Earth itself were but a theatre for human action. And we hear the songs of animals as if these songs emanated from alien creatures, as if animals themselves were of a biological order different from us and inferior to us. We hear the songs from a perspective that is alienated from animals."

I found myself that night nodding in assent with the Southern Baptist. As a United Methodist, my tradition, too, has been alienated from animals. I suspect that this alienation is characteristic of many urban industrial Christians: Protestant, Catholic, Orthodox, or Independent.

The alienation has been a loss for animals and for Christians. Animals have suffered because Christians have been silent and often accomplices to their abuse. Today this abuse takes two forms: (1) the violent manipulation of individual animals in science, sport, recreational hunting, trapping, and, not least, in commercial livestock operations, and (2) the massive disruption and destruction of habitats for wild animals. Christians have suffered because they, like other humans, need to be bonded with animals for the fullness of life. Indeed I submit that community with animals is a dream for which the God yearns. In the sections that follow I will elaborate upon this suggestion. First, however, a word about the word *animal.*

Heretofore I have been using the word *animal* in an unscientific and yet self-consciously biblical way. In the natural sciences the word refers to any living being that is not a plant. It refers to invertebrates as well as vertebrates, single-celled organisms as well as multicelled organisms. Paramecia are animals no less than ducks, amoebae no less than wolves. This is a legitimate way to use the word in certain contexts. Here *animals* refers to all members of what is traditionally called "the animal kingdom," or what I will call "the animal realm."

But in truth the word *animal,* like most other words, has different meanings in different contexts. I have been using the word to refer to those in the animal realm who are *most like us* both genetically and psychologically. This is how the Bible most often uses the word, and it is also the way in which animal rights advocates often use the word. In *The Case for Animal Rights,* for example, Tom Regan uses the word *animals* to name mammals over one year of age. For Regan, as for biblical authors, *animals* are those creatures in the animal realm who share with us not only the gift of life, but very *kind* of life that we know best: a life of feeling and awareness, of eros and the will to live, of social relations and play, of frustrated aims and suffering. *Animals* thus understood, are wolves and rabbits, cattle and pigs, cows and porpoises, dogs and cats: fellow beings endowed with what the Bible calls "the breath of life."

How, then, can those of us in Christian communities better appreciate these, our closest nonhuman kin? I believe we can take steps in the right direction by doing two things concurrently. The first is to think more deeply about God's relationship to creation, and the second is to think more deeply about the local congregation's relationship to creation. In the section that follows I focus on God, and in the final section I turn to the local congregation.

A God in Community with Animals

Let me divide my own proposals concerning God into three reflections. In the first I offer a distinctively "Christian" way of thinking about God that stresses the boundlessness of divine love, the luring character of divine influence, and the opportunity, on the part of Christians, to share in divine dreams. In the second I situate this way of thinking about God in terms of a creation-inclusive reading of the biblical story.[6] And in the third I offer an interpretation of the idea, found in Genesis, that God enters into covenant with animals.

First Reflection: Thoughts on a Distinctively "Christian" Understanding of God

In this reflection I do not pretend to offer *the* distinctively Christian understanding of God. No doubt there are many ways of thinking about

God that are "distinctively" Christian in that they emerge out of specific, though not necessarily unique, themes from the Christian heritage. What I will indicate is one way of thinking about God that is distinctively Christian in this sense and that has particular promise for helping Christians overcome alienation from animals and the Earth.

Let me also repudiate any pretense to an absolute knowledge of God. Most of us, save a few fortunate mystics, lack such knowledge. By virtue of socialization, bodily wisdom, or divine inspiration, we may feel that we are surrounded by an ultimate Mystery, that this Mystery is awesome and beautiful and terrifying, and perhaps even that this Mystery is trustworthy. We may hope, even trust, that the Mystery was revealed decisively in Jesus Christ. But if we are honest we also realize that the Mystery eludes our conceptual grasp and that we may be utterly wrong in what we say or feel about the Mystery. If we study other world religions and their history, we further realize that the Mystery has been, and can be, envisioned in many different ways, many of which diverge markedly from Christian-shaped intuitions. We realize that, as Christians, we live out of images and stories concerning the divine Mystery that we inherit from our traditions, and that we may well be wrong. Even the word *Mystery* has a Christian slant to it. I borrow it from the Catholic theologian John Haught (1986), who borrowed it from Karl Rahner. I use the word to remind myself that the word *God* rightly names something which eludes conceptual mastery and theological proclamation.

The texts from which Christians derive many if not most of our images of the Mystery are found in the Bible. Here I am thinking of the Bible not as a rule book or an inerrant authority, but rather as literature: as a rich, multifaceted anthology of writings written over many centuries by many people with many different interests. This anthology does not contain a single, self-consistent understanding of the Mystery, but rather myriad images. One cannot extract a single "theology of God" from the Bible. Nor, if we are faithful to the story-telling manner of so much biblical writing, ought we try to do so.

Nevertheless, most of us recognize that there is a dominant image of the Mystery in the Bible. It is that of a powerful male ruler presiding over his creation much as a king presides over subjects. Today many feminist and ecologically sensitive Christians are critical of this monarchical way of imaging the Mystery. They argue that exclusively male and monarchical conceptualities of deity wrongly legitimate the subjugation of women and others symbolically associated with women, such as animals and the Earth. Creation-inclusive feminists such as Rosemary Radford Ruether and Sallie McFague insist that, if male images are used in the future, these images must be complemented by radically alternative images, both female and organic, in order to offset the idolatry of rendering unto God that which belongs to Caesar. Those of us wishing to overcome alienation from animals can join them in this proposal.

But we can also join them in retaining the biblical view that the Mystery is in some sense a cosmic Thou, a subject rather than an object. If, as I have proposed elsewhere (McDaniel 1989, 76-79; 1990, 86-93) along with other process theologians, the universe itself is alive in its very depths, then it is plausible to imagine the Mystery within and beyond those depths not as lacking interiority altogether, but rather as possessing interiority, thou-ness, to an unlimited degree. It makes sense to imagine the Mystery not as less living, but rather as more living, than anything else we know.

The question then becomes: How shall we imagine the personality, the character, of this Life in whom we live and move and have our being? And here, of course, the Bible offers still further possibilities. God can be var-iously imaged as caring, wrathful, vengeful, compassionate, uncertain, faith-ful, repentant, jealous, vain, overwhelming, and tender. Because not all the images can be held together with ease, Christians inevitably select some among these images as central to "the Christian witness," interpreting the others in their light. One traditional approach, which those of us wishing to overcome alienation from animals share, is to take mercy and compassion as central. This is to take the spirit of Jesus' own life as an indication of what God is like; to risk believing that the Mystery is Jesus-like. Those who take this approach believe that, whatever else the Mystery is, it is inex-haustibly merciful and compassionate; it is Emmanuel, God-with-us. This claim, or more realistically, this hope, is the beginning of a distinctively Christian understanding of God.

The historic peace churches develop the proposal still further. Noting that Jesus was himself nonviolent, they suggest that, if God is Jesus-like, then God, too, must be nonviolent. In light of the history of religion—with all its images of a God of violence and power, or vengeance and blood-lust—this is a remarkable claim indeed. It is to suggest that the Mystery at the heart of the universe works through invitation rather than coercion, through the cross rather than the sword. This, too, I believe, is a feature of a distinctively Christian understanding of God.

But what can it truly mean to say that God acts through nonviolence? How might we humans actually feel the presence of a noncoercing God? In various other writings I have argued that, as individuals and as com-munities, we feel the presence of this God as an ever-present, ever-adap-tive, ever-changing, and yet ever-faithful Lure toward the fullness of life, toward *shalom*, relative to situations at hand. Here, as readers may well recognize, I am quite influenced by process theology. In much the same way that Quakers speak of an inner light within each of us, process thinkers speak of an inner Lure within each of us: a Lure that is within us and yet more than us and beyond us. Even as this divine presence is within human life, so process thinkers suggest, it is also in creation. Indeed, the Lure of God is within animals as well as people, being that motivating power in them by which they, in their own ways, are inspired toward their own forms of life's fullness. And the Lure of God is in the cosmos as well, influential in cosmic and biological evolution as well as in the particularities of life on Earth. It is that by which the universe as we know it was called into existence out of a primal chaos. As process thinkers understand it, the Lure has its origins in the Mystery itself and it is an aspect of the Mystery. It is the very reality whom Christians name "the Holy Spirit" and which, according to Genesis, was "moving over the face of the waters" on the first day of creation.

If, as process thinkers suggest, the Lure of God is always toward the fullness of life, the peace churches show that, in human life, the "fullness" toward which God calls is itself nonviolent. We are called by the very Heart of the universe to be gentle and caring in relation to one another, to be as forgiving and merciful, given our limitations, as is God. This special calling does not mean that we transcend creation or that we ourselves have not evolved. It does not mean that we are excluded from the animal realm. Rather it means that, over tens of billions of years of cosmic evolution, certain creatures have evolved on our planet who can mirror God's own love for creatures on our planet, and thus help realize a divine dream. We are those creatures. Though our four-legged relatives may not be able to live in full peace with one another or with us, we humans are "made in God's image." As empowered by God's Spirit, we can live in peace with one another and with them.

Clearly the peace churches have not generally recognized that peace extends to animals and the Earth as well as to humans. I will suggest shortly that the biblical story supports this claim. For now, however, let us note that other religions — particularly Jainism in India and certain forms of Buddhism — have been more open to this dimension of the Spirit's call than historical Christianity. Many Christians such as those I described in the introduction to this essay find themselves wishing that "being a Christian" could be a little more like "being a Buddhist" or "being a Jain." They recognize that the very God in whom they believe, a God who calls toward the fullness of life, has been present in other traditions as well as in Christianity; that a "distinctively" Christian understanding of God need not limit God's influence to historical Christianity. The people I described in opening this essay rightly sense that there are dreams and possibilities of the Spirit, at least partially realized in other religions, that are as yet unrealized by the church.

I have been using the words *dreams* and *possibilities* in order to offer still one more way of arriving at a distinctively Christian understanding of God. As individuals and as communities, we do not experience the Lure of the Spirit within our lives as a well-formulated creed or easily grasped concept. Rather we experience it as something we feel much more deeply at a prereflective, intuitive and imaginative level. It is a beckoning presence, a pull from ahead rather than a push from behind. As Walter Brueggemann points out in *The Prophetic Imagination* (1978), most of the biblical prophets — Moses, Isaiah, Jeremiah, and Jesus are his examples — seemed to experience God *through* imaginatively apprehended possibilities: possibilities that challenged the *status quo*, that were genuinely new relative to their historical situations, and that pointed to a still more shalom-filled way of dwelling in the world. Thomas Berry, one of the most visionary creation-inclusive theologians of our time and well-known author of *Dreams of the Earth*, might recast Brueggemann's point to say that God influences us through ever-adaptive and yet ever-faithful "dreams" relevant to the situation at hand. Berry would add that the Earth itself, understood as a subject in its own right, is a stimulus to our awareness of some of these divine dreams, and indeed that the Earth shares in these dreams. In feeling the callings of the Earth within our own lives, he says, we feel the numinous presence of the Divine.

Whether or not Berry is right that the Earth is a subject in its own right, I believe he is correct in saying that the Spirit of the Divine consists of dimly discerned, imaginatively apprehended dreams. These are dreams that belong to the Mystery itself, but which we may take as our own as well. At best, our dreams overlap with the Mystery's dreams such that "the will of God is done on earth as it is in heaven." We share and participate in the divine imagination. At worst, our dreams are mere projections of private interest, and we miss divine dreams altogether. We sin, oftentimes disastrously. Our very failure to live in community with the Earth and animals is an instance of such sin. The salvation emphasized by evangelical Christians lies in the fact that, quite undeservedly, we are forgiven.

For Christians seeking to overcome alienation from animals, then, I suggest that our first step is to think "Christianly" about God. This is to believe in a divine Mystery (1) who is Jesus-like, and hence with us in our trials and tribulations; (2) who is effective in our lives, and in the lives of other living beings as well, as an inwardly felt Lure toward the fullness of life; (3) who has beckoned the entire universe into existence through the very Lure we experience within ourselves; (4) who now beckons us, creatures made in God's image, to share in a dream for peace on earth; and (5) who, quite remarkably and on human standards unjustifiably, forgives us of our sins. As Christians we have no certainty that we are correct in viewing God this way. Amid what can often appear to be evidence to the contrary, we place our trust in a Mystery who is merciful and compassionate without limit, boundlessly loving.

Second Reflection: Understanding a God of Boundless Love in Light of a Creation-Inclusive Reading of the Biblical Story

The second step in overcoming our alienation from animals, at least insofar as this overcoming involves thinking about God, is to link the distinctively Christian understanding of God offered above with a creation-inclusive reading of the biblical story. In so doing, we realize that the love of God includes animals in a way rarely realized in more anthropocentric understandings of the biblical witness.

The point is made logically by Schubert Ogden: "Because God's love is subject to no bounds and excludes nothing from its embrace, there is no creature's interest that is not also God's interest and, therefore, necessarily included in the redeeming love of God" (quoted in Birch 1990, epigraph). If there is *no* creature's interest that is not also God's interest, then the interests of the battery hen are God's interests, the interests of the slain deer are God's interests, the interests of the AIDS-infected chimp are God's interests, the interests of the caged tiger are God's interests; the interests of the howling wolf are God's interests. The very Lure of God for well-being, the very Dreams of the Mystery for life's fullness, are present in some way in *these* creatures, relative to their lights, just as they are also present in us relative to our lights. God is with them just as God is with us.

In the context of most local congregations, however, such musing will be seen by many as mere flights of abstract philosophy, lest the musings be understood as in some way continuous with a significant strand of the biblical heritage. Thus the second step is to show that the imaginative amplification of the notion of an all-loving God offered above has its precedence in the Bible.

The aspect of the biblical heritage which I find most helpful is the notion of *covenant*, specifically the notion in Genesis that God has made a covenant with animals and with the Earth. But for this notion to have credibility, it must itself be understood in the broader context of one or another version of "the biblical story." Cognizant that the Bible itself is an anthology of diverse writings, the biblical story is best understood not as an indubitable narrative extracted from the texts, but rather as a narrative woven from the texts by contemporary interpreters who are, at best, guided by the Spirit. The texts are the threads, and the interpreters do the weaving, cognizant that no final version of the story is ever told and that various versions are imaginable. How, then, might the biblical story be woven in our time?

For many generations in the West, the biblical story has been woven in human-centered terms, as if it pertained only to human salvation alone. The dominant themes have been human sinfulness, human dominion over the Earth, and human redemption. But increasingly Christians are learning to read the Bible in another less-anthropocentric way, one that some biblical scholars argue is more faithful to the various texts, and one that, in any event, is more promising for Christians concerned with animals.

To be sure, the biblical texts are not unambiguous in their treatment of animals and the Earth. They generally image human beings as superior in value to the Earth and animals; they sometimes sanction practices we no longer deem desirable, such as the sacrifice of animals; and, in certain strands of the New Testament, they sometimes promote an otherworldly spirituality that seems to "leave the Earth behind" in a quest for spiritual ascent. Even as creation-inclusive theologies learn from the Bible, they must avoid the kind of biblicism that absolutizes all biblical points of view.

Still, many biblical writings are more creation inclusive than modern Western theology. This is particularly true of Hebrew Scripture. Though the New Testament has resources for ecological sensitivity and animal protection, Hebrew Scriptures are much more resourceful for ecological perspectives than is much of the New Testament. The reasons for this are manifold. John Austin Baker, the Anglican Bishop of Salisbury, includes the following: (1) the New Testament was written over a much shorter period of time (fifty years) than Hebrew Scripture (nine centuries), with much less opportunity on the part of the authors to develop the kinds of "general observations on life and the world-order" that are found in Hebrew Scripture; (2) the New Testament was written by urban peoples and directed to urban audiences who were not as close to their agricultural roots as were many authors of Hebrew Scripture; (3) many authors of New Testament documents expected the imminent end of the world, in which case speculations concerning nature were not that relevant; (4) many New Testament authors generally failed to draw upon ecological insights from Hebrew Scripture, since they approached the latter with the exclusive aim of showing that it pointed to Jesus. Baker puts it this way: "In seeking for any kind of theology of humanity and nature, the Christian cannot but be grateful that his or her Bible does not consist merely of the New Testament." A creation-inclusive reading of the biblical story needs to find its roots in Hebrew Scripture and then recognize, as are many today, that the New Testament is best understood by Christians as an addendum to, rather than a replacement of, Jewish insights. As appropriated by Christians, the stories of the New Testament are a way for Gentiles to be engrafted into a relationship with the God of Judaism.

What, then, does a creation-inclusive reading of the biblical story look like? Much work has now been done by biblical scholars in this regard (cf Anderson 1984a, 1984b, 1984c; Brueggemann 1976). I offer one illustration: a report produced by an ecumenical team of theologians brought together by the World Council of Churches to help the council interpret its own theme of "Justice, Peace, and Integrity of Creation." The team gathered in Annecy, France, in 1989, and consisted of approximately fifteen theologians from different parts of the world. The report is called "Liberating Life: A Report to the World Council of Churches" and appears in this book. It is instructive both because it contains the strongest statement to date by a Christian ecumenical body in support of animal well-being, to which I will allude in my subsequent discussions of church practice, but also because, in this context, it illustrates in broad strokes one way of telling the biblical story in a creation-inclusive way.

If we are to read the biblical story in a creation-inclusive way, so "Liberating Life" advises, we must take quite seriously the fact that the early chapters of Genesis position the very origins of human life in a cosmic context.

> Before and apart from the creation of human beings, God sees that
> the animals are good. When humanity is added the creation as a whole
> is very good. The command to human beings to be fruitful and to
> multiply does not nullify the identical command to animals. The image
> of God with its associated dominion is not for exploitation of animals
> but for responsible care. The plants that are good in themselves are
> given to both animals and human beings for their food. (Birch 1990)

This state of affairs was the original "integrity of creation."

Christians need not believe that such a state of affairs ever existed as
historical fact. A better option is to view this integrity of creation as a
dream of God, dimly discerned by biblical authors through the guidance of
the Spirit. Perhaps it is a dream from which creation itself has consistently
fallen short; hence the truth of a fallen creation. In any case it is a divine
dream, a divine hope. The first chapters of Genesis bespeak a primal yearning in the very heart of the Mystery, a yearning for a created order in which
humans live in harmony with the Earth *and with animals.*

It is strange that so little theological reflection has been given to the fact
that this primal dream of God involved a state of affairs in which human
beings were nonviolent in relation to animals. The primal dream seems to
have been for a vegetarian society, one in which humans would not kill
animals at all. As Genesis proceeds, we see that meat eating is sanctioned
by God only as a concession for human sin, not as something God ordained
at the outset. And indeed it was human sin, not the rest of creation, that
disrupted the primal integrity. Thus emerges what might be called the
interim period of creation: the period between the loss of the first dream
and the realization of the second.

In light of the fall, there emerges competition between pastoralists and
farmers.

> Injustice and strife proceed so far that God repents having created
> the world. Nevertheless God saves the Noah family from the deluge,
> and at God's command this human family exercises its rightful domin-
> ion in saving all the animals from a watery death. (Birch 1990)

It is noteworthy that dominion, rightly understood, is an act of kindly
stewardship, not exploitation. Noah exercises dominion by saving creatures
who, according to the first creation story, God hopes will "be fruitful and
multiply."

After the species are saved, a remarkable happening occurs. God makes
a covenant, not only with Noah and his family, but also *with the animals.*
This is the first explicit reference to covenant in the Bible. The text reads:
"I establish a covenant with you ... also with every living creature ... the
birds, the cattle, and every beast of the earth." The promise is reiterated
five times in the ninth chapter of Genesis. It is also described by God as a

covenant "between me and the earth" (Genesis 9:13). Even here, even in light of the fall and the subsequent strife between herders and farmers, the yearning of God for an integral creation could not be suppressed. It seems that God will not stop dreaming.

After the covenant, the whole of creation praises God, as the Psalms witness, yet it also groans in travail as a consequence of the fall. There gradually emerges a reconstituted dream, a hope for universal salvation. The latter hope is described most poetically by Isaiah as a time when the wolf will lie with the lamb, the leopard with the kid, the child will not be harmed by the snake. In a Christian context, it is also described by Paul as a time when the whole of creation that is "groaning in travail" as a result of human sin will be redeemed in Christ. The second dream is not exactly a duplication of the first; it is not exactly a return to the primal integrity of creation. Too much has happened in the interim. But it is an image of integral creation nevertheless. In it, at least in the version described by Isaiah and intimated by Paul, humans will again live in harmony with the Earth and animals as well as one another. The Dreamer cannot be stopped.

For the Christian, the incarnation of God in Jesus Christ opens up this possibility of a new beginning, a re-presentation of the original dream in the form of the new dream, to which humans can once again respond. More specifically, the incarnation effects a new covenant, one that lives in the heart and in Christian community rather than in codes and creeds. Christians rightly understand this new covenant as their opportunity to be faithful to God, to be grafted onto the history of Israel, and to share in God's dream by bearing witness to God's peace. In light of the Noachic covenant, which could as easily be called the Animal covenant, this "living in peace here-and-now" includes peace with creation, animals included. Such dwelling is a foretaste of an ultimate peace for which all hearts yearn, and which is itself realized in the end, when God is all in all. Such, I submit, is a creation-inclusive understanding of the biblical witness.

Third Reflection: An Interpretation of God's Covenant with Animals

It is in light of this creation-inclusive way of weaving the biblical story that the divine covenant with animals invites interpretation. What can this story mean for our time? Lest we seek the lost ark, I suggest that we understand it as if it describes not a relationship with animals that God established after an historical fall, but rather a relationship with animals that has been part of the divine Heart ever since animals evolved into existence. This is to understand the story mythically rather than historically.

But the mythic reading can itself be understood in one of two ways. On the one hand, it can be understood to imply that the divine Heart is timeless, that nothing occurs in God in a temporal way, because God is outside time altogether. This is the way of classical theism. By this reading, God dwells in an eternal present in which what we call "the future" is just as actual, and just as near to God's consciousness, as what we call "the pres-

ent" and "the past." *Future, present,* and *past* are our own arbitrary designations for happenings that are "already actual" in the divine Mind. There
is no narrative or story in the divine life, no before and after, because that
life contains no sequences of events.

This kind of mythic reading would be quite distant from many biblical
authors, who imagined the Mystery itself as having a history of relations
with creation and with Israel. Moreover, it leaves out something that is
explicit in the story and that is quite important for Christians seeking to
overcome alienation from animals. This something is that God *chooses* to
enter into covenant with animals *after* having first recognized and empa-
thized with their plight.[7] Here is a God who is moved to pity by animals
and who seeks to enter into deeper relationships with them — into a covenant with them — in light of being so moved. Here is a God who is more
affectionate and more vulnerable than the timeless God of classical theism.

What is needed, then, is a mythic reading of the divine covenant with
animals that retains this element of feeling and temporal transition in the
divine. Toward this end we can imagine God's covenant with animals not
as something that occurs timelessly, but rather something that occurs at
each and every moment in each and every animal's life. At each moment
in an animal's life, so I propose, we can imagine the Mystery at the heart
of the universe feeling the feelings of the animal at issue and seeking, in
light of those feelings, the well-being of that animal. At least this is the way
of thinking about God that has characterized process theology. In the goal-
directed dimension of their experience, so process theologians suggest, our
closest nonhuman kin — fellow mammals with psyches not dissimilar from
our own — experience God's aim for their well-being in the form of an aim,
a physical purpose, for satisfaction relative to the situation at hand. They
do not experience this aim as the presence of "the Holy Spirit," but they
are empowered by it no less than we are empowered by our aims. The
Spirit works in them, as in us, at a level far deeper than words.

Put in more general terms, I suggest that we imagine divine covenant
with animals as divine *communion* with animals. This communion can itself
be understood in two ways: as divine empathy for animals in their life
situations, and as divine eros for their well-being. As empathy, divine communion with animals can be imagined as an act of sharing, on the part of
the Mystery itself, of the very interiority of the animal. As the animal feels,
so God feels. As eros, divine communion can be understood as a divine
Lure, within each animal, to enjoy that particular form of satisfaction or
well-being that is possible and appropriate for the animal in the situation
at hand. As Christians, we can believe in a God who enters into community,
or communion with animals.

The Church as a Creation-Inclusive Community

In light of a creation-inclusive reading of the biblical story, we can also
believe in a God who invites us to enter into community with animals and

with the rest of life. Both as individuals and as communities, this is (1) to make the divine communion that now occurs at each and every moment a visible reality on Earth, and (2) to display the reconstituted dream of God, which is for a state of affairs in which the fullness of life is realized for all creatures. The implications of this are radical for both our personal and communal life-styles. I shall spell some of them out in terms of what it might mean for a reconception of Christian community.[8]

We best begin by distinguishing a community from a society. Whereas the word *society* often connotes a social group held together by legal and contractual relations alone, the word *community* suggests something more intimate, a social group held together by a shared self-understanding. Understood in this non-normative way, communities can be Christian or non-Christian, and large or small. They may be neighborhoods, small towns, professional organizations, nations, and cultures, as well as religions.

It is important to recognize that communities as thus defined are not necessarily "good" by Christian standards. They can be hierarchical or democratic in their internal organization, and they can be harsh or generous with respect to outsiders. It is also important to recognize that they occur in degrees. There is no sharp line between a community and a society. When the bonds among members of a community become tenuous, when their shared self-understanding becomes peripheral to their lives, they become more like societies.

Christianity did not emerge as a single community. Rather it emerged as a complex of communities that competed with one another for adherents, with the victors becoming "orthodox" and the vanquished becoming "heretics." Whether or not the Holy Spirit was influential in this victory is difficult to say. What seems even more evident, however, is that it is not a community today. Few Christians in North America feel a sense of intimacy with their sisters and brothers in Asia, Africa, and Latin America the way, for example, Jews and Muslims feel such identity. For this reason, it seems most honest to use the word *church* to refer to local congregations. In any case it is now in the local congregation, not in global ecumenism, where there is the greatest opportunity for the development of distinctively Christian community.

What might such a community look like, if it took God's love for animals as well as the Earth seriously? Here we are dealing with ideals to be approximated rather than realities to be fully actualized. Let me first describe the ideal Christian church in a somewhat traditional anthropocentric way, and then show how some of this traditional way might be recast in a more creation-inclusive way.

The Ideal Christian Community as a Human Community

For many Christians, a Christian community involves more than mutual self-understanding. It is a community in which the very Spirit of God, as revealed in scripture and in Jesus Christ, guides peoples' lives, inspiring them to enter into intimate communion with one another and bear witness to the presence and reality of God. Much depends, of course, on how the presence and reality of God are understood. In light of the understanding of God suggested in the previous sections, a Christian community would be one in which people dwell in peace in relation to one another, responsive to a Holy Spirit who beckons them to peace. The peace at issue would not be the absence of violence alone, though it would certainly include that. It would also be the fullness of life, *shalom*. They would exercise influence in relation to one another through persuasion rather than force or coercion, and in so doing they would dwell in mutual care for one another.

In light of the discussions in the previous section, mutual care can be seen to involve an empathy and eros that mirror the empathy and eros of God. The empathy among members of the community would lie in the fact that they share in one another's life situations, be they joyful or sorrowful, just as God shares in their situations. And their eros would lie in the fact, not that they seek self-gratification through the use of one another — as the word *eros* can sometimes imply — but rather that they desire the well-being of each and every member of the local congregation for his or her own sake, just as God desires the well-being of each one of them and of the community as a whole. Much as Paul described a local congregation in 1 Corinthians, they would be like different parts of a single body that are "members of one another."

To be sure, some forms of mutual membership can be smothering rather than freeing. However, a God who works through persuasion rather than coercion is one who enjoys rather than disdains the creative self-expression of creatures. Indeed, if the presence of the divine Spirit is Jesus-like, then it can be understood as empowering people, particularly those who have been marginalized, *into* creative self-expression, into a realization that they, the least of these, are "somebodies" rather than "nobodies." A Christian community that bears witness to this God would be similarly empowering. The community as a whole would take responsibility for its members, such that they all would be recipients of care. But it would do so in a way that is releasing rather than enslaving. There would be extensive participation of the members in the decisions that affect their lives, so that each person feels heard and appreciated in his or her creative capacities; and there would be respect for the diverse gifts and talents of the members, such that each person feels free to be different even as he or she enjoys membership in the community. Thus the three prominent traits of a genuinely Christian community, I suggest, are (1) care of the whole community for each individual, (2) allowance for participation on the part of individual members, and (3) respect for differences.

Needless to say, many Christian churches in North America today are a long way from being the kinds of communities just described. The ideal is a long way from being approximated in most settings, because most North American churches have been coopted by habits of individualism and self-centeredness that make them either social clubs or self-righteous enclaves of "forgiven sinners." In neither instance are they particularly caring communities in which the Spirit of God pervades.

The Ideal Christian Community as Creation-Inclusive Community

Even if the ideal was realized, this ideal of Christian community would be inadequate to the God who makes covenant with animals and the Earth. It neglects the question of how a Christian community bears witness to God's love for creation. To remedy the oversight, however, nothing from the ideal needs to be subtracted. Rather the ideal itself—that of a community in which empathy and eros prevail—needs to be expanded to include the Earth and animals. There needs to be a shift from the church as a human community in which the Spirit of God pervades to that of the church as a creation-inclusive community in which that Spirit prevails.

To move in this direction, we need to rethink the notion of who actually belongs to a local congregation. Normally we think of the members of Christian congregations as humans alone. We may think of deceased people as members of the congregation, and perhaps even of unborn people as members, but always the members are "people." The church is a "people" of God.

There is something very abstract, very unbiological, about this way of thinking. If we eat animals, for example, they do indeed become part of us. When we arrive for worship, we bring them with us, albeit in decomposed fashion. How is it that we should think of them as "outside our communities" even when they are "inside our bodies." And even if we do not eat animals, our bodies are inseparable from the Earth. We eat plants; we drink water; we breathe oxygen. Atmospheric gases will pass in and out of our bodies continually. When we arrive for worship, the Earth, too, arrives, at least in the form of the material elements that compose our bodies and nourish our psyches. The idea that there can be a community that is *simply* human and excludes the Earth exemplifies an atomized and disembodied understanding of human existence. It is oddly nonincarnational, at least if *incarnation* means that God affirms our very flesh, our very bodies, as part of who and what we are. It forgets that we are ourselves dimensions of the Earth.

There can also be something morally problematic about thinking of community as "strictly" human. Unfortunately, even ostensibly Christian communities often limit their spheres of moral concern to members of the community. They take as morally relevant what lies within the community, and as morally expendable what lies outside it. The results of this in historical Christianity have often been disastrous, as far too many Jews, Muslims, witches, heretics, and animals can attest. With regard to animals and the Earth, only if the intimacy implied in Christian community is expanded in a way that includes animals and the Earth, rather than excluding them, can this moral callousness be avoided.

This expansion can occur by taking the theme of covenant more seriously. The church needs to imagine itself as a community which "bears witness" to the God who enters into community with animals and the Earth and who yearns for peaceful relations between people and other living beings. Practically speaking, this is to reconceive the local congregation as a mixed community that attempts to be a microcosm of that cosmic communion — that communion with animals, Earth, and people — which is the Mystery itself.

The Church as Mixed Community

A "mixed community" is a community which includes animals among its inhabitants. The animals may or may not be called members of the community; they are nevertheless parts of the larger family. Many of us live in mixed communities, though we may not recognize them as such. If we have pets who enrich our lives, or if we are farmers with warm bonds with our farm animals, we enjoy mixed community. We think of our animals as parts of the family, even if we think them less important than the human members. And even as we exercise dominion over them, we do so by providing them with modes of satisfaction not unlike those enjoyed by human members of a Christian community.

Recall, for example, the three features of Christian community noted above: participation, responsibility, and respect for differences. In families with pets and in small farms that treat animals humanely, animals are often treated in just these ways: (1) their biological and social needs are taken into account, such that they indirectly participate in many of the decisions that affect their lives; (2) the human members of the family assume responsibility for their well-being, such that they are cared for in times of sickness and health; (3) and their unique qualities are appreciated, such that their differences from the human members are felt, by the human members themselves, to be viable contributions to the community as a whole.[9] To begin understanding what it might be like to participate in a church that is a life-community, some of us can look at our own homes and farms.

We might also wish that early Christians had looked in similar directions. It is fascinating to imagine how Christianity might have evolved if, in its very beginnings, the local congregation was conceived as a mixed community rather than a human community. At least with regard to farms, the models were available. But Christianity seems to have developed its original understandings of community on more urban models. Even land, such an important theme in Hebraic understandings of community, is absent from most Christian conceptions of church.

Even if the original models had developed in a more inclusive way, however, it is important to recognize that mixed communities are themselves morally ambiguous. The very emergence of mixed communities in human history was fraught with possibilities for violence as well as gentleness, both of which have been realized, not least in situations with domestic pets and farm animals.

For the longest period of human history, the paleolithic period, no animals were domesticated save the dog. There were no livestock and no pets, no mixed communities as we know them. For good and for ill, such communities emerged with the domestication of animals in neolithic times. The "good" is that these communities brought with them the possibility of a kind of intimacy between humans and animals not known in paleolithic times. Mary Midgley speculates on the origins of such communities in the neolithic age, and in so doing points out this new form of goodness. She writes:

> The animals . . . became tame, not just through fear of violence, but because they were able to form individual bonds with those who tamed them by coming to understand the social signals addressed to them . . . They were able to do this, not only because the people taming them were social beings, but because they themselves were social as well.

Her point is that mixed communities, at best, involve a kind of trust between animals and people from which both benefit. Stated in Christian terms, they involve a covenantal relation between the two.

The "ill" mixed communities brought is twofold. First, the very rise of plow agriculture wreaked havoc, and still does so, on wild animals because it destroys their habitats. Agriculture may well be good news for humans, but generally speaking it has been bad news for wild animals. What is needed in our time is the emergence of a humane, sustainable agriculture that simultaneously recognizes the ecological price of agriculture itself and therefore seeks to preserve wilderness.

Second, the rise of plow agriculture also introduced the possibility of a new kind of attitude toward animals. With the development of plow agriculture in the neolithic age, so Rosemary Ruether observes, wild animals were not simply tamed, they were enslaved. They were "yoked and put to the plow, driven under the whip," such that they were "in a new relation to humans," both "enslaved and coerced for their labor." Animals, she suggests, were the first slaves.

As Christians reconceive local congregations as mixed communities, it is important that they seek to maximize the good and minimize the ill. The ideal is for communities that are humane in their treatment of animals under their direct dominion, such that the animals enjoy a trusting relationship with humans, and for local congregations that are sustainable in relationship to the Earth. The local congregation is best reconceived as a humane, sustainable mixed community.

With regard to the sustainable dimension of church community, there are a host of activities upon which churches can embark. The National

Council of Churches of Christ has listed "Fifty-Two Weeks of Congregational Activities to Save the Earth."[10] Churches can stop using throwaway items for food services at congregational functions, become a recycling center; host a farmers' market, carpool, identify toxic products used by the congregation and its members; include "environmental stewardship" in the stewardship campaign; grow gardens and plant trees on their grounds; take ecological concerns as topics for sermons; develop Earth-sensitive liturgies; worship out of doors wherever possible, and so forth. Sadly, most churches in North America have not even taken these steps.

Even more sadly, almost nothing has been done by North American churches to address the humane dimension of a sustainable church community. Little if any thought has been given to those, our closest nonhuman kin, with whom, according to Genesis, God lives in covenant. How *would* the people in a church understand animals if they sought to be humane? I begin with theoretical considerations and turn to the practical.

Should animals be considered card-carrying "members" of the community? Should they be baptized? I realize, of course, that many readers will consider these questions ridiculous. Such is the legacy of conceiving the church as a strictly human affair. Let me say at the outset, however, that I do not recommend animal baptism. But the very idea raises some important points about how Christians should think of animals in relation to the church.

Let us note that some Christians may indeed wish for animal baptism, and that their wish has a logic. Consider a blind person with a seeing-eye dog, or a church for blind people. The people in this church experience God's grace through dogs in a way that supersedes many of their relations to humans. The dogs come to the worship services; they walk their owners to communion; they stand by their owners at the after-service potluck. In many respects, the dogs are indeed members of the community.

Why not baptize them? Just as some congregations baptize retarded children into their communities, despite the fact that these children will never understand themselves as members or become "believers," one can imagine the members of the congregation wanting a ritual to recognize the value of dogs to the people in the community and to God, even though the dogs would never understand themselves as members or believers. It might even occur to the members of the church for the blind to create a baptismal service for dogs. "Canine Baptism" would be a sacrament in which the human members of the community would recognize that the animals will receive care by the community as a whole, that they will be respected in their unique qualities, and that their needs will be met in sickness and health.

If we recommend against such a ritual — and I do — it is instructive to ask ourselves why. Is it because we believe the dogs are too lowly to be baptized? If this is the case, it violates the notion that God loves them for their own sake. Is it because we believe they are too alien? If this is the case, it violates the notion that they are in fact our fellow creatures. What, after all, are the legitimate reasons for recommending against an inclusion of animals within the church? I suggest that there are two reasons.

First, there needs to be some way to recognize the special kinds of intimacy people can have with one another that they cannot have with animals, simply by virtue of the fact that animals are members of different species. A restriction of the word *member* to human beings helps recognize this difference. Second, it is important to appreciate animals in their differences from humans, precisely because they have forms of goodness and value that humans lack. The use of the word *member,* and all that is associated with it, can co-opt animals in ways that violate their integrity. Both for us and for them, I believe, we best not baptize them.

But one need not be a member of a community in order to be a respected inhabitant of a community. In arguing that animals ought to be included within the church, I mean that those who are under the *dominion* of the people in the church ought to be included as beloved inhabitants of the community, such that the community bears witness to God's love for them. They ought to receive the care worthy of an inhabitant within one's household, in this instance a "household of faith," and their own needs for participation, care, and respect ought to be accordingly recognized.

The problem lies in identifying the animals under dominion. In our time, they are not simply the pets or farm animals owned by church members, the animals with names. They are also the animals Christians eat; those whose skins form their clothes; those on whose eyes their cosmetics and household products have been tested; those whom their children dissect in science classrooms; and those who have been killed in experiments paid for by a Christian's tax money. The faces of these animals are never seen, but their lives are quite directly affected by Christian actions. The animals may never set foot on the grounds of the church building, but their lives are profoundly affected by the building's human inhabitants. How might these communities understand *them* as part of the extended church family, and thus bear witness to a God who has made covenant with *them*?

"Liberating Life" suggests at least the following three steps. Churches can encourage their members to:

Avoid cosmetics and household produces that have been cruelly tested on animals, buying cruelty free products instead.

Avoid clothing and other aspects of fashion that have a history of cruelty to animals, products of the fur industry in particular, purchasing instead products that are cruelty free.

Avoid patronizing forms of entertainment that treat animals as mere means to human ends, seeking instead benign forms of entertainment, ones that nurture a sense of the wonder of God's creation and reawaken that duty of conviviality we can discharge by living respectfully in community with all life, animals included. (Birch 1990)

At the same time, churches can make sure that the products they purchase as a congregation are cruelty free and Earth friendly. The latter helps the congregation preserve habitats for wild animals even as it recognizes particular responsibilities to domesticated animals.

Still there is the question of eating. "Liberating Life" recommends that congregations can "avoid meat and animal products that have been produced on factory farms," purchasing instead "meat and animal products from sources where animals have been treated with respect" or abstaining "from these products altogether," depending on the situation. In light of the reflections made above, however, I find it difficult to understand how meat eating, if avoidable, can be justified at all. *If*, as a creation-inclusive reading of the biblical story suggests, the dream of God is for a state of affairs in which people live in nonviolent relations with one another and with animals; *if*, as seems the case to me, the very taking of the life of an animal, even if reared humanely, is a violent act, given the animal's predisposition to live; and *if* the taking of such life is avoidable, it seems to me that it ought to be avoided. Thus, for those who are able, the Christian way to bear witness to God's love for animals is not to eat them.

However, I realize that few Christians will immediately abandon meat eating. Custom and palate exercise at least as much power as theological argumentation. They may also exercise as much power as the divine Spirit. Thus the alternative recommendation of "Liberating Life" is a good, albeit lamentable, second best. Local congregations that seek to bear witness to the divine covenant with animals can commit themselves to the purchasing of meat from farmers who have given the animals a good life prior to slaughter and who have made sure that the slaughtering itself is done as humanely as possible. This commitment might itself assist those small farmers who now have to compete with factory farms and who wish to exemplify in their farming practices a genuinely Christian commitment. Congregations that commit themselves to responsible forms of purchase can help animals and small farms flourish.

Worship and Prayer

Practices such as those just named, however, will emerge only if sensibilities are changed. I conclude this essay with remarks about singing hymns and prayer. These remarks take us full circle back to the evening in the Ozarks described in the introduction.

With regard to singing hymns in church, it is interesting that we rarely acknowledge that the entire act of vocalizing is something we share with animals, and that it is utterly dependent on plants from which we receive the oxygen to breathe, much less sing. Singing hymns, no less than anything else we do in worship, is an Earth-dependent and animal-connected act. Music itself has its origins in forms of vocalization that predate human origins and belong to our animal ancestors.

Is it not possible, then, for congregations to have times in their worship service in which they hear the songs of animals and the Earth as hymns in their own right, as music for God, and, following Paul Winter, to explore forms of music that integrate human and animal sounds into collective hymns? I believe that we Christians that night in the Ozarks were wrong to think that howling with wolves was an un-Christian thing to do. Rather it was our own attempt to mirror or internalize the divine empathy for wolves and to inwardly affirm the divine eros for their well-being, a making audible of the divine communion. My recommendation is not that Christian worship services include howling. Rather it is that they find ways appropriate to their traditions to begin to hear the sounds of animals and the Earth as expressions of a different kind of music, a different kind of hymn singing, and to learn in their own ways, albeit with initial awkwardness, to sing along.

Finally, a word about prayer. Of course, we must learn to pray *for* the Earth and animals, to pray that they may flourish as we also flourish. But we must also learn to pray *with* animals. By this I mean that we need to become sensitive to the ways in which, in their interiority, they already pray to the Mystery. Of course, they do not pray with words we understand; they pray with feelings. Their "petitionary" prayers are implicit in their aspirations to be satisfied, to be free of pain, to enjoy a realization of their creative potential. In them, as in us, the Spirit is indeed at work "with sighs too deep for words" (Romans 8:26). Their prayers of "praise" occur when they do in fact realize their potential, when they move about and play, when, on resting, they enjoy their own "sabbaths" (cf. Exodus 20:10; 23:12) amid a difficult life. My suggestion is not that these animals have the concept of prayer. Rather it is that we recognize that their internal lives and struggles are heard by God and indeed embraced by God in an act of divine communion. By learning to hear animals ourselves, imaginatively entering into their own points of view as best we can, we join them in prayer. Here as well, I think we were wrong that night to understand howling with wolves as un-Christian. In praying with them, we were enjoying an act of corporate prayer.

In conclusion, the need in our time is for Christian congregations that can open themselves to a Spirit who calls for deep, profound solidarity with a creation that now groans in travail. The Bible calls us to this with its notion of a God (1) whose original dream for creation was for integral, nonviolent community; (2) whose ultimate dream for creation is for a similar kind of community; and (3) who, in the interim, enters into community with animals and the rest of creation, inviting people to do the same. What is needed is a church that takes the Bible more seriously. What is needed are people who, in community worship and action, can share in the divine imagination and join God in a covenantal relationship with life.

Notes

1. One of the most balanced studies of the history of Western theological approaches to nature—though it excludes the mystical traditions or Celtic Chris-

tianity—is H. Paul Santmire's *The Travail of Nature: The Ambiguous Ecological Promise of Christian Theology* (1985). Santmire suggests that two motifs have woven their way through classical Western theology: (1) a "spiritual" motif, in which the end of human existence is thought to lie either in a transcendence of creation or, in modern times, a humanization of creation; and (2) an "ecological" motif in which the end is thought to lie in community with creation, appreciative of the Earth's blessings and cognizant that creation has value apart from its usefulness to humans. Representatives of the "spiritual" tradition include Origen, Thomas Aquinas, Bonaventure, Dante, Karl Barth, and Teilhard de Chardin.

Despite the fact that some of these authors recognized the glorious fecundity of creation, their appreciation was blunted by an overly "spiritual" conception of the end of human life. Origen, for example, "depicted the goal of all things as the return of the fallen rational spirits to perfect union with God," in which the rest of creation is left behind. Thomas, after having affirmed the goodness of creation in a way that Origen never did, "nevertheless asserted . . . that the end of the whole creation is chiefly the beatitude of the saints (and the angels) alone in heaven with God." Dante and Bonaventure recognized the fecundity of nature, but they viewed nature primarily as a "ladder to heaven" which was no longer needed once heaven was attained. And in modern times Karl Barth and Teilhard both saw humanity as the whole point of creation. "Nature for Barth . . . is a kind of divine afterthought that allows God's primary purpose—redemption of the eternally chosen ones—to be fulfilled." Nature for Teilhard is important as a stepping stone to humanity, but it is "finally a field of conquest, especially with the instruments of modern technology," and the conquest itself is part of a divine process to humanize the entire universe. In the end, for both Barth and Teilhard, nature is not redeemed for its own sake; it is used for humans' sake.

Representatives of the ecological motif include Irenaeus, the mature Augustine, Francis of Assisi, and, to a lesser degree, Luther and Calvin.

With his vision of a good creation that will be redeemed as a whole at the end of time, "Irenaeus celebrates the flesh in this world and in the life to come . . . Nature for him is tangibly good and ultimately significant." With the mature (not the early) Augustine, "all things, the creatures of nature as well as human creatures, have their own integrity, their own value, their own necessary place in the greater history of the created order." And in Francis, we find "the ecological promise of the classical Christian ethos." Even Luther and Calvin, not generally known for their sensitivity to nature, have promising aspects for Santmire. Both reject the "spiritual" motif of ascent to God; emphasizing instead that God "descends" into the world. At points both speak of grace through nature and solidarity with nature. But their general attitude toward nature is much more ambivalent than that of Irenaeus, the mature Augustine, and Francis. They see nature primarily as a means to human ends and a stimulus to the human reception of grace. Luther stresses that it is oftentimes a hostile stimulus. Moreover, both Luther and Calvin are so preoccupied with issues pertaining to human salvation, such that themes of grace through nature and solidarity with nature remain at the periphery of their thought. Compared to Irenaeus, the later Augustine, and Francis, they only partially embody the ecological motif.

After tracing the two motifs, Santmire observes that the anthropocentrism implicit in the spiritual motif was secularized in the modern era, fueled by the rise of modern science and the Industrial Revolution. He concludes that there is a profound "ambiguity" in Western Christian attitudes toward nature, and that the negative side of this ambiguity reached prominence in the modern period. Concerning animals, consider the dominant teachings of the Roman Catholic Church, which stem from Thomas Aquinas. Though his own perspective was much more appreciative of animal life than, for example, modern mechanistic orientations, he nevertheless claimed that we have no duties toward animals in and for themselves, since God gave us complete dominion over them. We should be kind to them only inasmuch as such kindness will spill over into our relations with one another. Cardinal Newman repeated the view by saying the least human advantage compensates for any animal loss or suffering. And in the late nineteenth century, when Pope Pius IX was asked if a Society for the Prevention of Cruelty to Animals might be established in Rome, he replied that "a society for such a purpose could not be sanctioned in Rome."

2. On this point and much else besides, I am indebted to George L. Frear's "Caring For Animals: Biblical Stimulus for Ethical Reflection," published in this volume. My own telling of "the biblical story" in this essay is influenced by Frear's careful study of biblical sources as well as by the report to the World Council of Churches mentioned in the text.

3. Fairly typical of this neglect is the well-known anthology of essays in creation-centered theology: *Cry of the Environment: Rebuilding the Christian Creation Tradition.* As far as I know, the first and only anthology to date to include animal concerns within the horizons of creation-inclusive theology is *Liberating Life* (Birch).

4. The center at issue is "Meadowcreek" in Fox, Arkansas.

5. For a catalogue of Winter's music, including "Wolf Eyes," write Living Music Records, Inc., P.O. Box 72, Litchfield, CT 06745.

6. My approach here is a "canonical" approach in that I take the entire canon as a complex anthology from which a "story" relevant to a people can be woven.

7. Their "plight" of course, was that many of their ancestors had been killed in the flood and that even they could suffer such a fate. The matter is complexified by the fact that God caused the original flood, which would suggest that God himself feels a tinge of remorse at having done what he had done. (This would not be the first time that God repents in a biblical story.) In any event, I do not recommend imagining God as once having sent a flood to eliminate all but a few animals. But I do recommend imagining God as one who is sensitive to the plight of individual creatures — nonhuman as well as human — and who responds to the plights in which they find themselves.

8. My own interest in community has been stimulated by the work of Stanley Hauerwas (1981) in one way and John Cobb in another. It has seemed to me that Hauerwas's emphasis on the church and community can enrich, and be enriched by, the interest of process theologians in creation-inclusive understandings of community.

9. In the case of farm animals, the participation of the animal in its destiny, and the responsibility of the community for the animal, is limited to rearing. The animals seem to have little voice in how they are transported and no voice in whether they are slaughtered.

10. Contact the Eco-Justice Working Group, National Council of Churches of Christ, 475 Riverside Drive, New York, NY 10115.

Part III

SHOULD CHRISTIANS EAT ANIMALS?

Three Arguments for Vegetarianism

In the past, only in relatively obscure corners of Christendom has vegetarianism been thought to follow from the Christian gospel. Lately, with the rise of the animal liberation movement, moral vegetarianism has received increased attention. How should Christians regard this growing concern? Irrespective of the traditional silence in Christianity on the issue, might it not be appropriate for Christian theology to develop such an emphasis, having learned from other sources about the moral difficulties of consuming animal flesh?

The three essays of Part III each argue for a moral vegetarianism, although the form of their arguments is quite different. Each essay displays more than a theoretical concern for animals, for vegetarianism is a practice, not a theory. Hence, this part of the book illustrates the practical repercussions which might in fact follow for Christians as they rethink questions regarding the moral treatment of animals.

Chapter 7

Pigs and Piety

A Theocentric Perspective on Food Animals

Gary L. Comstock

It is not by mere chance that Virtue ... dwells in greatest proportions
precisely upon that same span of soil where hogs thrive in greatest abun-
dance. In Iowa, where people ... read the Bible in the bathtub, there is
approximately a full litter of pigs ... for every single citizen.

—William Hedgepeth[1]

Theological discussions can be abstract and hard to apply, but I do not
want this one to be. The reason is that I want to convince you to adopt a
specific stance toward food animals. The best way for me to do this is by
telling you my story.

I am a Mennonite, and we, typically, are rural folk. I do not know
whether other Christian sects or denominations have more farmers per
capita than we do, but I would be surprised if Presbyterians or Catholics
had a higher ratio. Mennonites aspire to live simply and peacefully, and
those who farm try to farm in a way that returns to the land as much as
we take out of the land. In Story County, Iowa, where I live, the simplest

Gary L. Comstock, Associate Professor of Philosophy and Coordinator of the Bioethics Program at Iowa State University, is the editor of *Is There a Moral Obligation to Save the Family Farm?* His areas of scholarly interest are philosophy of religion and agricultural ethics. He is married to actress Karen Werner Comstock, and they have three children, Krista, Ben, and Drew. Since 1982 the Comstocks have lived in Story County, Iowa.

This article is reprinted with permission of the editors from *Between the Species,* Vol. 8, No. 2 (Spring 1992). Research for this paper was generously supported by a faculty improvement leave grant from Iowa State University, and by the Center of Theological Inquiry in Princeton, New Jersey, where I was appointed a member in 1990. I would like to thank Steve Sapontzis, Ned Hettinger, Peter Singer, and Steve Holtzmann for comments.

and most sustainable way to farm is called family farming, where you raise grains in summer and feed them to livestock in winter. You use the manure to supply nitrogen fertilizer to your pastures and fields, and you sell your pigs and cows at auction when they are fat. On family, or mixed, farms, the rearing and selling of livestock is the *raison d'être* of the operation, and the operation is, in the current jargon, sustainable, ecologically balanced, and consistent with principles of Christian stewardship.

Three initial confessions. I am not a farmer; my theological convictions are informed as much by the Reformed tradition as by the Anabaptist; and I am not nearly as virtuous as William Hedgepeth's paean to hog-surrounded Iowans would lead you to believe. I know something about the way mixed farms operate, and I know something about the way Mennonites think. I know, too, that Hedgepeth is right; there are eight times as many pigs in my state as people. But, contrary to what my mother thinks, I am not a moral virtuoso. Neither am I interested in defending received traditions about family farms; or sectarian theology; or the supposed angelic effects of boars and sows on people. I am interested in drawing on the wisdom invested in the practice of family farming and the reasoning of theologians and philosophers in order to answer this question: Is it in God's will to raise and eat pigs? In the conclusion to a book called *Is There a Moral Obligation to Save the Family Farm?* I argued in 1987 that mixed farms are the most politically viable institution for meeting obligations concerning food production, rural economies, and future generations.[2] The burden of proof is on those who think we should get rid of family farms and replace them with large industrial farms. My brother-in-law read the book and then asked me what an ideal farm would look like. I had no answer, and not only because I did not know enough about the daily operation of farms. I did not know what to say about the practice of raising and slaughtering animals, the cornerstone of the family farm's economy. I was sure that factory farms were not the answer, because it is clearly inhumane to confine four chickens to floorless cages and to keep anemic veal calves in narrow chutes.[3] But the question for me went beyond "What constitutes humane care?" to "Is it right to raise and slaughter animals?"

Several years after beginning to champion the virtues of family farms, and a few months after converting to the Mennonites, I became convinced by philosophical arguments that eating meat is morally wrong. This made for a dilemma. How can someone who loves family farms reject the central practice on which they are based? How can someone of my Anabaptist and Reformed theological proclivities reject the time-honored tradition of Christian stewardship in which the domestication and humane use of animals is not only permitted but encouraged? And yet, there I was, newly convinced that domestic animals had at least a *prima facie* right not to be killed and eaten at a young age, but without a clue as to how to square this belief with my theological and agricultural convictions. Did I mean to say that the actions of generations of Mennonite farmers in raising and slaughtering hogs were sinful?

How I Became a Vegetarian

I have told you that philosophical, not theological, arguments convinced me to abandon meat eating. Abandoning it was not an easy thing to do, because meat eating is not an abstract philosophical issue. You cannot just make up your mind to oppose meat eating the way you might make up your mind to oppose apartheid. If you make up your mind on this subject, you cannot really defer acting on your resolution until the next faculty meeting. You have to decide, before your stomach growls—probably within the next four hours—whether you are going to act on your new belief. The concreteness of the issue was a barrier for me.

I did not have a hard time deciding whether pigs experience pleasure and pain, or whether they have emotions, desires, wishes, preferences, and a family life. All of this seemed evident to me from watching the pigs on my uncle's farm. Reflecting on a pig's life will probably convince you, too.

Consider: Pigs are not, as common knowledge has it, dirty, dumb, or solitary animals. If given a sufficient amount of room, pigs will invariably defecate in the same area, teach their young to keep away from this area, and establish the area at a considerable remove from the sleeping area. Contrary to popular belief, pigs prefer to wallow in clean water, not mud, and will not play with toys soiled by feces.[4] Pigs are intelligent, affectionate, and social animals. The only thing they seem to love more than having their stomachs and ears rubbed is lying next to their neighbors after having run playfully in circles around them, squealing and barking all the while.

What is it like to be a pig? No one can get inside a pig's mind, of course, but we can think carefully about how they appear. Here is William Hedgepeth's perspective on his day spent in a pig pasture:

Idling hogs amble and squat. Some root. One sneezes. The sleeping hog beside me wags his ear a twitch or two and otherwise remains removed from the milieu. A Hampshire bites a Yorkshire's ear. A Poland China bites my foot. A white hog with a black face and black spot on his side executes a galloping gleeful leap into the vacant pond. A wandering rooter pussyfoots up the hill and sneezes right into the face of the one asleep, who responds merely with another quick ear-wag and continues his snooze (p. 125). . . . A hog [taking a] siesta on the hilltop has just jumped up to bump an intruding rooter down the slope, somersaulting to the bottom with a tumbling eruption of high-pitched squeals. Most of the hogs are up now, moseying about, perfectly unhurried: gambol and squat awhile, browse in the dried mud, drift in bulky serenity among the stumps and stubble and birds, call a sudden halt to it all every so often to look up at a sound or nudge another in the loin. Probe, poke, trot, root. Ah, hogs! They have unquenchably inquiring minds, each with a vast capacity for sustained wonder. And such a beatific quality—a certain handsomeness, really (p. 128).

Aristotle believed each animal has a telos or purpose to which it is directed, a "that for the sake of which" it exists. If Hedgepeth is right, the telos of a hog is the will to root, to find his food at least three inches underground, and to get his snout into every tractor tire, hole, and crevice within reach. Not forgetting sleeping and investigating and eating and mating and playing, rooting must be one thing for the sake of which God made hogs.

The daily activities of hogs clearly suggest that they possess desires, preferences, pleasures, pains, and social lives. You may also now have some idea of what the telos of this mammal may be. The hog: Kingdom, *Animalia*; Phylum, *Chordata*; Class, *Mammalia*; Order, *Artiodactyla*; Family, *Suidae*; Genus, *Sus*; Species, *Sus scrofa*; Subspecies, *S.s. scrofa* (the Central European wild boar), *S.s. leucomystax* (Japanese wild boar), *S.s. vittatus* (Southeast Asian pig), and *S.s. domestica* (domestic). These are some of the facts about hogs, but facts alone, no matter how many, would never add up to the moral judgment that it is wrong to kill and eat *Sus scrofa domestica*. For that, we need a general moral principle or two.

Here's one: It is wrong to deprive a being of its right to life. When I first started thinking seriously about the one-and-one-quarter-inch-thick Iowa chops I so loved to barbecue, I thought I had to decide whether pigs had rights and whether I was depriving them of that most basic right, the right to life, by paying other people to carve them up for me. I was impressed by arguments like Joel Feinberg's and Michael Tooley's that it is impossible for an entity to have a right to life unless that entity has interests in the sense of "able to have an interest in x."[5] Clearly, it is in the pig's interest to be able to sleep, eat, and root. But this is a different, weaker, sense of "interest" than the one required, for there are things that have interests that cannot take an interest in anything. It is in a hay baler's interest to be kept full of baling twine, but the machine does not possess the conscious awareness necessary to take an interest in seeing that it does not run out of twine in the middle of a row. Having things that are in its interest, and even having things that are good for it, nonetheless a hay baler is clearly not a bearer of moral rights. The machine does not have the *right* to be well maintained.

In order to have moral rights, something must be conscious, *capable of taking an interest* in what is good for it. We are capable of taking an interest in food, freedom, and the future, and we each have a basic moral right to food, freedom, and a future existence. Do pigs? According to R. G. Frey's analysis, an animal has to be able to possess concepts in order to have interests in the relevant sense, because without concepts the animal cannot represent its interests to itself. If the animal cannot represent its interests to itself, it cannot *take* an interest in anything. To have concepts, the animal must possess language, because that is the medium in which beings frame concepts. Here the argument reaches rock bottom, and I found myself asking, Do pigs possess language?

We, I reasoned, surely possess language, although I knew that talking about our mental life in this way committed me to a specific psychological paradigm, the paradigm philosophers call the belief and desire framework. To interpret ourselves in terms of beliefs and desires is not the only way to explain what goes on inside, but it is a powerful and well-developed way, and it coheres with the picture we typically use to think about ourselves. So I was prepared, and am still prepared, to accept the belief and desire schema. Humans have both beliefs and desires. We have already established that some higher mammals — pigs — have, at least, desires. When my uncle's barrows and gilts lift the lids on their feeder bins, I see no simpler or more efficient way of interpreting their behavior than to say that they *desire* to eat. When Hedgepeth's piglets chase each other around the pasture, there is no better explanation than that the pigs *want* to play. The central question is not whether pigs have desires, but whether they have beliefs. If they *believe* that there is food under the lid, or that by hiding behind the tire they will surprise their buddy, then they must possess language and concepts, because beliefs are made of language and concepts. If they have beliefs, they may be capable of *taking an interest* in their eating and playing. And if they can take an interest in those things, they may have a moral right to food, freedom, and a future. Frey is convinced, however, that animals do not have language because, he asserts, they are not capable of making assertions or lying. If Frey is right that animals do not have language, then animals cannot have concepts, beliefs, or interests in the sense required for having moral rights. If animals cannot take an interest in their future, they cannot have a right to that future. It follows, according to Frey, that painless slaughter does not violate a pig's right to continued existence, because pigs do have a right to continued existence.

This line of argument, if sound, would constitute a powerful philosophical justification for the historical Mennonite practice of slaughtering and eating pigs, and would buttress theological positions emphasizing ecological harmony and stewardship of nature. But do pigs lack language? They may not have the ability to make or entertain declarative sentences, Frey's way of interpreting what it means to be capable of language. But it seems to me that pigs communicate with each other, and they can, if they so desire, communicate with us in certain limited but distinctive ways.[6] Pigs, moreover, appear to many observers to reflect in a self-conscious way about their environment. Some, including me, think they have seen pigs trying to deceive each other. Pigs may indeed possess language, and may have the conceptual ability to take an interest in their future. But if they can take an interest in their future existence, they may have a moral right to that future. And if they do, our killing them violates their most basic right. If my factual claims about pigs' lives are correct, and if the moral principle that it is wrong to deprive a being of its right to life is true, and if I have made no mistakes in reasoning to the conclusion, then it may be wrong to deprive a pig of its right to life. So I reasoned for several months.

A Problem with Animal Rights Talk

According to this line of reasoning, pigs have the right to life because they have beliefs and can take an interest in their future. But what about beings without beliefs who cannot take an interest in their future? What about fetuses, very young infants, and adults in irreversibly comatose states? Lacking beliefs, language, and the ability to take interest in their future, so-called marginal human beings also lack the equipment necessary to have a right to life. But do we really want to say *that* — that newborn babies do not have a right to life because, as Tooley puts it, they do not "possess any concept of a continuing self"? Tooley candidly, if somewhat coolly, admits this line of thought leads to the conclusion that killing infants does not violate their moral rights. Any chain of reasoning ending with that conclusion may be mistaken. I began to see that trying to think about morality solely in terms of rights may lead to counterintuitive results. And I was soon convinced that the consequences of thinking about which beings we may and may not justifiably kill solely in the language of individual rights may itself be a *reductio* of such a narrow approach. As one philosopher has pointed out, "we have to take seriously the possibility . . . that some actions are wrong for reasons other than that they violate rights."[7] And as another adds, "we may have *duties* to entities which don't have rights."[8] To think there is a single simple criterion according to which we may decide whether we are justified in killing a being is to think in excessively constricted terms. And to think that "the way is open" to killing any being that lacks moral rights is to think in terms of an unacceptable conceptual paradigm.[9] I decided to rethink my approach.

A Theocentric Perspective

There I was, converted to the view I should not eat animals with interests but no longer persuaded by the arguments that had brought me to that point. I wanted a more substantial and holistic grounding for my conclusions, so I returned to my teacher, James Gustafson, for his theocentric perspective. Gustafson argues that ethics as traditionally construed is excessively anthropocentric in that it concentrates only on what is good for the human species. Gustafson wants those in religious traditions, at least, to take into account the wider patterns of God's governance and care for all of Creation, and he urges his reader to search for rules cohering with the natural relations of all things. Adapting a command from Paul's letter to the Romans, Gustafson summarizes his approach this way: "Be enlarged in your vision and affections, so that you might better discern what the divine governance enables and requires you to be and to do, what are your appropriate relations to God, indeed what are the appropriate relations of all things to God."[10]

If we relate to all things in ways that show respect for the relations of all things, will we eat meat? Let us agree to judge our practices by the criterion of whether a practice fits with the natural relationships of plants, animals, and humans, as these relationships can be discerned from the study of science, philosophy, and theology. Suppose, further, that "Man, the measurer, can no longer be the measure of the value of all things," and that, instead, "all things" are now the measure of us. May farmers continue to buy and sell feeder hogs?

Gustafson himself seems to have little interest in this question, and offers no guidance. To figure out what a theocentric perspective on food animals might be, then, I turned to Scripture. You will not be surprised to learn that I found a thoroughly ambiguous answer. The Bible implies here that God wants lions and lambs to lie down together in peace; in the first chapter of Genesis we are told that God gave us only plants and fruits for food.[11] Yet the Bible implies elsewhere, in passage after passage, that it is all right to be carnivores. After the Fall, God explicitly issues permission for us to eat animals. How can a Mennonite reconcile these biblical permissions with moral vegetarianism?

An Interlude: Christmas Meditation

As I think about the Bible and animals toward the end of 1990, Christmas approaches, and I am reminded of my earliest memories of Christmas. There is my mother's manger scene: the stable made of wood, the angel hung from the peak, baby Jesus wrapped in swaddling clothes and lying in the manger. There is Mary, hovering over the infant, attentive to his slightest movement, and there, a step behind her, are Joseph, the wise men, and the shepherds. I could end my description there, but I would have skipped the animals, of course. For there, behind the holy baby and the Virgin and in front of the shepherds, are the wise men's camels, looking gangly and out of place; the shepherds' dogs, asleep at their masters' feet; the cow, chewing her cud; and the sheep, woolly and white. Over here is the donkey, shaggy and brown. Jesus Christ comes to earth in human form, and we witness and rejoice at his birth. But he was born not in one of our houses, but in an animal shed. It is not insignificant that animals witnessed and rejoiced at his birth, for God put animals around the manger just as God put them at the scene of every major event in salvation history. Think of the scene at the Garden of Eden. Before God made women and men and boys and girls, God made cows and donkeys and dogs and sheep. Think of God's first words to humans. When God first laid down the law for how we are to treat each other, God did not overlook our relations to animals, making a point of instructing us *only* to eat plants. Originally, we were vegetarians, and God did not want us to raise and slaughter animals. As the author of Genesis 1:29-30 puts it,

> God also said, "I give you all plants that bear seed everywhere on earth, and every tree bearing fruit which yields seed: they shall be yours for food. All green plants I give for food to the wild animals, to all the birds of heaven, and to all reptiles on earth, every living creature."

And think of the scene at the future New Creation. The biblical story begins with humans as vegetarians, and it ends that way, too. When the Lord comes in power, when the poor are judged with justice and the knowledge of the Lord fills the land, then, we are told by Isaiah,

> the wolf shall live with the sheep,
> and the leopard lie down with the kid;
> and the calf and the young lion shall grow up together,
> and a little child shall lead them;
> and cow and the bear shall be friends,
> and their young shall lie down together.

One day, all animals will stop doing harm to each other, and "the lion shall eat straw like cattle." And if the "infant shall play over the hole of the cobra," what excuse will we have for killing cobras, or lions, or cattle? For on that day, no living thing will "hurt or destroy in all my holy mountain" (Isaiah 11:5-9).

Or think of the stories Jesus liked to tell. If the number of times someone refers to lambs and sheep and goats and vipers and asses is any indication of their affection for animals, then our Lord must have loved nonhumans as much as St. Francis of Assisi loved them. Jesus' parables are full of animals. So, pick any major biblical scene, and you will find animals there. The menagerie at the manger scene is not a biblical anomaly. Why all the biblical concern with animals? Because, in the words of my mother's favorite hymn, God's eye is on the sparrow. In the very first covenant God makes with us after God has destroyed the world in the flood, God makes an agreement with Noah and his family that includes animals in it. The covenant is not, as we ordinarily think of it, between the Deity and humankind, but rather between the Deity and all of creation, human and animals included. Genesis 9:13 renders it like this: "My bow I set in the cloud, sign of the covenant between myself and the earth." And five times in the ninth chapter of Genesis, God promises never again to destroy creation. The promise includes humans, but it extends to "every living creature that is with you, all birds and cattle, all the wild animals with you on earth, all that have come out of the ark" (Genesis 9:8-10).

If the biblical story begins and ends with humans as vegetarians, why do most Christians, unlike Brahmins, adherents of the Jain religion, and many Buddhists, eat meat? The reason is that we believe God gave us permission to do so. When and where? At the same time God made the covenant with Noah. God tells Noah to "be fruitful and increase, swarm throughout the earth and rule over it" (Genesis 9:7), adding "The fear and dread of you shall fall upon all wild animals on earth, on all birds of heaven, on everything that moves upon the ground and all fish in the sea; they are given into your hands. Every creature that lives and moves shall be food for you; I give you them all, as once I gave you all green plants" (Genesis 9:2-3).

This is the divine permission on which the nomadic and agrarian economies of the West are based. To me, the passage reads less as divine permission, more as divine curse; less as God's preferred norm for human-animal relations, more as God's grim prediction of what will happen to human-animal relations. Be that as it may, there are plenty of other passages recording God's commands to sacrifice animals. The world's three major western religions, Judaism, Christianity, and Islam, all condone meat eating, and all support economies founded on the domestication, slaughter, and consumption of animals.

And yet, there by Jesus' crib, are the animals. Are they there only to serve us? Well, they do serve us, and some have said we have rigorous covenants to keep with them because they serve us. We have a covenant with the donkey, it is said: You carry the mother of our Lord, and we will care for your every need. We have a covenant with the dog, it is said: You provide us companionship, and we will give you exercise. And we have a covenant with the horse, it is said: You pull our plow, and we will give you a warm stall and oats. We signed different terms with sheep, cows, turkeys, chicken, fish, and hogs: They serve us by dying for us at a premature age. For modern breeds of hogs, whose life expectancy might conservatively be put at ten years, the contract runs out at six months. Of course, we provide them with plenty of food and water while they are with us. But they pay, early, with their lives.

Are these fair contracts?

The Bible indisputably approves of them. The authors of Scripture recognize the intrinsic value of animals in the original and final creations but, in the meantime, in the between times, God seems to have made a concession to our sinful condition by relaxing the law against the eating of animal flesh. For hard after describing the Garden of Eden, the author of Genesis describes the post-Fallen world as one in which the animals are "meat for us," and in which we are to rule over, have dominion over, all forms of plant and animal life.

What about Jesus? Even though animals often serve as examples in his parables, he said nothing to our knowledge about vegetarianism. There are no recorded instances of him eating red meat in the New Testament, but it seems reasonable to suppose, given the Mediterranean culture of his time, that he ate fish. And he said nothing about restoring the original herbivorous condition of the original and final creation. So I must ask again: In the face of the strong biblical permission to raise and slaughter animals for food, can a Mennonite argue for moral vegetarianism if she takes the Bible and its tradition of interpretation seriously?

This is a difficult question for me. My tentative answer has two parts. The first part is that vegetarianism is not required for all people at all times. When the eating of meat is the only way to sustain human life, then I believe it is permissible to do so. The Bible was written by largely nomadic or pastoral peoples who may not have been able to flourish without raising the flocks of sheep that appear throughout the Bible. So, on the one hand, the Bible may originally have been addressed to an audience in which a limited diet of animal flesh was required for existence. Notice, however, what does not follow from this concession. It does not follow that affluent Americans in the twentieth century may eat meat. We can easily have our need for protein met in ways other than eating pork chops and hamburgers.

The second part of my reply to the Bible's explicit permission of meat eating is this: While the Bible does address many sins, it does not address all sins. For example, the Bible does not explicitly call discrimination on the basis of age or sex a sin. Nor does it call slavery a sin. Jesus said nothing about the practice of buying and selling people with skins darker than ours. Are we to conclude that God would have us continue to own slaves or that Jesus Christ, the Savior and Liberator of all people, would not disapprove of our beginning once more to conduct slave raids on poor developing countries? Even though the Bible says nothing that could be taken as a direct condemnation of slavery, slavery is still wrong. The reason is because the overall themes of the Bible are freedom, liberation, justice, and mercy. The nineteenth-century American Methodists and Quakers who led the abolitionist movement knew this. Even though Christian slave owners in the nineteenth century could point to a multitude of specific biblical passages that explicitly permit slaveholding, the abolitionists had the stronger argument, and we now acknowledge their point of view as most in keeping with the trajectory of whole biblical narrative.

I have come to interpret the Bible's views on the killing of animals in the way I interpret its views on the owning of slaves. Even though each practice is implicitly, if not explicitly, condoned, the practice is still shown to be wrong by the larger story of salvation in Jesus Christ. How could the biblical authors have been so wrong on this point of morality? I do not believe they were wrong on a point of morality. I believe they were wrong on a point of fact. Regarding slaveholding, they were wrong to think that darker-skinned humans were not conscious, rational individuals. Once this perception of the facts was corrected, darker-skinned humans could no longer be thought to fall outside the Bible's moral protection.

Analogously, the biblical authors were wrong about mammals. They thought animals were not conscious, sentient individuals. Once this misperception is changed, nonhuman animals no longer fall outside the Bible's moral protection. To argue this point effectively would require me to say why I think some animals are conscious and sentient beings. That involves the philosophical argument I made earlier, which turns on the claim that mammals aged one year and older have beliefs, desires, emotions, social and family lives, and interests in the strong sense of "able to take an interest in" something. Having that, they are entitled to basic moral rights, including the right to life. To my mind, Tom Regan makes this argument persuasively.[12]

Just as early abolitionists had to fight both the wider slave society and the power of slave-owning Christians who rested their case on a selective reading of Scripture, so Christian defenders of animals must fight both the wider meat-eating society and the power of carnivorous Christians who rest their case on a selective reading of Scripture. No easy chore. I find encouragement in the scene around the manger. There we see a picture of creation in the peaceful coexistence God originally intended and finally wants. Around the manger, we see the truth of God's admission that God "desires steadfast love and not sacrifice, the knowledge of God rather than burnt offerings" (Hosea 6:6). And we see what it means for God to have shown us what is good. God shows us in the manger scene that what the Lord requires of us is "to do justice, and to love kindness and [to] walk humbly with [our] God" (Micah 6:8).

Scripture gives an ambiguous answer to the animal question. As I mentioned previously, the text implies here that God wants lions and lambs to lie down together, while it states explicitly, elsewhere, that all animals are to be food for us. I concluded, in my journey, that I could no more convince myself to be a vegetarian on the basis of the Bible alone than I could convince myself to be a vegetarian on the basis of rights talk alone.

I did not find clearer advice when I turned to other religious traditions. Consider Hinduism, in which Brahmins revere all animals, practice vegetarianism, and adhere to the doctrine of *ahimsa*, noninjury. Like Albert Schweitzer and the Jains, Brahmins in principle will not even swat a gnat. Around the corner, however, lower castes behead a goat in pious sacrifice to the goddess Kali. Within Hinduism, there is no consensus about the propriety of universal abstention from meat. Consider Native American traditions, where you find ambiguous attitudes. There is an attitude of respect for the buffalo's power and immensity, and warriors pause to pray to the beast, imploring it to lend them its noble spirit. But then they proceed to slaughter it, eat it, and wear its skin. Surely it is better to use all of the animal if you are going to kill it, but wouldn't it be better just to eat corn and beans and squash, and wear cotton?

I have not, in short, found unambiguous guidance about how God would have us relate in a natural way to domestic pigs from Gustafson, from Scripture, from Christian theology, or from the world's religions. Every argument that the Christian tradition should be read as sanctioning humane treatment and slaughter of food animals may be met by one that the tradition should really be read as pointing proleptically toward vegetarianism. So even if my theologian colleagues will not forgive me, they may at least understand why I turned back at this point to my philosophical colleagues.

An Environmental Theory of Respect for Nature

Gustafson insists that correct actions flow more from the possession of proper affections than from the following of proper rules. Paul Taylor believes that character is the heart of ethics, too, and I read his philosophical theory of respect for nature as a complement to, and development of, certain aspects of Gustafson's theology. Taylor makes the attitude of respect for nature the basis of all moral reflection about the environment, and identifies four dimensions of that attitude. Two of them are relevant here. The first is the valuational dimension, "the disposition to regard all wild living things in the Earth's natural ecosystems as possessing inherent worth."[13] The second is the affective dimension, "the disposition ... *to feel pleased about* any occurrence that is expected to maintain in existence the Earth's wild communities of life, their constituent species-populations, or their individual members."[14]

Taylor believes we owe the attitude of respect toward wild living things. He avoids the language of animal rights, but he insists we follow the principles of proportionality and minimum wrong. The first principle means that we should never act disproportionately, for example, violating an elephant's basic interest in life simply to satisfy our nonbasic interest in having ivory carvings on our mantlepiece. "Greater weight is to be given to basic than to nonbasic interests, no matter what species, human or other, the competing claims arise from. Nonbasic interests are prohibited from overriding basic interests."[15] The second principle states that "the actions of humans must be such that no alternative ways of achieving their ends would produce fewer wrongs to wild living things."[16] From these two principles you may see how protective Taylor is of wildlife. His attitude toward domestic animals is less than clear, however. The reason is that Taylor is impressed by the fact that pets and food animals have been purposefully bred to serve a human purpose. Unlike wild animals whose existence does not depend on their fulfilling our needs, domestic animals exist only because we have exercised dominance over them and their environment. Taylor puts the matter forcefully:

[The practice of rearing food animals depends, first,] on total human dominance over nonhuman living things and their environment. Second, [it involves] treating nonhuman living things as means to human ends ... The social institutions and practices of the bioculture are, first and foremost, exercises of absolute, unconditioned power. They are examples of the way humans "conquer" and "subdue" nature. (The conquest of nature has often been seen as a key to the progress of civilization.) When we humans create the bioculture and engage in its practices we enter upon a special relationship with animals and plants. We hold them completely within our power. They must serve us or be destroyed. For some practices their being killed by us is the very thing necessary to further our ends. Instances are slaughtering animals for food, cutting timber for lumber, and causing laboratory animals to die by giving them lethal dosages of toxic chemicals.[17]

Taylor does not explicitly draw the conclusion that it is morally permissible to continue to subdue nature in this way, but that conclusion is implied by his remarks. Other environmental philosophers such as J. Baird Callicott and Mary Midgley have a similarly bifurcated attitude toward animals.[18] They think wild animals should be left alone, whereas domestic animals should be treated humanely—that is, maintained in good health until they are to be killed painlessly.

It began to look as if my turn to environmental philosophy and the theocentric perspective might cause me to overturn my decision against meat eating. If there is an absolute difference between wild and domestic animals, and if this difference means that wild animals have intrinsic value while domestic animals have only instrumental value for humans, then it might be permissible to raise and slay hogs and yet impermissible to kill wild warthogs. To decide whether the difference between tamed and untamed was really this decisive, I had to read some animal science. Just how different are Minnesota Number Threes from wild boars?

I immediately ran into a problem. To my knowledge, there are no scientific studies comparing the physical or behavioral traits of specific domestic pigs with wild pigs.[19] Nonetheless, on the basis of certain generalizations scientists have proffered in the literature on swine production, some observations about the difference can be offered tentatively.[20] Feral swine tend to have aggressive dispositions. They often live in herds of four to twenty foraging animals consisting of one to four females and their young. Wild boars range freely in forest settings throughout the year, staying close to the herd during the reproductive season, when they become territorial and protective. Omnivorous and voracious eaters, sows and boars alike, spend the majority of their waking hours walking, rooting, and eating. The courtship of an oestrus female by a wild boar takes several days, with the male grunting a soft rhythmic mating song and having to overcome a last-minute rebuttal from her when she wheels and faces him just before he tries to mount her. The wild sow may spend days making a nest for her young. The boar seems to enjoy the presence of piglets, tolerating them as they wiggle on top of him as he rests.

Domestic swine tend to be larger, less fatty, more docile toward humans, and less agonistic toward each other. As you might guess, we have little information about how large a "domestic herd" might be, because pigs in confinement are not allowed to form natural social groups. Boars are kept away from the sows, feeder pigs are thrown together according to age, and sows are kept in maternity pens before parturition and during nursing. Even though they are usually denied the space and freedom to form natural relations with other pigs, domestic pigs are still known to adapt rapidly to new conditions. They exhibit a high degree of intelligence and have, for example, been trained to hunt truffles and indicate targets like pointer dogs.

The sexual relationships of confined pigs are noticeably different from their wild counterparts. When a sow in heat is presented to a boar, copulation occurs quickly. There is very little behavior corresponding to the long courtship of wild sows and boars, as domestic sows usually allow boars to mount immediately, and boars are selected, in part, for their virility and promiscuity. Boars kept away from sows sometimes form stable homosexual relationships. Their behavior toward young piglets is hard to observe, for reasons noted above.

There are, in sum, significant differences between the physical, psychological, and social characteristics of domestic and wild pigs. Wild pigs tend to be smaller, fattier, more romantic, less promiscuous, and more ferocious. Domestic pigs tend to be larger, leaner, less romantic, eager to mate in season or out of season, and more docile. The differences stem from the influence of human intervention as farmers have consciously selected individual pigs for the traits now possessed by sows and boars. Breeders have weakened the pig's natural defenses and rendered them dumber, less agile, and more meaty than their wild relatives. Differences are undeniable. And yet we may ask, how great are the similarities? Are the differences significant enough to justify claims that we have exercised "absolute power" over the domestic animals?

The differences in physical appearance of African bush pigs and Duroc hogs are noticeable, but both look more like the other than they look like other species. Both adapt quickly to changed environmental conditions. Both exhibit tremendous behavioral plasticity in the face of fluctuations in weather, diet, and physical threats. Both exhibit attitudes of defiance, pride, and affection. Both are extremely social. Both prefer not to leave the company of others, except for the case of older males, who sometimes prefer occasional solitude. Both like to root in soil and water, to wallow in pools. Both exhibit distinctive territorial behavior, keep separate areas for elimination of urine and feces, and train their young to do the same. Both are curious about new objects, and will sniff and nibble any protrusion or hole. Both have a complex range of vocal snorts and whoofs for communicating a variety of emotions, signals, and alarms. Both have nearly identical olfactory and auditory capacities. Neither is able to regulate body temperature for at least two days after birth. Neither is receptive to newcomers to the herd. Both are gregarious animals, huddling together against cold weather and enjoying warm weather in close proximity.

The list could go on, but I have made the point. The differences between domestic and wild pigs pale in light of their similarities. May we then continue to believe that we have exercised "unconditioned" power over the being of the production hog? The scientific evidence fails to support the claim, because the identity of the production hog is as much a product of natural forces as it is of human intervention.

May we at least claim responsibility for the distinctive features we have selected in our hogs? For example, domestic pigs are diurnal creatures, whereas wild pigs sleep during the day and are active at night. Is this trait a human mark stamped on the pig? It may be, just as the sexual promiscuity, docility, and physical size of the domestic hog may be marks of human intervention. Still, we must ask whether these traits are really of our doing or whether they are not responses that may be equally attributed to the hog. Consider that domestic hogs tend to be diurnal creatures whereas wild hogs tend to be nocturnal; hunting is easier in the evening hours. Did humans cause this difference? I doubt it. Hogs are highly adaptable creatures, and there is not much stimulation in hog pens at night. The domestic hog's preference for daylight activity may be a tribute to their own plasticity of behavior, a trait caused as much by the pig's own initiative as by the breeder's selections. Being diurnal, in short, may be a learned response to environmental conditions, and it may be a characteristic pigs would abandon if turned out of their pens or if stimulated at night. This suggests that certain behavioral differences between domestic and wild species may not only not be permanent but may be reversible.[21]

Based on a review of the empirical differences between undomesticated and domesticated hogs, we may conclude that Taylor's claim is unjustified, as is his implication that domestic animals are human artifacts we may regard the way we regard tools.[22] There is no question that today's breeds are expressions of human power and control over nature, the result of invasive, repeated, and sustained manipulations of generations of animals. The Durocs and Hampshires and Yorkshires now on Mennonite family farms would almost certainly not be there were it not for humans. Hogs are part of our moral community in a way wild animals never have been, because their evolution is intricately connected with our own. They depend on us for their existence. But it does not follow that we are justified in continuing to intervene in their histories by encouraging them to inbreed and by slaughtering their young.

If Taylor's views about food animals are not entirely clear, other environmental philosophers' views are clear. Midgley and Callicott seem to condone meat eating as part of the long history of relations between humans and domesticated animals. The view gains credence in light of the fact that the history of a being is relevant to deciding what that being is and what our natural duties toward it are. Consider Midgley's view. She approaches ethics from a biosocial perspective, and points out that we are members of nested communities, each of which has a different structure. According to our various roles in the various communities, we have various duties. The central community for many of us is an immediate family. We have duties not only to feed, clothe, and shelter our children, but to bestow affection on them. Bestowing similar affection on our neighbors' children is not similarly required of us, however. Not only is it not our duty, but "it would be considered anything from odd to criminal were [we] to behave [toward neighborhood children the way we behave toward our own]." At the next level, we have "obligations to [our] neighbors which [we] do not have to less proximate fellow citizens—to watch their houses while they are on vacation, for example, or to go to the grocery for them when they are sick or disabled." We have obligations to those in our state which we do not have toward human beings in general, and we have "obligations to human beings in general which [we] do not have toward animals in general."[23]

These subtly shaded social-moral relationships are complex and overlapping. Thinking of animals, Midgley argues that pets are surrogate family members and merit treatment not owed either to less intimately related animals—for example, to barnyard animals—or to less intimately related human beings. Following Midgley's biosocial line of thinking, the narrative history of each animal defines its identity. Since hogs have been bred to play a certain role in our community, our duties toward them derive from understanding what their role naturally is.

Like Midgley, Callicott argues that the welfare ethic of the mixed community enjoins us to leave wild or "willed" animals alone, while caring humanely for domestic species. This means that we are justified in using domestic animals in the ways they have been bred to be used. It is not inhumane to use a Belgian draft horse to pull a wagon, as long as you do not abuse her in the process. It is not inhumane to kill pigs and chickens and steers for food, as long as you care for them in a way that does not violate the unspoken social contract we have evolved with them.[24]

Well, reading environmental philosophy made me wonder whether my decision not to eat meat had been divorced from narratives, history, and common sense in the worst way. If the history and social role of a being plays a decisive role in determining what that thing is, and if today's pigs would not be here if it were not for the long history of human intervention in the mating patterns of hogs, then the raising and slaughtering of pigs is the very practice necessary for Durocs, Hampshires, and Minnesota Number Twos to exist at all. Who was I to condemn these creatures?

Callicott seemed to press the point on me. Those who condemn meat eating thereby condemn the "very being" of the animals they are trying to defend. For without the long historical practice of meat eating, Callicott writes, these particular animals would not exist. My moral vegetarianism weakened.

Then I started thinking critically about the biosocial environmentalist claims. Do we condemn the very being of something if we disapprove of the life-style that being is forced to lead? Surely not. To condemn the way something is treated is not to condemn that thing. When we condemn slavery we do not thereby condemn the existence of the slaves. Far from it. In the interest of the good of the slave, we condemn the social contract that has evolved to rationalize the restriction of their freedom. Analogously, I came to see that I could condemn the practice of domesticating and slaughtering pigs without thereby condemning the existence of *these* pigs.

Having answered Callicott's challenge, I went back to Taylor's rigid differentiation between the respect owed wild animals and his quasi-instrumentalist view of domestic animals. I discovered on second reading that Taylor is more insistent on vegetarianism than I had thought at first, "even though," he writes, "plants and animals are regarded as having the same inherent worth."[25] The principle of fairness, captured in the metaphor of sharing the earth, draws attention to "the amount of arable land needed for raising grain and other plants as food for those animals that are in turn to be eaten by humans when compared with the amount of land needed for raising grain and other plants for direct human consumption ... In order to produce one pound of protein for human consumption, a steer must be fed 21 pounds of protein ... [a pig must be fed] 8.3 pounds ... [and a chicken] 5.5 pounds."[26] The land now in cultivation to grow grains for cows and pigs could be returned to wildlife refuge.

Taylor argues for vegetarianism by pointing out that humans have taken over much more than their fair share of the globe. To return land to wild animals, we should cultivate less ground, shrink our farms' size, and probably concentrate them in one location so as to leave large tracts of wilderness. His reasoning seemed sound to me then, as it does now. And that is where I have come to rest, for the moment. There are good reasons of an environmentalist and theocentric sort for opposing the eating of meat.

I still had two questions: Would it be wrong, if we pulled in our plows and chemical sprays and shared the earth equitably with other species, to eat an occasional future pig raised on one of the small nonfactory farms? And if in that ideal world some of us revert to hunting and gathering as a permanent life-style, would it be wrong for us to kill and eat one of the millions of wild pigs?

To answer this question, I went back to Taylor's five priority principles. When the requirements of human ethics compete with those of environmental ethics, Taylor tells us to follow principles exhibiting the attitude of respect for nature. The fundamental criterion is fairness, read as species impartiality. According to Taylor, both plants and animals deserve respect, even though neither one is a primary moral rights holder. The first priority principle is the principle of self-defense. "It is permissible for moral agents to protect themselves against dangerous or harmful organisms by destroying them" (pp. 264-65). This principle "condones killing the attacker" only if that is the only way to protect the self. We must "choose means that will do the least possible harm" (p. 265).

The second principle is the principle of proportionality, and it deals with conflicts "between *basic* interests [for example, food, water, and continued existence] of animals/plants and *nonbasic* interests [for example, air conditioned offices] of humans." "Greater weight is to be given to basic than to nonbasic interests, no matter what species, human or other, the competing claims arise from. Nonbasic interests are prohibited from overriding basic interests" (p. 278).

This principle prohibits such practices as:

• Slaughtering elephants so the ivory of their tusks can be used to carve items for the tourist trade.
• Killing rhinoceros so that their horns can be used as dagger handles.
• Hunting and killing rare wild mammals, such as leopards and jaguars, for the luxury fur trade.
• All sport hunting and recreational fishing (p. 274).

The third principle is the principle of minimum wrong. Like the second principle, it concerns conflicts "between basic interests of animals/plants and nonbasic interests of humans." "The actions of humans must be such that no alternative ways of achieving their ends would produce fewer wrongs to wild living things" (p. 283).

Plants and animals and humans have equal inherent worth, in Taylor's estimation, but he recognizes that rational people may decide to engage in activities involving harm to wild living things. As long as these people are "rational, informed, and autonomous persons *who have adopted the attitude of respect for nature*," then "it is permissible for them to pursue [their] values only so long as doing so involves fewer wrongs (violations of duties) than any alternative way of pursuing those values" (pp. 282-83).

Taylor's fourth principle is the principle of distributive justice, and applies to "conflicts between *basic* interests, in which nonhumans are not harming us." The cases in question, then, are cases where the principles of self-defense, proportionality, and minimum wrong do not apply. "When the interests of parties are all basic ones and there exists a natural source of good that can be used for the benefit of any of the parties, each party must be allotted an equal, or fair, share" (p. 292).

The fifth principle is the principle of restitutive justice: "When harm is done to humans, animals, or plants that are harmless, some form of reparation or compensation is called for. The greater the harm done, the greater the reparation required" (p. 304).

Using these principles, I was able to answer my two questions. Consider the second question first. If I lived in a place or a time where I could not survive without hunting wild goats and sheep, or fishing for tuna and whales, then it would be permissible for me to kill and eat those animals. Why? Because the first principle enjoins self-defense and, *per hypothesis*, the only way to protect myself from death under the circumstances of my thought experiment would be to eat meat or fish. As long as I hunt and fish in a way that respects the principles of fairness, minimum wrong, and proportionality, I will be justified in my carnivorous behavior. There is, Taylor points out, no principle requiring me to sacrifice my life for the sake of animals.

Consider now my first question, whether raising and slaughtering animals would not be permissible in the ideal world, in the world where the number of humans and farms is dramatically reduced. If there were, say, only 500 million of us instead of 5 billion, and only 50,000 small farms instead of half a million corporate farms, then other species might flourish. Under those conditions, couldn't rational autonomous persons who have adopted the principle of respect for nature decide to raise pigs in such a way that the animals were allowed maximal freedoms and long unhurried lives? And wouldn't it then be the case that those animals would be better off living *that* life-style than never having the opportunity to be born at all?

This question is more difficult, but it seems to me we should answer it negatively. The principle of self-defense could not be enjoined to sanction such activity, because slaughtering the pigs in question, even toward the end of their lives, would not serve any *basic* interest of ours; we can get our protein elsewhere. The principle of proportionality also offers little support, because our nonbasic interest in enjoying a good set of barbecued back ribs is prohibited from overriding the pig's basic interest in continued existence. The principle of minimum wrong would also argue against even a low level of meat eating, since there are alternative ways of achieving our interest in experiencing robust gustatory pleasures.

Careful consideration of the natural relations of all things and rigorous adoption of the attitude of respect for nature inclines strongly toward moral vegetarianism. And thus was I moved, against the historical practices of my religious tradition and my personal convictions about the virtues of family farms, to think some mammals have mental lives roughly analogous to ours; that killing them for food, even in a painless fashion, does harm to them; and that I should stop having bacon for breakfast. I then had to explain this to my evangelical, Iowa-farm-raised mother, who did her best to feed her four children meat three times a day. I also had to explain it to my Iowa farm relatives, Mennonite dairy acquaintances, and Colorado ranch buddies, all evangelical Christians, all outfitted with Bible verses describing God's permission to eat meat in Genesis, and Jesus' story of the prodigal son ending with the killing of the fattened calf and—well, you fill in the blank. I have, as I have admitted, no definitive response to what I perceive as the most convincing interpretation of what the biblical authors thought about this matter, and I have conceded the Bible for the present. But I hasten to add that I am not happy about this situation because the text has authority for me and my community, and I am not prepared simply to abandon it.

Three Theological Arguments for Meat Eating

In conclusion, I want to say something against three theological arguments for meat eating. The first is that meat eating is a concession to sin, and that God granted us permission to eat animals because of our fallen condition. The idea here is that we could not reasonably be expected to control our carnivorous instincts once our taste buds had been debased and we had been exposed to the Tree of the Knowledge of Good and Evil. So God no longer required truly moral behavior of us.[27]

This argument is not convincing, for two reasons. First, we know from experience that humans are capable of controlling the instinct to eat flesh. Many former meat eaters have changed their habits, difficult as it may have been to overcome the fear they would not find anything sufficiently full of protein to eat at the next meal. Second, if God really thought the Fall had so weakened us that God had henceforth to permit certain acts as a concession to our pitiful condition, wouldn't a merciful God decide to permit something less violent than bloodletting? How about allowing us not to respect our parents occasionally, or not keeping every fourth Sabbath, or gossiping during the cold month of February? These would seem more reasonable concessions to sin than allowing us to slit the throats of billions of God's good animals.

The second argument for meat eating follows on the heels of Midgley's view that the domestication of animals is a mutual covenant evolved between us and animals. The idea here is that animals do not simply serve us; we have a contract to provide them with food, water, shelter, care, and comfortable lives. But what is their responsibility? To pay us back with their lives. The contract seems a bit one-sided. The argument would make more sense if it was generally understood to mean "Let the animals live in their natural social groupings, provide them with conditions under which they can pursue their interests, and let them live until a ripe old age before backing up the truck." But that is not the way the alleged covenant is generally understood. We squeeze hogs together into pens not large enough for them to establish their own area for defecating, we throw them together into new social groupings every few weeks, we control their reproductive cycles with manufactured drugs, and we kill them before they are six months old. If the terms of the agreement were to support hogs into comfortable retirement and then take the carcasses of animals dying of natural causes for sausage, the covenant argument would be more persuasive. I suspect, however, that not many meat consumers would want to sign it.

The third argument is that killing animals is permissible as long as we take the minimal number, and in a pious spirit. Native Americans kill the buffalo with a tragic sense for the loss of its life, and they kill only the number they need. They either eat or use the entire animal, and they do all of this with a humble and grateful spirit, demonstrating respect for the harmony and balances of nature.

Isn't it permissible to kill and eat animals this way? My response is Taylor's response: If it is a question of survival, if it comes down to the Native American's life or the buffalo's life, then the principle of self-defense will justify the killing. I do not know how many Native Americans still fall into this category, but I am confident few of my readers face such dire circumstances.

I have tried to write concretely, telling you my story about my particular religious pieties and my evolving attitude toward pigs. Philosophical considerations moved me to give up meat, but the environmental and theocentric perspective that warrants my view now is different from the animal rights perspective with which I began. My position is somewhat softer now, and does not amount to an absolute proscription against the taking of animal life. Yet, I regret to say, it offers little moral support to those farmers struggling to hold onto their land by raising animals to be led to slaughter.

Notes

1. William Hedgepeth, *The Hog Book* (New York: Doubleday, 1978), pp. 54-55.

2. Gary Comstock, ed., *Is There a Moral Obligation to Save the Family Farm?* (Ames, Ia.: Iowa State University Press, 1987).

3. For a description of modern techniques of swine production on factory farms, see James Mason, "Brave New Farm?" in Peter Singer, ed., *In Defense of Animals* (New York: Basil Blackwell, 1985), especially pp. 93-94.

4. Cf. Kathy and Bob Kellogg, *Raising Pigs Successfully* (Charlotte, Vt.: Williamson, 1985), p. 23.

5. Michael Tooley, discussing the alleged right to life of fetuses, gives what he calls the "particular-interests principle," which draws on Joel Feinberg's general "interest-principle." Tooley's principle states, "It is a conceptual truth that an entity cannot have a particular right, R, unless it is at least capable of having some interest, I, which is furthered by its having right R." Michael Tooley, "In Defense of Abortion and Infanticide," in Joel Feinberg, ed., *The Problem of Abortion*, 2nd ed. (Belmont: Wadsworth, 1984), p. 125. Tooley's example of the principle is that "an entity cannot have a right to life unless it is capable of having an interest in its own continued existence" (p. 132).

6. Cf. Hedgepeth's informal survey of the meanings of hog sounds such as *groonk, rah, wheenk,* and *Wheeeeeeeiiiiiii* in *The Hog Book,* p. 137.

7. S. I. Benn, "Abortion, Infanticide, and Respect for Persons," in Feinberg, ed., *The Problem of Abortion,* p. 136.

8. Susan Leigh Anderson, "Criticisms of Liberal/Feminist Views on Abortion," *Public Affairs Quarterly* 1 (April 1987): 87.

9. In "Autonomy and the Value of Animal Life," *The Monist* 70 (January 1987), Frey argues that "the way is open to infanticide or the killing of severely handicapped newborns" because they are not autonomous beings. "Obviously," he concludes, "the way is also open to the killing of animals" (p. 51). I respond to Frey's argument in "The Moral Irrelevance of Autonomy," *Between the Species* (forthcoming).

10. James M. Gustafson, *Ethics from a Theocentric Perspective*, 1 (Chicago: University of Chicago Press, 1981), p. 327, drawing on Romans 12: 1-2.

11. "All plants that bear seed everywhere on the earth, and every tree bearing fruit which yields seed: they shall be yours for food" (Gen. 1:29, NEB). Quoted in Tom Regan, "Christianity and Animal Rights: The Challenge and Promise," *Liberating Life* (Maryknoll, N.Y.: Orbis Books, 1990), p. 82.

12. Tom Regan, *The Case for Animal Rights* (Berkeley, Calif.: University of California Press, 1983).

13. Paul Taylor, *Respect for Nature: A Theory of Environmental Ethics* (Princeton, N.J.: Princeton University Press, 1986), p. 81.

14. Ibid., p. 83.

15. Ibid., p. 278.

16. Ibid., p. 283.

17. Ibid., p. 55.

18. See, for example, J. Baird Callicott, *In Defense of the Land Ethic: Essays in Environmental Philosophy* (Albany, N.Y.: S.U.N.Y. Press, 1989), esp. pp. 33-36; and Mary Midgley, *Animals and Why They Matter* (Athens, Ga.: University of Georgia Press, 1983), esp. pp. 112-24.

19. A brief history of pig breeding for those who are interested: We have been intensively breeding sows and boars for about two hundred years. Until the sixteenth century, there were very few differences between the wild and domestic pigs, except for the fact that the wild boar was slightly larger. In the eighteenth century, Englishman Robert Bakewell decisively broke any cultural prohibitions outlawing incest among animals when he bred his Leicester rams and longhorn bulls back to their daughters, and the way was open for intensive hog breeding. Farmers selected for desirable characteristics—characteristics such as physical size and fitness, size of litter and ease of reproduction, resistance to disease, ability to gain weight quickly and efficiently, and tenderness of flesh. As they did, the pedigreed herds came to exhibit more and more physical uniformity, reflecting a narrowing of the genetic pool. Pigs selected for characteristics desirable to humans lost their agility (Irish Greyhound pigs were once known to jump five barred gates), their ability to survive in the wild, and pedigreed herds soon came to require increasingly skilled care from farm managers, veterinarians, nutritionists and husbandmen. The ratio of the length between the wild boar's intestine and its body length is 9 to 1. The boar puts its protein into making bone and a big head. The ratio for today's improved American breeds is 13.5 to 1, allowing the pig to consume more feed and convert it into meat along its sides and quarters.

20. Much of the following information is taken directly from a study by E. S. E. Hafez and J. P. Signoret, "The Behaviour of Swine," in Hafez, ed., *The Behaviour of Domestic Animals* (Baltimore: Williams and Wilkins, 1969), pp. 349-390.

21. On this point, Klaus Immelman argues that it is very difficult to conclude a specific behavioral trait has been caused by the process of domestication. Immelman writes: "the development of many structural and physiological characteristics also

depends to a large degree on environmental factors, the artificial conditions in which the animals live can also lead to modifications that are superimposed on any possible genetic changes." Klaus Immelman, *Introduction to Ethology*, tr. Erich Klinghammer (New York: Plenum, 1980), p. 197. The reason is that changes in behavior can result from the animals' responses to environmental conditions. Such changes would have to be considered modifications made by the animal itself, not by human selection of specific genetic arrangements.

22. Taylor refrains from saying food animals have a right to life. At one point he seems to imply the history of domestication has reduced food animals from the status of beings deserving respect to the status of "machines, buildings, tools, and other human artifacts" (*Respect for Nature*, p. 56). But he immediately adds we must treat them in ways that are good *for them*, and "this is a matter that is quite independent of whatever usefulness [they] might have to humans" (p. 57). He writes, further, that "the question of how [domestic animals] ought to be treated could not be decided simply by seeing what sort of treatment of them most effectively brings about the human benefit for which they are being used" (p. 57). Taylor's view is not unambiguous, but this is because his primary concern is with our duties toward wild living things and not with our duties toward domesticated animals.

23. Callicott, *In Defense of the Land Ethic*, pp. 55-56.

24. J. Baird Callicott, "Animal Liberation and Environmental Ethics: Back Together Again," *Between the Species* 4 (Summer 1988): 167.

25. Taylor, *Respect for Nature*, p. 295.

26. Ibid., p. 296. The reference for Taylor's figures is Francis Moore Lappe, *Diet for a Small Planet* (New York: Ballantine, 1971).

27. The rabbinic tradition contains such an argument in *Sanhedrin* 59b: "Rav Judah stated in the name of Rav, 'Adam was not permitted meat for purposes of eating as it is written . . . But when the sons of Noab came [God] permitted them [to eat the beasts of the earth]. . .' "

David J. Bleich, in *Contemporary Halakhic Problems*, vol. 3 (New York: KTAV, 1989), p. 238, offers this restatement of the position: "Primeval man was denied the flesh of animals because of his enhanced moral status. Permission to eat the flesh of animals was granted only to Noah because, subsequent to Adam's sin, his banishment from the Garden of Eden and the degeneration of subsequent generations, man could no longer be held to such lofty moral standards."

See "Animal Experimentation," (pp. 194-236) and "Vegetarianism and Judaism," in Bleich, *Contemporary Halakhic Problems*, pp. 237-50. Bleich does not agree with this interpretation of the text: "In point of fact, [Rav Judah's] talmudic dictum is simply a terse statement of the relevant law prior to the time of Noah but is silent with regard to any validating rationale" (p. 238).

Bleich notes that Rabbi Abraham Isaac Kook also maintains that humans are unable in their fallen state to overcome their desire for meat, and refers to Kook's *"Afikim ba-Negev,"* *Ha-Pales* vol. 3, no. 12 (Elul 5663), p. 658.

Chapter 8

The Vampire's Dilemma

Animal Rights and Parasitical Nature

Andrew Linzey

Imagine that you are a twenty-five-year-old living in New Orleans, called Louis. The date is 1791. You suffer a terrible bereavement due to the untimely death of your brother — a death for which you blame yourself. You spend nights drinking in New Orleans in a state of near despair. One night, just a few steps from your door, you are attacked by an unknown assailant. To experience family bereavement, to be consumed by guilt and remorse, to verge on the abyss of despair — surely these are terrible things. Even more terrible when one is violently attacked — without provocation — to boot. And yet such is the way of life that as terrible things are happening to us, even more terrible things are just round the corner.

In the case of Louis, he woke up, not only battered and bruised, but bled — almost to death. The assailant was not just an ordinary eighteenth-century New Orleans mugger, but a vampire, and what is more, a vampire-making vampire. Louis regains consciousness not as an ordinary mortal but as a member of an immortal species. Some of you of a more inquiring disposition may be curious as to how one vampire propagates its species. Alas, I cannot claim any expertise in vampirology, but I am led to believe that the process happens like this: the propagating vampire sucks the blood from his or her would-be progeny almost to the point of death, but then instead of letting him or her actually die, fills the person with blood mingled

Andrew Linzey is IFAW Senior Research Fellow, Mansfield College, Oxford, and also Special Professor of Theology, University of Nottingham. Amongst his pioneering works on animals and theology are: *Animal Rights: A Christian Assessment* (SCM Press 1976), *Christianity and the Rights of Animals* (Crossroad & SPCK 1987), *Animals and Christianity* (Crossroad & SPCK 1989).

from his own. Looked at purely dispassionately, we could liken the process to a blood transfusion with a certain extra factor supplied. For ease I will refer to this in due course as the "X" factor.

Doubtless you will be aware that one salient feature of a vampire's existence is the need to kill for food, or, to be more precise, to suck blood. It is important to understand that this is no optional gastronomic extra but essential for vampire life. Indeed, technically, I was wrong to describe Louis as a vampire made so simply by the process of transfusion. Louis became a vampire only as he recognized the deep hungering thirst for blood and in particular learned how to kill. Lestat, his propagator, had to teach him. As the deep hungering thirst grew within Louis, he finally consented to drink human blood. A victim was selected, Lestat completed the preparatory work, and Louis was invited to drink from the victim's wrist. This is how Louis relates this first experience:

> I drank, sucking the blood out of the holes, experiencing for the first time since infancy the special pleasure of sucking nourishment, the body focused with the mind upon one vital source.

As Louis drew blood, he heard sound:

> A dull roar at first and then the pounding like the pounding of a drum, growing louder and louder, as if some enormous creature were coming up on one slowly through a dark and alien forest, pounding as he came, a huge drum. And then there came the pounding of another drum, as if another giant were coming yards behind him, and each giant, intent on his own drum, gave no notice to the rhythm of the other. The sound grew louder and louder until it seemed to fill not just my hearing but all my senses, to be throbbing in my lips and fingers, in the flesh of my temples, in my veins. Above all in my veins, drum and then the other drum ... I realized that the drum was my heart, and the second drum had been his.[1]

I venture to relate this first experience, not in any way for ghoulish purposes, but in order that we may understand Louis's predicament correctly. Those who are apt to be rather superior in their attitude to vampires frequently forget that sucking blood was no mere satisfaction of the appetite, rather it was a profound life-engaging experience involving not inconsiderable ecstasy.

Now I have called this paper "The Vampire's Dilemma." But some of you may legitimately query whether Louis's predicament should be classed in these terms. After all, a vampire is a vampire. He or she does what he or she does, notwithstanding mystical ecstasy, because of necessity. No blood, no vampire. And yet Louis's experience is rather unusual in this regard. He certainly needs blood, indeed, without it he would die. He even craves for it, and, like all vampires, is physically distraught without at least one such bloodsucking encounter every day. And yet through some fortuity of circumstance, Louis is not happy about being a vampire. Not that he feels nostalgic for his mortal origins; after all, he was desperately unhappy, at least immediately prior to his vampirehood. Neither is Louis's unhappiness principally because of his lack of vampire colleagues. It is certainly true that his one close vampire acquaintance, even would-be friend, Lestat, is not always charming company, and yet solitude for a vampire may not be the grievous blow it is for us simple mortals. Vampire life, and especially its increased powers of movement, perception, sensibility — not to mention flight — does have some compensating factors. It would be wrong, as some high-minded vampire commentators have suggested, to suppose that immortality under such conditions is necessarily disagreeable.

Nevertheless, Louis is unhappy. We should allow him to describe his sorry predicament in his own words:

> Am I damned? Am I from the devil? Is my very nature that of a devil?
> I was asking myself over and over. And if it is why then do I revolt
> against it ... turn away in disgust when Lestat kills? What have I
> become in becoming a vampire? Where am I to go? And all the while,
> as the death wish caused me to neglect my thirst, my thirst grew
> hotter: my veins were veritable threads of pain in my flesh: my temples
> throbbed and finally I could stand it no longer. Torn apart by the wish
> to take no action — to starve, to wither in thought on the one hand;
> and driven to kill on the other — I stood in an empty, desolate street
> and heard the sound of a child crying.[2]

For those who are already wondering what happened to the child and what Louis decided to do, I should report that Louis bled the mother of the child and made the child a vampire. Together they travel the world, ostensibly in search of other vampires who will help them to understand why they are as they are.

By now the point to which this elaborate metaphor is leading must be becoming increasingly obvious. But before I state the point or dilemma, I must acknowledge my debt to Louis and in particular his literary creator, Anne Rice. For it is from her book, *Interview with the Vampire*, that I have taken the basic plot. This book, I understand, is only the first of three volumes which explore the nature of contemporary vampirehood.[3] I cannot claim to have read the other volumes, but it is clear from what I have read that the human species is in debt to Anne Rice's imagination. If, as Charles Morgan once remarked, there is no failure except failure of the imagination, Rice's work richly deserves both her reputation and her readership, the latter of which I am assured runs into tens of thousands.

The full extent of Louis's dilemma should now become clear. Should he go on living at the expense of other mortal creatures? Does it matter that he kills to live, and if it doesn't matter, why should he feel so stricken about it? Likewise we may ask: does it matter that the human species exists today only by the mass slaughter of billions of other creatures as food? Six to nine billion nonhuman animals are slaughtered in the United States every year; approximately 500 million in the United Kingdom. In comparison with this annual carnage, consumption even by the most rapacious of all vampires is rather slight. The average American eats more than the average vampire.

If we return to Louis's story for a while, we find that some features of his predicament show uncanny similarity to our own. In the first place, almost all Louis's fellow vampires do not see that there is a moral problem at all. When he raises with his propagator, Lestat, whether there might be something less than desirable about sucking blood, Louis is chided for his emotional immaturity. He was simply chasing the "phantoms of [his] former self." "You are in love with your mortal nature," argues Lestat. In other words, Louis had not yet grown up. He didn't yet see that the issue of killing was no moral issue at all. As Lestat puts it:

> "Vampires are killers . . . Predators whose all-seeing eyes were meant to give them detachment. The ability to see human life in its entirety not with any mawkish sorrow but with a thrilling satisfaction in being the end of that life, in having a hand in the divine plan."[4]

Although Lestat here seems to suggest that killing is actually to be commended theologically, I think it is fairest to characterize Lestat's overall view of killing as amoral. Since death for each mortal individual is inevitable, the process of hastening that inevitability is as devoid of moral significance as is the blowing of the wind or the pouring of the rain.

And it is this idea that brings us to the second, and by far the most significant, similarity between almost all vampires and almost all humans. Eating animals by humans is thought to be as natural as sucking blood is for vampires. The argument is quite explicit: "Do what it is your nature to do," argues Lestat. "This is but a taste of it. Do what it is your nature to do."[5] This claim seems to sum up the dilemma of both vampires like Louis and mortal vegetarians like myself who would rather live without killing. Are we not simply opposing the nature of things as given, or indeed our own natures? Aren't non-bloodsucking vampires and non-meat-eating humans similarly anomalous in the history of our respective species? Is it not true that both are seemingly incapable of facing the world as it is without emotion or moral squint?

Considerations such as these lead Louis and his child colleague to a series of journeyings, one might even say pilgrimages, in search of knowledge — both of how they came to be — and more decisively still to the Creator of all things which be. In the middle of his European voyage by ship, Louis nurtures the hope that somewhere in this new continent he might find "the answer to why under God this suffering was allowed to exist—why under God it was allowed to begin, and how under God it might be ended."[6]

In the same way that Louis was led to God in order to explain and understand the "X" factor that makes vampires bloodsucking, so too have many previously wrestled with the morality of carnivorousness in the sight of God. Louis is by no means alone in the history of moral deliberation. Plato seems to have envisaged a world, almost a Golden Age, in which all creatures lived harmoniously, and only after humans had been given God-like power over animals, did those harmonious relationships degenerate into strife and violence.[7] Genesis 1 similarly depicts a state of perfect Sabbath harmony within creation where humans and animals are both prescribed a vegetarian diet.[8] This fundamental insight that parasitical existence is incompatible with the original will of God has to be grasped if we are to understand the subsequent attempts in Genesis both to limit and accommodate killing. The Fall and the Flood are the great symbols of why humanity can no longer live at peace either with itself or with other creatures.

And yet the insight that parasitical existence is incompatible with the designs of the Creator still does not answer the problem of how vampires or carnivores must live today. If God can tolerate such a system, are we not in the end to resign ourselves to it, or abandon the notion of a holy, loving Creator altogether? Most humans have followed the reasoning of Samuel Pufendorf, who argued in 1688 that

> [I]t is a safe conclusion from the fact that the Creator established no common right between man and brutes, that no injury is done brutes if they are hurt by man, since God himself made such a state to exist between man and brutes.[9]

At first sight, religious people would appear to be impaled on the horns of a dilemma. Either they accept that God did not ordain a just state of affairs, in which case we can no longer postulate a loving, just deity, or otherwise they have to accept that God is not—as claimed—the sovereign Creator of all things. But are Christians obliged to take either of these two options? I think not. There is a third and theologically much more satisfying option. It begins by asking us to consider that the world really is *creation*. It is the work of a loving and holy God, yes, but it is also creation, and not Creator. Because the world is creation and not Creator, it cannot be anything other than less than divine. To be a creature is necessarily to be incomplete, unfinished, imperfect. If creation was wholly perfect, it would have to be, like God, perfection itself. From this standpoint the very nature of creation is always ambiguous; it points both ways; it both affirms and denies God at one and the same time. Creation affirms God because God loves and cares for it, but it also necessarily denies God because it is not divine. It follows that there can be no straightforward moral or theological appeal to the way nature is. Note the way in which Pufendorf deliberately takes the state of nature as a yardstick or measure of what God wills or plans for creation. I argue rather that the state of nature can in no way be an unambiguous referent to what God wills or plans for creation.

The issue may be clarified by reference to the traditional theological notion of natural law. We turn to what has been one of the most enlightened of attempts to rehabilitate natural law theory. In his essay, "Rethinking Natural Law," John Macquarrie argues that it is essential to distinguish natural law as an ethical concept from any scientific law of nature: "The expression 'natural law' refers to a norm of responsible conduct, and suggests a kind of fundamental guideline or criterion that comes before all rules or particular formulations of law."[10]

Now at first sight such a redefinition would seem to support Louis's position. After all, does not Louis experience a prerational, intuitive conception of what is right? Something parallel to what Macquarrie calls a "norm of responsible conduct" — a "criterion" that comes before all formulations of law? The problem is, however, that Macquarrie — like so many ethicists before him — is unable to develop and justify such a notion of natural law without reference to what he calls the way things are. "Natural Law too claims to be founded in '*the way things are*,' in ultimate structures that are explicitly contrasted with the human conventions that find expression in our ordinary rules and customs."[11]

Again: "[Natural law] safeguards against moral subjectivism and encourages moral seriousness by locating the demand of moral obligation in the very way things are."[12] In contrast, I suggest that if we can use the term "natural law" at all in this context, it can properly, perhaps only, be discovered *not* in *the way things are* but in the sense of *what should be*. In short, so much natural law theory rests upon an unqualified "naturalism." What we have witnessed almost by sleight of hand is a developing "naturalism" within moral theology which fundamentally limits the redeeming capacities of God to what humans perceive to be "the way things are" in nature itself. The result has been an almost total failure to grasp the possibility of redemption outside the human sphere.

One example must suffice. John Armstrong, in a sensitive and perceptive discussion of Hebrew attitudes to animals, nevertheless castigates the Isaianic vision of the lion lying down with the lamb as an attempt "to get rid of the beasts of prey or change their nature beyond recognition."[13] He does not see the point of Isaiah's vision, which is not that animality will be destroyed by divine love but rather that animal nature is in bondage to violence and predation. The vision of Isaiah is directly relevant here: It invites us to the imaginative recognition that God's transforming love is not determined even by what we think we know of elementary biology.

If there can be any rehabilitation of natural law, we must reiterate that we are speaking neither of "law" nor "nature" in any recognizable sense. There is nothing in creation which of itself can give us an unambiguous understanding of the moral purposes of God. To return to Louis's dilemma for a moment, I am suggesting that he is right to be vexed and troubled. He is right to rail and thunder against a kind of nature which forecloses on the moral option. Louis is right to seek a way out; even against all appearances of necessity, he is right to go on searching, and not least of all, he is right to place the question mark at God itself. Louis's deep, prerational, intuitive sense that sucking blood is not right is what we should call not "natural law" but rather "transnatural moral imperative." To have grasped such an insight is an implicitly theological act. The world does not explain itself; either there is explanation outside creation or creation remains enigmatic and inexplicable.

But if it is right that Louis should strive, even against all odds, to realize this moral imperative, even more should the human species seek to live without killing to eat. This is the obvious point of this paper. The vampire has a dilemma because it seems — at least at present — that he cannot choose to live without recourse to blood, but we humans do now have such a choice. Whether humans have always been so free is something which at worst I am doubtful about, at best I have an open mind. When theologian Dean Inge, deeply committed to animal rights as he was, argued as recently as 1926 that we could not give up flesh because "we must eat something,"[14] I do not believe that he was being disingenuous. Inge really believed, as did many of his compassionate forebears, that one could not live without eating animals. Rumors of vegetarians existed, but like the rumors themselves did not — it was thought — persist. Most people until comparatively recently were incredulous that real vegetarians both existed and prospered. Despite all the vegetarian literature produced by George Bernard Shaw, popular commentators still claimed that only secret consumption of liver kept him alive. Again only comparatively recently have dietitians accepted that vegetable protein is, like meat, "first-class protein," and even now it seems there are some nutritionists determined to expose what they see as the dangers of veganism. For the first time in the history of the human race, vegetarianism has become a publicly viable option — at least for those who live in the Western world. This is not of course to overlook all the many pioneers and prophets, but all of these have been just that: pioneers, protesters and prophets against the stream. But that mainstream has now to contend — in the United Kingdom at least — with something approximating four million vegetarians, demi-vegetarians and vegans. For humans there is now no dilemma compounded through ignorance. We can live free of meat; there are now numerous examples of people who do so and who are alive and well. When we know that we are free to do otherwise, eating meat constitutes what Stephen Clark calls "empty gluttony."[15]

To this conclusion, I anticipate four objections. The first argues that my insistence upon the "fallen" nature of creation, and its inherent ambiguity, mitigates against contemporary environmental ethics and with it an increased respect for animals in particular. After years in which nature and materiality have been devalued within Christian theology, do we not need a new theology of the inherent goodness of all creatures? Was Gerard Manley Hopkins wrong when he claimed that the "world is charged with the grandeur of God"?[16]

It is certainly true that in recent years observers of the theological scene have witnessed the growth of a body of writing concerned to reestablish what is called the "sacralization of nature." Such writing must be construed as a valuable protest against the kind of unqualified appeal to human supremacy articulated by, for example, Charles Davis, in 1966. Davis argues that nature is no longer regarded by "scientific man" as "sacred and untouchable," and he proclaims that such a view of nature is in full harmony with the Christian faith, indeed required by it. "Any other view of nature is, in the light of Christian teaching, idolatrous, superstitious or magical."[17] Davis may well have reason to regret his utterances at a time when it is precisely unremitting human domination of the earth that seems to threaten even human survival. It is not difficult to see how, in the light of contemporary environmental destruction, individuals want to posit a relocation of value which includes all natural objects. Slogans such as "the world is all good" or "the earth knows best" are quite understandable as protests to the massive contemporary devaluing of creaturely life.

And yet, understandable as this protest is, when it is combined with a view that all "natural" structures of life are themselves good or perfect in every way, the whole possibility of a theological ethic is eclipsed. Certainly we need to recover a sense of the original blessing of creation, but if we suppose that all in creation is indiscriminately good, then we have no room left to establish the best. One may be forgiven for thinking that the task left to humanity is—on some ecological accounts—simply to emulate the structures of parasitical existence. We are supposed to glory in the economy of existence whereby one species devours another with consummate efficiency. It may not be surprising then that some recent commentators have seen a potentially sinister relationship between far right philosophy and some forms of green political theory. Whether such a connection can be responsibly made is a matter I cannot pursue here, but it cannot be doubted that an appeal to pure "naturalism" opens up a pathway to a rebirth of brutalism in which humans are invited not to morally transform the cosmos but to imitate its worst manifestations. If the legacy of Genesis is sometimes thought to be disadvantageous to animals, even more so the contemporary legacy of Darwinism.

And yet some may surely question whether we now have gone too far on the other side. Are we not to celebrate the life of creation with all its beauty, magnificence and complexity and therein with Hopkins to perceive signs of the grandeur of God? Is not the biblical material right to point us to the ways in which some animals at least appear to provide moral examples for our own behavior? Isn't the story of Balaam's ass a sign of how morally advanced are the beasts compared to the mindless Balaams of our

world? I have no desire to deny the force of any of these arguments. Theologian Karl Barth is right to speak eloquently of how creation should be
construed as "justification," that is, as divine beneficence, benefit, grace.[18]
That there is beauty, value, goodness in the created order is judicious
Christian doctrine; that the whole creation is right as it is, or in the way it
is—that it is in no way incomplete or unfinished—is not. To maintain that
creation is *all* alright is to make God the Redeemer redundant. In short:
"the earth is all good" slogan fails to recognize the X factor.

The second objection is that Jesus was—as far as we know—no crusading
vegetarian. While there are no precise biblical accounts of him eating meat,
the canonical Gospels leave us in no doubt that he ate fish. And if this is
true, on what grounds can we claim him as the revelation of an alternative
nonparasitical existence?

At first sight this appears a pretty cast-iron objection. As Stephen Clark
asks: "Shall not the Judge of all the earth do right?"[19] There seem, however,
to be two principal grounds on which this argument founders. The first is
in its implicit assumption that the demands of contemporary Christian discipleship can be met simply by the imitation of the Jesus of first-century
Palestine. If this is really taken to its limit, there would be hardly any scope
for moral theology at all. The purpose of ethical reflection would be invalid.
Ethical striving would simply center upon the need to imitate Jesus as he
then was in that situation. In contrast, what Christian discipleship requires
is summed up well by John Macquarrie:

> The Christian . . . defines mature manhood in terms of Jesus Christ,
> and especially his self-giving love. But Christ himself is no static figure,
> nor are Christians called to imitate him as static model. Christ is an
> eschatological figure, always before us; and the doctrine of his coming
> again "with glory" implies that there are dimensions of christhood
> not manifest in the historical Jesus and not yet fully grasped by the
> disciples. Thus discipleship does not restrict human development to
> some fixed pattern, but summons into freedoms, the full depth of
> which is unknown, except that they will always be consonant with self-
> giving love.[20]

The second way in which this argument founders is in failing to grasp
the necessary particularity of the incarnation. To be God incarnate as a
human being does not mean being some kind of Superman. The traditional
affirmation about Jesus is not that he is God, but that he is God and human.
The point is no mere technicality. God incarnates himself or herself into
the limits and constraints of the world as we know it. It is true that one of
the purposes of the incarnation was to manifest something of the transnatural possibilities of existence, but no one human life can demonstrate,
let alone exhaust, all the possibilities of self-giving love. To those who argue
that Jesus was deficient or limited either in his lack of crusading power for

feminism, for the abolition of slavery, or for veganism—not to mention home rule—miss the central point that to confess Christ crucified is to confess a Christ inevitably and profoundly limited by the fact of incarnation. To be in one place at one time means that one cannot be everywhere.

In the light of this, it is all the more significant that early reflection upon the work and person of Christ is determined to spell out its eventual cosmic dimension and meaning. The line from Ephesians expresses it well: "[God] has made known to us his secret purpose, in accordance with the plan which he determined beforehand in Christ, to be put into effect when the time was ripe: namely that the universe, everything in heaven and on earth, might be brought into a unity in Christ."[21]

And likewise in Colossians, where God chose Christ "and through him to reconcile all things to himself, making peace through the shedding of his blood on the cross—all things, whether on earth or in heaven."[22]

This concept of cosmic reconciliation provides the framework in which we may grasp the transnatural moral imperative glimpsed in the actual historical life of Jesus. For the revelation of God in Jesus is such as to intensify rather than diminish the puzzle of the created order. For Jesus stands against as much as for the order of nature as we now know it. The natural processes of sickness and death and disease, even indeed the vagaries of the weather, are subject to the power of God in Jesus Christ. If we follow Jesus, we are set upon a course of transnatural transformation whereby the sick do not suffer and die but are healed and restored; the poor are not downtrodden but become the first among equals; and even the winds which blow us to the four corners are gathered together. The so-called "nature miracles" of Jesus are signs among many that in Jesus is a birth of new possibilities for all creation. I suggest that what we have in Jesus is a model not of the accommodation of nature but rather of the beginning of its transformation. Not that all things were transformed by Jesus, nor that all of his life in every aspect was so transforming, nor that every part has even yet been transformed, but that to follow Jesus is to affirm, and seek to actualize, the fundamental possibility of world transformation.

The third objection to my thesis is that even if eventual peace and harmony is God's will in Christ for all creation, we can't achieve it now. Humans do face a dilemma. Even if there is no natural law requiring us to eat flesh, there is a psychological one. Humans cannot be expected to forego the enormous pleasures of consuming flesh. Gluttony it may be, but we humans can do no better. As vampires need their mystical fix of blood, so we humans need our finger-licking good chicken or juicy steak.

Some may think that I have already caricatured this objection, but I have put it in such a crass form because in this way it expresses well a fundamental kind of despair about moral self-improvement which is a great deal more widespread than is often supposed. There are all kinds of reasons why Christians should be wary of schemes for moral perfectionism. Gran-

diose moral and social hopes often create incapacitating disappointment
when it is discovered that they cannot be realized. In particular it follows
from my overall argument that humans are themselves simply creatures:
limited, finite, incapable of seeing things whole, incapable indeed by themselves of becoming whole. Moral burdens incapable of being relieved can
create anger, frustration, even violence. We do well to realize what a frail
and limited vessel the human creature is. If we cannot prevent greed, stupidity, cruelty, deceit, violence, envy, hatred, culpable acts of wickedness
performed by members of our own species against other members of our
species, what chance can we have of behaving any better to other, nonhuman, creatures? It is worth noting that Karl Barth opposed vegetarianism
on the grounds that it represents "a wanton anticipation of . . . the new
aeon for which we hope."[23] Not that living nonviolently in peace with all
creation was not God's will—rather that this vision of peaceableness could
not be even approximated now.

Those of us who may sometimes feel encouraged to an optimistic view
of life need to take cognizance of the lyrical protest of political philosopher
William Godwin:

> Let us not amuse ourselves with a pompous and delusive survey of
> the whole, but let us examine parts severally and individually. All
> nature swarms with life. This may in one view afford an idea of an
> extensive theatre of pleasure. But unfortunately every animal preys
> upon his fellow. Every animal however minute, has a curious and
> subtle structure, rendering him susceptible, as it should seem, of
> piercing anguish. We cannot move our foot without becoming the
> means of destruction. The wounds inflicted are of a hundred kinds.
> These petty animals are capable of palpitating for days in the agonies
> of death. It may be said with little licence of phraseology that all
> nature suffers. There is no day nor hour, in which in some regions of
> the many peopled globe, thousands of men, and millions of animals,
> are not tortured to the utmost extent that organized life will afford.
> Let us turn our attention to our own species. Let us survey the poor;
> oppressed, hungry, naked, denied all the gratifications of life and all
> that nourishes the mind. They are either tormented with the injustice
> or chilled into lethargy. Let us view man writhing under the pangs of
> disease, or the fiercer tortures that are stored up for him by his breth-
> ren. Who is there that will look on and say "All is well; there is no
> evil in the world"?[24]

Notwithstanding the beauty and goodness and magnificence of the created world, no sane person, it seems to me, could simply say "All is well;
there is no evil in the world." And I agree with Godwin that the "creed of
optimism," as he puts it, "has done much harm in the world."[25] But it seems
precisely because one cannot say in truth that all is well with the world,

and further that the creed of optimism speaks truthfully of how the world is, that the case for believing in world-transforming Christian theism is so strong. The choice is clear: Either there is at the heart of being unredeemed or unredeemable suffering and misery and death, or there is actually a pattern of transformation, glimpsed in Christ, which is actually capable of bringing about a new world order.

Now there can be little doubt that such a perception is demanding and burdensome and itself flies in the face of not inconsiderable evidence. But it should be clear that such a perception is consistent with, even required by, Christian faith. To the objection that this invites otiose, even harmful, perfectionism, there can only be one answer. The God who demands is also the God who enables. Even by the power of the Holy Spirit it may be that the world cannot be made well at a stroke given the necessary self-limitations imposed by the Creator. Nevertheless, it is possible and credible to believe that by the power of the Spirit new ways of living without violence can be opened up for us, even within a world which is tragically divided between the forces of life and the forces of death. We should celebrate the possibility that through the Spirit we can today live in some way freer of the X factor with regard to animals than many of our forebears. Optimism may well be facile; despair, however, is not a Christian option.

The fourth and final objection questions the rational and theological basis for obeying this prenatural intuition in what I have called the "trans-natural moral imperative." Is it self-evident that we should live in peace, or that peace is itself better than violence? Can anything be self-evident in our confused and contradictory creaturely world? I do not suppose that my own tentative answer will satisfy all, as explanations of moral imperatives seldom do. But I suggest that there may be one sense in which the notion of so-called natural law can help us. It is found in the notion of Heraclitus that "all human laws are nourished by the one divine law; for this holds sway as far as it will, and suffices for all and prevails in everything." This law is identified by Heraclitus with the *logos*, "the primordial word or reason in accordance with which everything occurs." Before it is protested that I am merely returning to a notion of natural law previously rejected, let it be clear, as one commentator makes explicit:

A "law of nature" is merely a general descriptive formula for referring to some specific complex of observed facts, while Heraclitus' divine law is something genuinely normative. It is the highest norm of the cosmic process, and the thing which gives the process its significance and worth.[26]

It will not be overlooked that the concept of *logos*, here defined in a Greek context, has obvious affinities with Jewish and Christian ones. It is, I suggest, in the doctrine of Christ as the *Logos* that we are given the revelatory principle that peace is better than violence and that reconciliation is better than disintegration. The Cosmic Christ through whom all things come to be is the source and destiny and well-being of all creatures. To affirm the Cosmic Christ is to embrace a new possibility of existence within our grasp now. It will be clear that this view gives a high place to humans in nature; not because they are so worthy in themselves but because they are — as no other species, as far as we know, at least — capable of focusing the forces of life and death, of being vampires or vegetarians.

It is for this reason that I also want to conclude that vegetarianism, far from being some kind of optional moral extra or some secondary moral consideration, is in fact an implicitly theological act of the greatest significance. By refusing to kill and eat meat, we witness to a higher order of existence, implicit in the *Logos*, which is struggling to be born in us. By refusing to go the way of our "natural nature" or our "psychological nature," by standing against the order of unredeemed nature, we become signs of the order of existence for which all creatures long.

I end as I began, by asking you to consider the plight of our morally stricken vampire called Louis. I am sorry to say that I cannot report a happy ending. Despite his searches all over the world and his encounter with fellow vampires older and wiser than himself, and despite all his moral strength, he is unable to free himself from his own parasitical nature. There is one saving grace for Louis, however. His story will not have been told in vain if it has helped us to recover a sense of the responsibility of our own moral freedom.

Notes

1. Anne Rice, *Interview with the Vampire* (New York: Ballantine Books, 1976) pp. 19-20.

2. Ibid., p. 83.

3. The other titles are *The Vampire Lestat* and *The Queen of the Damned*, both published by Ballantine Books.

4. Rice, p. 83.

5. Ibid., p. 88.

6. Ibid., p. 169.

7. Plato, "The Statesman," in Harold N. Fowler and W. R. M. Lamb (tr.) *Plato* (London: Heinemann, 1925) 271d -4c; extract in P. A. B. Clarke and Andrew Linzey (eds.) *Political Theory and Animal Rights* (London and Winchester, MA: Pluto Press, 1990), pp. 53-55.

8. See Gen. 1:29.

9. Samuel Pufendorf (1632-92), *The Law of Nature and Nations* (1688) trs. C. H. and W. A. Oldfather (New York: Oceana, 1931) Vol. II, pp. 530-1, extract in Clarke and Linzey (eds.), *Political Theory and Animal Rights*, pp. 116-119.

10. John Macquarrie, "Rethinking Natural Law," in *Three Issues in Ethics* (London: SCM Press, 1970), p. 92.

11. Ibid., p. 97; my emphasis.

12. Ibid., p. 110.

13. John Armstrong, *The Idea of Holiness and the Humane Response: A Study in*

the Concept of Holiness and Its Social Consequences (London: George Allen & Unwin, 1985), p. 44. I make the same point in my *Brother and Sister Creatures: The Saints and Animals*, forthcoming.

14. W. R. Inge, "The Rights of Animals," in *Lay Thoughts of a Dean* (New York and London: The Knickerbocker Press, 1926), p. 199; cited and discussed also in my *Christianity and the Rights of Animals* (London and New York: SPCK and Crossroad, 1987), p. 145 f.

15. Stephen R. L. Clark, *The Moral Status of Animals* (Oxford: The Clarendon Press, 1977), p. 83.

16. Gerard Manley Hopkins, "God's Grandeur," in Andrew Linzey and Tom Regan (eds.), *The Song of Creation: An Anthology of Poems in Praise of Animals* (London: Marshall Pickering, 1988), p. 119.

17. Charles Davis, *God's Grace in History* (London: Fontana Books, 1966), p. 21f; the reference to Davis is lifted from my *Animal Rights: A Christian Assessment* (London: SCM Press, 1976), p. 16.

18. Karl Barth, "Creation as Justification," in *Church Dogmatics*, Vol. III/1 (Edinburgh: T & T Clark, 1960), p. 348 f.

19. Clark, *The Moral Status of Animals*, p. 196.

20. Macquarrie, "Rethinking Natural Law," p. 109.

21. Ephesians 1:9-10 (REB).

22. Colossians 1:20 (REB).

23. Karl Barth, "The Command of God the Creator," *Church Dogmatics*, Vol. III (Edinburgh: T & T Clark, 1961), p. 256.

24. William Godwin (1756-1836), *Enquiry Concerning Political Justice and Its Influence on Modern Morals and Happiness* (1798) (London: J. Watson, 1842), pp. 216-18; extract in Clarke and Linzey, (eds.), *Political Theory and Animal Rights*, pp. 132-4.

25. Ibid.

26. Werner Jagger, *The Theology of the Early Greek Philosophers*, trans. E. S. Robinson (London: Oxford University Press, 1967), p. 36 and pp. 115-16. The translation from Heraclitus is from Jagger, cited and discussed in Macquarrie, "Rethinking Natural Law," pp. 93 f.

Acknowledgments

I am grateful to Marly Cornell for first bringing to my attention the theological significance of Anne Rice's work—as well as for many hours of illuminating theological conversation. I also acknowledge my debts to Professor Daniel Hardy of Princeton University and Professor Colin Gunton of King's College, London, who have helped me, both by their conversation and writings, to understand something of the Christian doctrine of creation. I am especially grateful to Professor Stephen Clark of Liverpool University, whose paper "Is Nature God's Will?" helped me to think through this topic in a fundamental way.

Chapter 9

Feeding on Grace

Institutional Violence, Christianity, and Vegetarianism

Carol J. Adams

Better a dish of vegetables if love go with it than a fat ox eaten in hatred.

—Proverbs 15:17 (NEB)

Introduction

The day after I arrived home from my first year at Yale Divinity School, an urgent knocking summoned me from my task of unpacking. It was a distressed neighbor reporting that someone had just shot one of our horses. We ran through the pasture to discover that indeed, one of my horses was lying dead, a small amount of blood trickling from his mouth. Shots from the nearby woods could still be heard. One horse lay dead and the other frantically pranced around him.

That night, upset and depressed, I sat down to a dinner of hamburger. Suddenly I flashed on the image of Jimmy's dead body in the upper pasture, awaiting a formal burial by backhoe in the morning. One dead body had a name, a past that included my sense of his subjectivity, and was soon to be respectfully buried. The other dead body was invisible, objectified, nameless, except in its current state as hamburger, and was to be buried in my stomach. At the time I realized the hypocrisy of my actions. The question

Carol J. Adams is the author of *The Sexual Politics of Meat: A Feminist-Vegetarian Critical Theory* (Continuum 1990), which won the 1989 Continuum Women's Studies Award. She is editing an anthology on ecofeminism and the sacred, forthcoming from Crossroad, and completing a book on pastoral care and sexual terror.

142

confronting me was: "If Jimmy were meat would I, could I, be his meat eater?" And the answer was "of course not." Having recognized his individuality, his subjectivity, having been in relationship with him, I could not render him beingless. So why could I do this to another animal, whom, if I had known her, would surely have revealed her individuality and subjectivity? The invisible became visible: I became aware of how I objectified others and what it means to make animals into meat. I also recognized my ability to change myself: Realizing what meat actually is, I also realized I need not be a meat eater.

This experience in 1973 catalyzed the process by which I became a vegetarian slightly more than a year later. It also catalyzed a theoretical and theological search to understand why our society invests so many economic, environmental, and cultural resources into protecting the eating of animals. It is my position that the eating of animals is a form of institutional violence. The corporate ritual that characterizes institutional violence deflects or redefines the fact that the eating of animals is exploitative. This is why conscientious and ethical individuals do not see meat as problem. It is fair to say that the most frequent relationship the majority of Christians have with the other animals is with dead animals whom they eat. Because of institutional violence, meat eating is conceived of neither as a relationship nor as the consuming of dead animals. It is not often while eating meat that one thinks: "I am now interacting with an animal." We do not see our meat eating as contact with animals because it has been renamed as contact with food. We require an analysis of institutional violence to identify just why it is that Christians ought to reconceptualize meat eating. This essay offers such an analysis and reconceptualization.

The Institutional Violence of Eating Animals

Through an understanding of institutional violence we will come to see the dynamics of exploitation vis-à-vis the other animals, and begin to recognize their suffering as morally relevant in determining our own actions.

For something to be *institutional* violence it must be a significant, widespread, unethical practice in a society. As an industry, meat production is the second largest in this country. It is both widespread and vitally important to our economy. Though meat eating is now the normative expression of our relationship with other animals, a close examination of the functioning of institutional violence will reveal why I call it unethical.

Institutional violence is characterized by:

1. An infringement on or failure to acknowledge another's inviolability
2. Treatment or physical force that injures or abuses
3. A series of denial mechanisms which deflect attention from the violence

4. The targeting of "appropriate" victims
5. Detrimental effects on society as a whole
6. The manipulation of the public (e.g., consumers) into passivity

Meat eating fits this definition of institutional violence. In fact, the word *"meat"* itself illustrates several of these components. It renders animals appropriate victims by naming them as edible and deflects our attention from the violence inherent to killing them for food. Because the word "meat" contributes to minimizing the implications of institutional violence, it will be enclosed in quotation marks in this essay. At times the more accurate term "flesh" will be used.

Institutional violence toward animals at its core denies their inviolability. Its function is to uphold and act upon the violability of animals. It works at the individual level by wrenching any notion of inviolability from one's sense of Christian ethics. Even if many children object to eating animals upon learning where "meat" comes from, this objection is rarely respected. And even if adults are discomforted by some form of flesh—whether it be because of the animal it is stolen from, a dog, a horse, a rat, or the part of the animal being consumed, the brain, the liver—they have no Christian ethical framework into which these objections might be placed. The absence of such a framework means that any reminders that animals have to be killed to be consumed, experienced by children explicitly and by adults implicitly, remain unassimilated and repressed. Institutional violence interposes an ethics of exploitation for any burgeoning ethic of inviolability.

We become firmly and persuasively convinced that the eating of animals is not only acceptable but necessary for survival. This deviates from the representation of our corporate beginning in Genesis as vegetarians, when God/ess says in Genesis 1:29: "Behold, I have given you every plant yielding seed which is upon the face of all the earth, and every tree with seed in its fruit; you shall have them for food.'"[1] This corporate and personal beginning as vegetarians seems to be confirmed by anthropological sources that indicate that our earliest hominid ancestors had vegetarian bodies. In the records of their bones, dental impressions, and tools, these anonymous ancestors reveal the fact that "meat," as a substantial part of the diet, became a fixture in human life only recently—in the past 40,000 years. Indeed, it was not until the past two hundred years that most people in the Western world had the opportunity to consume "meat" daily.

Our bodies appear better suited to digesting seeds and fruits than muscle and blood, suggesting again our personal origins as vegetarians. From this perspective, ingesting flesh is an act against our own body as well as against another animal's body, a double violation.

We have fallen from this state of grace with the other animals represented in Genesis 1:29 and substituted institutional violence for respect for their inviolability.

The Institutional Violence of Eating Animals Is an Infringement on or Failure to Acknowledge Another's Inviolability

Some individuals recognize the inviolability of animals. In other words, they believe that animals are not ours to use, abuse, or consume. They believe that if animals could talk, farmed animals, vivisected animals, fur-bearing animals, circus, zoo, and rodeo animals, hunted animals, would all say the same thing: "Don't touch me!" In the absence of a language that animals can speak that proclaims their inviolability, some human beings are searching for a language that speaks this on their behalf. So far most of these efforts could be grouped under the general heading of animal rights theory. Elsewhere in this volume, this approach is called to task. Here, let me say that the notion of animals' inviolability is a deep belief in search of a language. Because we have no adequate language for emotions or intuitions, we have no framework into which our misgivings about animals' current violability can be fit. In the absence of such language, it is important that we widen Christian ethical discourse to address the problem of the use of animals.

I believe that flesh eating is an unjust use of another for one's own profit or advantage. It is unjust because it is *unnecessary* (people do not need to eat animals to survive), *cruel*, and perpetuates inauthentic relationships among people and between people and the other animals. As such, it enacts the first component of institutional violence—the failure to honor another's wholeness and the interposition of your will against another's self-determination. Through the term "inviolability" I am claiming "Don't touch me" on behalf of animals, or to put it otherwise, "Animals should be inviolable!" Institutional violence tramples these claims and arrogates to humans the right to dominate and violate animals' bodies.

Institutional Violence Involves Treatment or Physical Force That Injures or Abuses

By treatment I mean *ongoing* conditions that are abusive or injurious. Factory farming involves such treatment. Intensively farmed animals fare poorly, being raised in enclosed, darkened, or dimly lit buildings. Their lives are characterized by little external stimulus; restriction of movement; no freedom to choose social interactions; intense and unpleasant fumes; little contact with human beings; ingestion of subtherapeutic doses of antibiotics to prevent diseases that could tear through an entire population of imprisoned animals, sometimes 70,000 in one building. Laying hens live with two to four others in cages slightly larger than this opened book. When being cooked in an oven, the chicken has four or five times more space than when she was alive. "Veal" calves are kept in crates that measure 22 inches wide by 54 inches long, where they cannot turn around, since exercise would increase muscle development, toughen the flesh, and slow weight gain. Standing on slatted floors causes a constant strain. Diarrhea, a frequent problem because of their improper diet which is meant to keep their flesh pale, causes the slats to become slippery and wet; the calves often fall, getting leg injuries. When taken to slaughter, many of them can hardly walk.

Factory farming is inevitable in a "meat" advocating culture, because it is the only way to maintain and meet the demand for flesh products. Thus, those who argue that factory farming is immoral but alternatives to obtaining animal flesh are acceptable, are attempting to deny the historical reality that has brought us to this time and place. Moreover, no matter where the animals to be slaughtered have been raised, it is the custom to withhold feed for the last twenty four hours of their life. As the authors of *Raising Pigs Successfully* reveal:

> Withholding feed is usually done for the sake of the butcher (less mess when the intestines and stomach are empty) and to save wasted feed. Some raisers don't do it because they say that it upsets the animal to miss feedings and adds to the stress level on butchering day. (Kellogg, 110)

This is clearly abusive treatment.

By physical force, I mean *specific* actions that cause injuries, in this case death by violence. While raising an animal in a loving family farm situation may mean that the conditions described above are not present, this condition – that of force that injures or abuses – will always be present, for an animal does not become "meat" without being violently deprived of his or her life. This violence can come in one of three ways: death at the hands of the family farmer, death by a hired gun who comes to the farm, or, as with animals intensively farmed, death at a slaughterhouse. This last option requires the transporting of the animals – often the only time that an animal will travel – a strange, sometimes uncomfortable, and perplexing if not alarming experience. At the slaughterhouse, smells and sounds alert the animal that something frightening is happening.

Clearly, animals prefer to live rather than to die, and when given the opportunity they tell us so.

As a child growing up in a small village, I lived down the street from the town butcher. We were allowed to watch him kill and butcher the animals. These animals did not go merrily to their deaths. Several times, rather than face his rifle, cows escaped from the truck and went running down the street. Pigs let out high squeals, moved frantically, and upon having their throats slashed, continued to toss and turn until yanked heavenward so that bleed-out could begin.

The killing of animals is physical force that injures and abuses animals against their will.

Institutional Violence Requires a Series of Denial Mechanisms

Denial of the extent and nature of violence is an important protective device for maintaining institutional violence. It communicates that the violence that is an integral part of the existence of some commodity, some benefit, is neither troublesome nor severe. In the language of "meat" and "meat eater" the issues of animal suffering and killing are neutralized. This language reveals that we have difficulty *naming the violence*. Why are we unable truthfully to name the eating of animals as such? Why do we eat animals and yet, through language, deny that this is what we are doing? Adrienne Rich offers one answer:

> Whatever is unnamed, undepicted in images. ... whatever is mis-named as something else, made difficult-to-come-by, whatever is bur-ied in the memory by the collapse of meaning under an inadequate or lying language – this will become, not merely unspoken, but unspeakable.

The truth about raising and slaughtering animals is both unspoken and unspeakable. We are especially not to discuss it when animals' bodies are being consumed. As a consequence *false naming* is a major component of institutional violence. Indeed, false naming begins with the living animals. Whether they are to be found on family farms or in factory farms, the advice is the same: Do not give animals to be eaten by human beings any names that bestow individuality. Family farmers advise: "If you're going to eat it [*sic*], don't give it [*sic*] a pet name. Try something like 'Porky' or 'Chops' or 'Spareribs' if the urge to name is too strong" (Kellogg, 13).

Factory farmers advise: "Forget the pig [or a cow, a chicken, etc.] is an 'animal.' Instead, view them as 'a machine in a factory' " (Byrnes in Mason and Singer, 1).

Do not name animals you are going to consume; don't call them Mary, Martha, or Paul, or even a pig, chicken, or cow, but a food-producing unit, a protein harvester, a computerized unit in a factory environment, an egg-producing machine, a converting machine, a biomachine, a crop, a grain-consuming animal unit.

False naming means that we can avoid responsibility. False naming cre-ates false consciousness. We communicate something different about our relationship to animals when we speak about "meat" than when we speak either about living animals who enjoy relationships or about the eating of slaughtered, cooked, and seasoned severed animal muscle and blood.

False naming means that "meat" eaters are people of the lie. They are lying about their actions, which they do not see as actions. Through lan-guage, we lose sight of the fact that someone must be acting as a perpetrator of violence for there to be someone else called "meat."

Language removes agency and cloaks violence: "Someone kills animals so that I can eat their corpses as meat" becomes "Animals are killed to be eaten as meat" then "Animals are meat" and finally "Meat animals" thus "Meat." Something *we do to animals* has become instead something that is a part of animals' nature and we lose consideration of our role as eaters of animals entirely. False naming about "meat" is an integral aspect of eating animals.

False naming enacts what I have called the structure of the absent referent. In *The Sexual Politics of Meat* I argue that animals in name and body are made absent as animals for "meat" to exist. If animals are alive they cannot be "meat." Thus a dead body replaces the live animal and animals become absent referents. Without animals there would be no flesh eating, yet they are absent from the act of eating flesh because they have been transformed into food. Animals are also made absent through language that renames dead bodies before consumers eat them. The absent referent permits us to forget about the animal as an independent entity and enables us to resist efforts to make animals present.[2] False naming and the structure of the absent referent create the permission for institutional violence and announce that *there is no call to accountability* for the eating of animals. In the absence of accountability, abuse continues.

The lack of any direct involvement with or consciousness of the violence of the slaughterhouse keeps us unaccountable. Again, as the family farmers reveal:

> We usually send our hogs out to be slaughtered simply because we don't want the work of preparing the meat ourselves and because, emotionally, we tend to grow attached to the porkers. It is far easier to pat them good-bye as they leave in the truck and welcome them back in white paper wrappers. The act of killing something [*sic*] you have raised from a baby is not an easy task. (Kellogg, 109)

Killing, except for the ritual of the hunt, remains distasteful to most consumers. Since the institutional violence of meat eating requires killing, at the rate of some 15 million a day, a cloud of denial surrounds this.

Denial is enacted at the financial level as well. "Meat" eaters do not have to pay the true costs for the "meat" that they eat. The cheapness of a diet based on grain-fed terminal animals exists because it does not include the cost of depleting the environment. Not only does the cost of "meat" not include the loss of topsoil, the pollution of water, and other environmental effects (see below), but price supports of the dairy and beef "industry" mean that the government actively prevents the price of eating animals from being reflected in the commodity of "meat." My tax money subsidizes war, but it also subsidizes the eating of animals. For instance, the estimated costs of subsidizing the "meat" industry with water in California alone is $26 billion annually (Hur and Fields 1985a, 17). If water used by the "meat" industry were not subsidized by United States taxpayers, "hamburger" would cost $35 per pound and "beefsteak" would be $89. Tax monies perpetuate the cheapness of animals' bodies as a food source; consequently "meat" eaters are allowed to exist in a state of denial. They are not required to confront "meat" eating as a "pocketbook issue." Federal support of an animal-based diet protects it from scrutiny from budget-conscious house-holds. As much as we bemoan the war industry that is fed with our tax monies, we might also bemoan the support our tax monies give to the "meat" industry that wars upon animals and the environment.

Institutional Violence Targets "Appropriate" Victims

I have referred to two different experiences I myself have had with the violence of "meat" eating. In one, I watched with fascination and dispassion as animals were slaughtered, bled, dunked into boiling water to rid them of their hair, skinned, disemboweled, and halved. In the other, I became upset by the death of my horse and connected that to the "hamburger" I was about to eat. How could I go home as a child each day from watching the bloody slaughter and eat flesh foods nonplussed, but as a young adult, greet the knowledge about eating animals with horror? Several answers come to mind; they all revolve around the notion of the appropriate victim. When cows and pigs were butchered, they had no names and no prior relationship with me. I had not affectionately combed their hair, bestowed upon them attention, recognized their individuality and personality. While their deaths were very vivid, indeed, the reason for our attendance at this ritual of slaughter, they remained absent referents. Images in our culture construct pigs and cows as appropriate victims—their sociability denied, given neither a past, present, nor future upon which we base our knowledge of them. I had little other understanding of them, except that as pigs and cows they were meant to be killed and eaten in our culture. As children, my friends and I recognized this and accepted it. I honestly cannot remember meeting with any qualms the pork chops or t-bones served at home the same night as the butchering we had watched. It was all a part of acceptable reality in our culture. Why else did cows and pigs exist?

However, horses are not generally meant to be killed and eaten in our culture. As a child, I begged that dog food made from horses be banned from our home.

Through my identification with Jimmy's death I came to see the meaning of institutional violence *for the victims rather than the consumers*. This painful experience allowed an ethic of inviolability to surface in my consciousness. There were no longer any appropriate victims.

Ideology makes the existence of "appropriate victims" appear to be nat-ural and inevitable. Everything possible is done to keep us from seeing terminal animals as subjects of their own lives, and to keep us from seeing ourselves in any sort of relationship with a living, breathing, feeling being. Such animals are objectified in life and death. We ignore our radical bio-logical similarity with these animals.

A logic of domination accompanies the making of appropriate victims. Differences have been deemed to carry meanings of superiority and infe-riority. According to a logic of domination, that which is morally superior is morally justified in subordinating that which is not (Warren 1990, 128-

33). The other animals are appropriate victims for "meat" eating simply because they are not humans. Once their inferiority is established through species differences, their subordination to humans' interests then follows. They become appropriate victims because they are not like us; they are not like us, in part because we dominate them.

Institutional Violence Has Identifiable Detrimental Effects on the Society as a Whole

A remarkable aspect of institutional violence is that it is culturally protected and seen as beneficial, even though it is actually harmful in several ways besides the killing of billions of sentient beings. There are three areas of concern here: the consequences to the environment, to the health of eaters of animals, and to the workers who produce dead animals for consumption.

Consequences for the environment: Millions of acres are deforested to convert land to grazing and croplands to feed farm animals. Then overgrazing or intensive cultivation causes these lands to become desert. Eighty-five percent of topsoil erosion—the loss of the organic soil layer which provides plants with nutrients and moisture—is due to livestock raising. Because of conversion of land to feed animals, wildlife are losing their habitats, and are often crushed or wounded during the clearing operations.

Animal agriculture is the major industrial polluter in the United States. Feedlots and slaughterhouses are responsible for more of the country's water pollution than all other industries and households combined. A pound of animal flesh means that 100 pounds of livestock manure had to be disposed of, often in our waterways. Slaughterhouse waste—fat, carcass waste, fecal matter—is several hundred times more concentrated than raw waste, yet it is dumped into our rivers at the rate of more than two tons an hour. It is estimated that 125 tons of waste are produced every second by animals raised for human consumption; more than half of this waste is not recycled. "American livestock contribute 5 times more harmful organic waste to water pollution than do people, and twice that of industry" (Lappé 1982, 84). Agricultural crops—more than half of which are harvested to produce livestock feed—are the source of most of the pollutants such as pesticides, nutrients, leachates, and sediment that plague our water resources.

A by-product of livestock production is methane, a greenhouse gas that can trap twenty to thirty times more solar heat than carbon dioxide. Mainly because of their burps, "ruminant animals are the largest producers of methane, accounting for 12 to 15 percent of emissions, according to the E.P.A" (O'Neill 1990, 4).

The land and water needs of a vegetarian diet are substantially less than those of a "meat" based dietary: The same land that can be used to produce meat for 250 days would provide sustenance for 2,200 days if cultivated with soybeans. An animal-based diet requires about eight times more water than a plant-based diet. Over half the water used in this country is used to irrigate feed crops. "The fact is, a vegetarian diet is about the most ecologically efficient thing *anybody* can do."[3]

Consequences for "meat" eaters' health: A study of the eating habits of 6,500 Chinese revealed that a flesh-eating and dairy-product consumption diet increases the risk of developing disease. Some of its findings include:

- While the Chinese consume 20 percent more calories than Americans, Americans are 25 percent fatter. The difference is attributed to the source for these calories. The Chinese eat only a third the amount of fat as we do, but twice the amount of starch, since the majority of their calories come from complex carbohydrates rather than from flesh foods.
- Over-consumption of protein, especially protein from animal flesh, is linked to chronic disease. Americans not only consume more protein than the Chinese (a third more) but 70 percent of that protein comes from flesh foods; only 7 percent of protein for Chinese is derived from dead animals. Those Chinese who increase their protein intake, especially animal protein intake, have the highest rates of "diseases of affluence": heart disease, cancer and diabetes.
- Chinese cholesterol levels are much lower than ours, so that "their high cholesterol is our low," according to Campbell (Brody 1990). Animal foods, including dairy products, are implicated in Americans' high cholesterol level. (A diet rich in fat also increases the risk of breast cancer, which strikes at least one out of every nine women.) Jane Brody notes a five-fold to ten-fold difference in death rates between countries with high-fat diets and those with low-fat diets such as Japan (Brody 1981, 71).
- The Chinese diet contains three times more dietary fiber than the average American diet, because of the Chinese reliance on plant foods. Those with the highest fiber intake had the most iron-rich blood.

T. Colin Campbell, who oversaw the Chinese dietary study, concludes that "We're basically a vegetarian species and should be eating a wide variety of plant foods and minimizing our intake of animal foods" (Brody 1990).

Consequences for the workers who produce flesh foods: One of the basic things that must happen in the institutional violence of slaughtering is that the animal must be treated as an inert object, not as a living, feeling, breathing being. Similarly workers on the assembly line become treated as inert, unthinking objects whose creative, bodily, and emotional needs are ignored. They must view the living animal as the "meat" everyone outside the slaughterhouse accepts it as, while the animal is still alive.

Also, the "meat" packing industry has become increasingly centralized. A few large corporations that are strongly antiunion have driven down industry wages and benefits. Increased technology has permitted an industry-wide speedup, and resulted in some of the most dangerous jobs in America, jobs which, if they had a preference, most would choose not to hold. As Beverly Smith commented to Andrea Lewis: "It's not like they decided ... 'I'll go cut up chickens though I could go and be a college professor.' Those people don't have freedom of choice" (Lewis, 175-76). Smith was referring to "lung gunners" who must each hour scrape the insides of 5,000 chickens' cavities and pull out the recently slaughtered chickens' lungs. Ninety-five percent of these poultry workers are black women who face carpal tunnel syndrome and other disorders caused by repetitive motion and stress (Clift 1990; Lewis 1990, 175).

The Final Condition of Institutional Violence Is That Consumers Are Manipulated into Passivity Regarding This Practice

This manipulation occurs in several ways. As children we became convinced that eating animals was good and proper. Any objections were quelled at the dinner table. Since the 1950s the four basic food groups have contributed to our passivity as beneficiaries of the institutional violence of "meat." Because of the four basic food groups and their emphasis on flesh foods and dairy products, many people continue to believe erroneously that they need to eat "meat" to survive. Free recipes sent to newspapers around the country by the Dairy Council, the Egg Council and the Beef and Pork lobbies keep the idea of eating animals firmly in place, so firmly that many who perceive its deficiencies despair of changing it.

It may seem to be a tautology to say that if we believe some other beings are meant to be our "meat" (the appropriate victims) then we are meant to be "meat" eaters. Conversely, if we are meant to be "meat" eaters then we also believe that someone else is meant to die to be our "meat." These are interlocking givens, ontologies that become self-perpetuating and breed passivity. Most of us think there is no problem, and those few who might initially detect one are encouraged to dismiss it as unsolvable.

Christianity and the Institutionalized Violence of Eating Animals

I have demonstrated the nature of institutional violence and how it is that "meat" eating is a form of institutional violence. With this framework established, we can now turn to the Christian dimension to the institutional violence of eating animals.

One reason that many Christians do not see animals as inviolable is because they believe that only humans are in the image of God, and thus only humans are inviolable. Animals become the appropriate victims because they are not in God's image, but instead consumable entities: lambs of God, sacrificial lambs, fatted calves. The same passage that establishes the relationship of humans to God's image appears to bestow legitimacy on the exploitation of the other animals. Genesis 1:26 reads: Then God said, "Let us make man in our image, after our likeness; and let them have dominion over the fish of the sea, and over the birds of the air, and over the cattle, and over all the earth, and over every creeping thing that creeps upon the earth."

Genesis 1:26 is seen to be God's permission to dominate the other animals and make them instruments for human's interests, thus de facto allowing "meat" eating. By interpreting "dominion" to mean God gave us permission to exploit animals for our tastes, several denial mechanisms are enacted. We are deflected from concern about animals by believing that we are absolved from the action that has cast animals as "meat." The comforting nature of this belief derives from the fact that the onus of the decision to eat animals is shifted from individual responsibility to divine intent. (Someone, but not me, is responsible for these animals' deaths. If I am not responsible, I do not need to examine what I am doing and its consequences.) In this viewpoint, God as the author of and authority over our lives has created us as "meat" eaters. In one act of authorization two ontological situations are created simultaneously: "meat" eater and "meat." As Bowie, the commentator in *The Interpreter's Bible*, remarks on this passage: "Fish and fowl and animals have been his [sic] food."

This interpretation of Genesis 1:26 requires associating dominion with exploitation. Some believe that the clue to this association is found in the choice of words in this passage. Von Rad opines that "[t]he expressions for the exercise of this dominion are remarkably strong: *rada*, 'tread,' 'trample' (e.g., the wine press); similarly *kabas*, 'stamp' " (60). But others see a less harsh meaning to the concept of dominion. Barr suggests that *rada* was generally used about kings ruling over certain areas. "For instance in 1 Kings 5:4 the verb is used to express Solomon's dominion (expressly a peaceful dominion) over a wide area." He believes that *kabas*, "subdue," refers not to animals but to the tilling of the earth (Barr, 22). C. Westermann has suggested that the use of *rada*, "have dominion, govern," "can be compared with what is said in 1:16 about the sun and moon, which are to 'govern' the day and night" (Barr, 23).[4] According to this viewpoint, dominion carries no idea of exploitation, indeed, "man [sic] would lose his 'royal' [sic] position in the realm of living things if the animals were to him [sic] an object of use or of prey" (Barr, 23).

When dominion is equated with exploitation, people are conferring their own preconceptions concerning their relationship with animals upon the Bible, for an exploitative interpretation of Genesis 1:26 cannot be reconciled with the vegetarian passage quoted above found in Genesis 1:29. The *Interpreter's Bible* notes the difficulty of reconciling these two passages when it exegetes Genesis 1:29: "Man [sic] is thus to be a vegetarian. This is something of a contradiction to verse 26, according to which he was to *have dominion over* all living creatures" (Simpson, 486).[5] For others:

the human "dominion" envisaged by Genesis 1 included no idea of using the animals for meat and no terrifying consequences for the animal world. Human exploitation of animal life is not regarded as an inevitable part of human existence, as something given and indeed encouraged by the ideal conditions of the original creation. (Barr, 21)[6]

Genesis 1:26 does not supersede the meaning of creation that extends to include Genesis 1:29. When severed from the meaning of creation and the direction to be vegetarian, the scriptures are used as a historically justificatory defense of actions. This a denial mechanism at the theological level.

These defenses continue when considering God's explicit permission to consume animals in Genesis 9:3, "Every moving thing that lives shall be food for you; and as I gave you the green plants, I give you everything." On a certain view of Genesis, one must argue that "meat" eating is a consequence of the fall. The end of vegetarianism is "a necessary evil" (Phillips, 48), and the introduction of flesh eating has a "negative connotation" (Soler, 24; see also Kook). In his discussion of the Jewish dietary laws, Samuel H. Dresner argues that "the eating of meat [permitted in Genesis 9] is itself a sort of compromise" (21), "a *divine concession to human weakness and human need*" (26). Adam, the perfect man, "is clearly meant to be a vegetarian" (22). In pondering the fact that Isaiah's vision of the future perfect society postulates vegetarianism as well, Dresner observes:

At the "beginning" and at the "end" man [*sic*] is, thus, in his ideal state, herbivorous. His [*sic*] life is not maintained at the expense of the life of the beast. In "history" which takes place here and now, and in which man [*sic*], with all his [*sic*] frailties and relativities, lives and works out his [*sic*] destiny, he [*sic*] may be carnivorous. (24)

What is interposed between Genesis 1:29 and Isaiah is human history. In this sense, history is the concrete, social context in which we move. Moreover, history becomes our destiny.

We come to believe that because an action of the past was condoned by the ethical norms of the time, it may continue unchanged and unchallenged into our present time, history becomes another authority manipulating and extending our passivity. It allows us to objectify the praxis of vegetarianism: it is an ideal, but not realizable. It is out of time, not in time. When Genesis 9 is used to interpret backward to Genesis 1 and forward to our own practice of "meat" eating, history is read into creation, and praxis is superseded by an excused fallibility. History will then immobilize the call to praxis — to stop the suffering, end institutional violence, and side with the oppressed animals. If vegetarianism is out of time, in the Garden of Eden, then we need not concern ourselves with it.

Objectifying the praxis of vegetarianism makes it ahistorical, outside of history and without *a* history. This may explain why vegetarianism throughout the ages has been called a fad despite its recurrence. "Meat" eating has not constituted a large part of the diets of humankind and, I believe, each individual at some point experiences some discomfort with the eating of animals. In the light of what I have called "the sexual politics of meat" — i.e., women, second-class citizens, are more likely to eat what are considered to be second-class foods in a patriarchal culture, vegetables, fruits, and grains rather than "meat" — the question becomes who exactly has been eating the "meat" after Genesis 9? Consider, for instance, this terse comment on Leviticus 6 by Elizabeth Cady Stanton, a leading nineteenth-century feminist: "The meat so delicately cooked by the priests, with wood and coals in the altar, in clean linen, no woman was permitted to taste, only the males among the children of Aaron" (Stanton, 91).

Perhaps we should ask of Genesis 9 and the notion that we are unable to avoid eating flesh: Is this true for us now? In light of the health, environmental, and ethical consequences of eating animals, do we cling to such an authorization that some find in Genesis 9? Do we continue to believe that our relationship with God/ess endorses a clearly exploitative relationship with the other animals? Do we affirm God/ess and creation by denying relationship with terminal animals? And what then do we do about this? Isn't, rather, reconstructing these relationships the most authentic and ethical response available to us?

Resisting Institutionalized Violence

We are estranged from animals through institutionalized violence and have accepted inauthenticity in the name of divine authority. We have also been estranged from ways to think about our estrangement. Religious concepts of alienation, brokenness, separation ought to include our treatment of animals. Eating animals is an existential expression of our estrangement and alienation from the created order.

Elisabeth Schüssler Fiorenza reminds us that "The basic insight of all liberation theologies, including feminist theology, is the recognition that all theology, willingly or not, is by definition always engaged for or against the oppressed" (6). To side with history and posit vegetarianism as unattainable is to side against the oppressed animals; to side with the praxis of vegetarianism is to side with the oppressed and against institutional violence. Insofar as Christians are called to live in the reign of God initiated by Jesus, they cannot legitimately take the "practical" fallen history of Genesis 9 as authority.

It is here, in the conflict between history and eschatology, that I would place a Christology of vegetarianism. This Christology is not concerned with whether Jesus was or was not a vegetarian just as feminist theology rejects the relevance of the maleness of the twelve disciples. This is not a quest for historical duplication but for the acquisition of an ability to discern justice-making according to the Christological revelation. With this perspective we should come to see that a piece of "meat" turns the miracles of the loaves and fishes on its head. Where Jesus multiplied food to feed the hungry, our current food-producing system reduces food sources and damages the environment at the same time, producing plant food to feed terminal animals.

A Christology of vegetarianism would argue that just as Jesus challenged historical definitions such as Samaritan, or undercut identities such as the wealthy man, so we are equipped to challenge the historical and individual identity of a food habit that fosters environmental and ethical injustice. We are not bound by our histories. We have been freed to claim an identity based on current understanding of animal consciousness, ecological spoilage, and health issues. A Christology of vegetarianism would affirm that no more crucifixions are necessary, and insist that animals, who are still being crucified, must be freed from the cross. The suffering of animals, our sacrificial lambs, does not bring about our redemption but furthers our suffering, suffering from preventable diseases related to eating animals, suffering from environmental problems, suffering from the inauthenticity that institutionalized violence promotes. In the following quotation feminist ethicist Beverly Harrison contributes important insights into this process of Christians resisting institutional violence, which can be readily connected to the eating of animals. (I add these connections in brackets.)

> Each of us must learn to extend a critical analysis of the contradictions affecting our lives in an ever-widening circle, until it inclusively incorporates those whose situations differ from our own [such as animals]. This involves naming structures that create the social privilege we possess [to eat animals and make them appropriate victims] as well as understanding how we have been victims [manipulated into passivity so that we believe that we need to eat dead animals]. . . . Critical consciousness and, therefore, genuine social and spiritual transcendence, do not and cannot emerge apart from our refusing complicity in destructive social forces and resisting those structures that perpetuate life-denying conditions [including eating animals]. (235-36)

Perhaps our greatest challenge is to raise the consciousness of those around us to see the institutional violence of eating animals as an ethical issue. But how does something become an ethical issue? Sarah Bentley has described the process by which wife beating has become an ethical concern.[7] She does so by drawing on Gerald Fourez's *Liberation Ethics* which demonstrates that " 'concrete historical struggles' " are the basis for the development of "the discipline called 'ethics.' " For something to become an ethical issue we need " 'a new awareness of some oppression or conflict.' " This is critical consciousness.

I would suggest that an example of this critical consciousness is the animal liberation movement and its identification of the eating of animals as inhumane and exploitative. As Bentley explains, after a time of agitation by a group living with the critical consciousness of this oppression, others besides the group with the critical consciousness begin to question the oppression as well. The social consciousness of a community or a culture is transformed by this agitation. "Ethical themes, therefore, are *historically specific*, arising from 'the particular questions that certain groups are asking themselves.' "

Christians responding to the insights of the animal liberation movement must ask questions about the institutional violence that permits them the personal satisfaction of eating flesh. "In effect, the [particular] questions represent 'problems *raised by practices* that have to be faced.' " Farming and slaughtering practices such as caging, debeaking, liquid diets for calves, twenty-four-hour starvation before death, transporting and killing animals are all troublesome practices. We must stop denying them. But of course, denial is necessary when concrete practices are challenged. Indeed, ethical statements "always evolve 'as particular ways of questioning in which people, individually or in groups, *stake their lives* as they decide what they want to do and what their solidarity is.' Thus, *if no one questions*, if no *practical engagement* takes place, no problem exists."

This can be linked with the success of false naming and other denial mechanisms we have mentioned. They cannot be overcome at a merely theoretical level. Unless we acquaint ourselves with the *practice* of farming and slaughtering animals, we will not encounter the *problems* raised by these practices, such as the abuse of animals, the environment, our health, and workers in the "meat" industry. If the problem is invisible, in a sense mirroring the physical invisibility of intensively farmed animals, then there will be ethical invisibility.

A Christian ethics adequate to challenging the institutional violence of eating animals and modeled on this understanding of the evolution of an ethical stance involves three connected parts: certain practices raise problems; practical engagement and solidarity ensues when these problematic practices are perceived; an ethical position arises from this ongoing solidarity that forges critical community consciousness. As we become personally aware of the contradictions between Christianity and the practice of eating animals, we find that we must enter into a struggle regarding our own and this culture's practice.

To overcome our failure to acknowledge another's inviolability we need to find alternative ways of relating to animals rather than eating them. Beverly Harrison proposes that "We know and value the world, *if* we know and value it, through our ability to touch, to hear, to see" (13). We have not known and valued the domestic animals that are eaten because we have not touched, heard, or seen them. To most of us, animals are disembodied entities. Disembodied animals have little potential of being touched, heard, or seen, except as "meat."

Demonstrating Harrison's sensual understanding of how we know the world, Alice Walker describes what happens when she touches, hears, and sees an animal. With Blue the horse she sees the depth of feeling in his eyes and recalls something she feels adults fail to remember: "human animals and nonhuman animals can communicate quite well" (Walker 1988, 5). Shortly after having that insight, Walker experiences the injustice of a steak: "I am eating misery" she thinks. Walker touches, hears, sees, and describes interactions with very specific animals, and she is changed by this, called to authenticity.

We all have an option to dispense with the consumption of misery: We can feed instead on the grace of vegetables. Virginia de Araujó describes such a perspective, that of a friend, who takes the barrenness of a cupboard, filled only with "celery threads, chard stems, avocado skins" and creates a feast

> & says, On this grace I feed, I wilt
> in spirit if I eat flesh, let the hogs,
> the rabbits live, the cows browse,
> the eggs hatch out chicks & peck seeds.

The choice is institutionalized violence or feeding on grace. One cannot feed on grace and eat animals. Our goal of living in right relationships and ending injustice is to have grace *in* our meals as well as *at* our meals. Socially responsible persons, justice-oriented persons, must recognize that we are violating others in eating animals, and in the process wilting the spirit. There are no appropriate victims. Let the hogs, rabbits, cows, chicks live. In place of misery, let there be grace.

Notes

1. I use the term God/ess after Rosemary Radford Ruether in *Sexism and God-Talk: Toward a Feminist Theology.* Ruether explains: "when discussing fuller divinity to which this theology points, I use the term God/ess, a written symbol intended to combine both the masculine and feminine forms of the word for the divine while preserving the Judeo-Christian affirmation that divinity is one. . . . [I]t serves here as an analytic sign to point toward that yet unnameable understanding of the divine that would transcend patriarchal limitations and signal redemptive experience for women as well as men" (Ruether, 46).

2. The structure of the absent referent is fulfilled in intensive or factory farming, but did not originate with it. Indeed, in *The Sexual Politics of Meat*, I gave little attention to factory farming per se because I see the problem as the objectification of animals, not any single practice of producing flesh foods. On the problem of the hunt as the way of obtaining flesh foods, see Adams 1991.

3. Paul Obis, 4. This information was gathered from material including Fund for Animals, 1990; Robbins; Akers, Hur and Fields, 1984; 1985a, 1985b; Hur, 1985; Krizmanic, 1990a, 1990b; Lappe, O'Neill, Pimental, 1975, 1976.

4. James Barr adds parenthetically, "a different Hebrew word indeed, but there

is no reason to suppose that this makes much difference" (Barr, 23).

5. Cuthbert Simpson's explanation is that verse 29 may have been an addition to P's original narrative, containing the classical conceptualization of the Golden Age—which was seen as vegetarian and peaceful between humans and animals—and so it is more linked to the visions of Isaiah 11:6-8; 65:25; Hosea 2:18. Thus it posits potentiality rather than reality.

6. Jean Soler agrees with Barr's conclusion, stating "meat eating is implicitly but unequivocally excluded" and that the reason for this has to do with the way that God and humans are defined in Genesis 1:26 by their relationship to each other (Soler, 24). See also Cohen.

7. The quotations which follow about the development of an ethical issue are from Sarah Bentley, pp. 16-17. Those quotations with both single and double quotation marks are Bentley's references to Gerard Fourez's *Liberation Ethics* (Philadelphia: Temple University Press, 1982), pp. 93, 108-109. Italicized words within the quotation marks contained this emphasis in the original source.

Part IV

HOW SHOULD CHRISTIANS RESPOND TO CURRENT CONCERNS FOR ANIMALS?

Theoretical and Practical Considerations

The marked rise of the animal rights movement as well as the new environmentalism is a central theme in the development of the moral consciousness of Western democracies in the past decade. It would be surprising and lamentable were Christians wholeheartedly to resist this development. Nonetheless, it should not be strange to find Christians criticizing certain of its facets: its inconsistencies, perhaps, its failure to go deep enough, or its emphasis upon moral notions that Christians might regard with some suspicion, such as "rights."

The essays by the theologians in this final part of the book ask critical questions of current trends from a theological perspective, even while supporting the basic thrust of the movement. In each case, an attempt is made to be constructive as well, tempering certain features of the movement while emphasizing other alternative features. Included as well is an essay by Tom Regan, a philosopher and articulate spokesperson for the animal rights movement, who responds to at least one set of criticisms of the movement while at the same time noting crucial points of commonality that can and should carry Christians forward with others as they continue to think and act upon questions regarding the moral treatment of animals.

Chapter 10

African-American Resources
for a More Inclusive Liberation Theology

Theodore Walker, Jr.

Black theology is a form of liberation theology which holds that we are morally obliged to contribute to the well-being of all, and most especially to the well-being of the poor and oppressed. Black theology, on account of its appropriation of this philosophy of black power, sometimes describes contribution to the well-being of others in terms of empowerment. And most often, black theology's main social ethical concern is with the well-being and empowerment of people, i.e., "power to the people." This essay emphasizes what is occasionally but not frequently emphasized by black and other liberation theologians, that our moral obligation to contribute to the well-being and empowerment of others includes obligation to plants and animals.

In the foreword to Jay B. McDaniel's *Of God and Pelicans: A Theology of Reverence for Life*, John B. Cobb, Jr., notes that until recently the church was largely silent in regard to environmental issues. Cobb accounts for this "deafening silence" in terms of churchly fear that "attention to ecological issues would distract from that given to justice" (p. 11). But, as Cobb notes, "this has changed" because the church is coming to see that both justice and ecological sustainability "are essential and that in fact neither is possible without the other" (p. 11).

Like other churches and theologies, black churches and black theologians have been less than consistently outspoken about support for ecological and animal rights issues. Again, it would be correct to account for this

Theodore Walker, Jr., is Assistant Professor of Ethics and Society at Perkins School of Theology, Southern Methodist University. He has taught at Bethune-Cookman College and at Hood Theological Seminary at Livingstone College. He is the author of *Empower the People: Social Ethics for the African-American Church* (Orbis 1991).

163

relative silence by reference to the need for increased attention to human rights issues, and while it is true that John Cobb, Jay McDaniel, Sallie McFague, Thomas Berry, Tom Regan and others have done much to increase the conceptual and moral ground for unity between concern with justice and concern with the environment, there are some causes of black churchly and theological reluctance to adopt ecological and animal rights agenda which have yet to be overcome. From the perspective of many black and colored peoples, there are racial and racist aspects of modern white ecological/animal rights thinking which make it somewhat more difficult for us to adopt their ecological/animal rights agenda as our own. One recent example from the literature of environmental and animal rights/protection will serve to illustrate our difficulty.

Douglas H. Chadwick's "Elephants—Out of Time, Out of Space," in *National Geographic* (vol. 179, no. 5, May 1991) includes a photograph of two white persons shooting a family of elephants in Zimbabwe (pp. 44-45). In the text we are told that the riflemen are members of a "culling team," and: "Culling, unlike poaching and trophy hunting, attempts to maintain the herd's natural age and gender balance. Still, critics emphasize the inevitable loss of genetic diversity and the horror of slaughtering great and intelligent beings" (p. 45).

Here it is reported that regard for the well-being of elephants and a sense of horror over their slaughter, produces criticism of shooting elephants, even when killing individual elephants is thought to benefit elephant life in general. In this very same article, there is a photograph of black men shooting black men. The text tells us this is Richard Leakey's "anti-poaching unit in Kenya," and that they are armed with automatic rifles, helicopter gunships, and "shoot-to-kill orders" (pp. 30-31). And we are told that as a result of Leakey's command; "more than a hundred poachers have been killed, giving Kenya's elephants a fighting chance" (p. 31). *National Geographic* reports nothing horrible, regrettable, or even critical of killing more than a hundred humans.

Obviously, this example of animal protection policy is morally problematic. Moreover, the fact that Mr. Leakey's anti-poaching unit has shoot-to-kill orders that pertain to predominantly if not exclusively black poachers in Africa, but no such homicidal power over the predominantly nonblack buyers and distributors of ivory, indicates that this valuing of elephant life over human life is helped by the fact that the humans being shot are black. This uncritical valuing of elephant life over black human life is helped by the fact that the modern West is victim of a racist heritage that regards black and colored humans as less than fully human. For instance, at one point in United States legal history, a black man was counted as "three-fifths of a man." This racist heritage no doubt helps to enable white environmentalists and animal rights advocates to experience no horror when Mr. Leakey's unit shoots to kill black humans for the sake of elephants, when in fact they do experience horror when elephants are shot for the sake of elephants, and when in fact they would be much horrified if Mr. Leakey's antipoaching unit were to start shooting to kill the white consumers, investors, and distributors who profit from this and other destruction of wildlife.

From our perspective, many calls by white persons for an extension of the range of moral concern so as to include regard for the well-being of plants and animals are morally suspect on account of failure to include adequate regard for the well-being of black and colored humans—such as, for example, the more than one hundred persons killed by Mr. Leakey's antipoaching unit. When those who value the lives of black humans less than they value the lives of elephants, and less than they value the lives of white humans, ask us to join them in expressing their newfound concern for the well-being and rights of animals, we are not overly eager to join them. When we see environmentalists and animal rights proponents expressing criticism and concern with the well-being of elephants and other life while at the same time being utterly unconcerned about human life, just as when we see "right-to-life" activists showing much concern for the well-being of the unborn and no concern for the already born, we find it difficult, even impossible at times, to adopt their social ethical agenda as our own. Too often what passes for a wider concern inclusive of the environment is in fact a white racially gerrymandered concern which reaches out to include plants and animals while continuing to exclude black and colored peoples. These difficulties have yet to be overcome, and they must be overcome if white environmentalists and animal rights activists expect to receive the support of black and colored peoples.[1]

In the meantime, it is important for black theologians to consult non-racist traditions and resources in order to develop our own independent black churchly environmental agenda. Moreover, we must work to help our white sisters and brothers in the various environmental and ecological movements overcome the racial exclusions that continually retard the development of more inclusive efforts to contribute to ecological sustainability and liberation of other life. Katie Geneva Cannon has an essay in a book titled *Inheriting Our Mothers' Gardens*, the language of mothers' gardens being an inheritance from Alice Walker's black womanist *In Search of Our Mothers' Gardens*. In her essay, Katie Cannon speaks about "surviving the blight" of hard times and oppression by attending to the inheritance from our mothers' gardens.[2] When black theologians attend to the inheritance from the gardens of Mother Africa, we learn that righteous social ethical reflection must take due account of the cross-generational character of human existence.

According to traditional African thought, we are morally obliged to remember and venerate the contributions of previous generations, most notably the ancestors; we are morally obliged to contribute to the well-being of our neighbors in this generation, and our neighborhood includes other life, human and nonhuman; and we have a moral responsibility to contribute to the well-being of future life (including our own future lives) and future generations. Traditional African social ethical reflection is characterized by a strong emphasis upon the need to contribute to the well-being of future life, including especially the well-being of those who are called "the beautiful ones" by Ayi Kwei Armah in his classic novel *The Beautiful Ones Are Not Yet Born*.[3] We have a moral responsibility to contribute to the well-being and empowerment of the beautiful ones who are not yet born.

This cross-generational vision of social ethical obligation is an important resource for black theological social ethical reflection. It is also a very much needed resource for modern western ethical thought. For it is clear that much of modern western ecological irresponsibility is a function of the failure to consider the well-being of future life and future generations. The well-being of other life and of future generations is regularly sacrificed for the sake of immediate monetary gain. Modern western ethical calculus seldom reaches beyond consequences which obtain for the present generation. Let us, then, cultivate among ourselves and others the habit of being explicitly attentive to the cross-generational aspects of human existence and social ethical responsibility. This is essential to the development of more ecologically responsible social ethical reflection and behavior.

Another insight essential to more ecologically responsible social ethical reflection and behavior which we can glean from traditional African sources is a more holistic vision of life and of our place within the web of life. Harvey Sindima's essay "Community of Life: Ecological Theology in African Perspective" teaches us that traditional African thought offers an alternative to the traditional western "mechanistic perspective that views all things as lifeless commodities to be understood scientifically and to be used for human ends."[4] Sindima describes the African alternative to this western-mechanistic-commodity-oriented way of seeing the world as "a life-centered way" which "stresses the bondedness, the interconnectedness, of all living beings" (p. 137). According to this African alternative, the non-human world of nature is not merely a collection of exploitable lifeless commodities; instead, the whole world (including nonhuman animals, plants, the earth, and its ecosystem) is seen as a living and sacred part of one divine life. Specifically, Sindima says that for Malawians, "nature and persons are one, woven by creation into one texture or fabric of life, a fabric or web characterized by an interdependence between all creatures. This living fabric of nature—including people and other creatures—is sacred" (p. 143).

For Sindima, this traditional African perspective upon the community of life calls for a more inclusive understanding of justice. Sindima defines justice in terms of "how we live in the web of life in reciprocity with people, other creatures, and the earth, recognizing that they are part of us and we are part of them" (p. 146).

Also among the important resources inherited from the gardens of

Mother Africa are the ancient and antiquitous religions of North Africa, greater North Africa, and the Afro-Mediterranean world, including ancient Egyptian, Hebrew, Christian, and Moslem religions. Scripture scholars and historians of religion are already teaching us that according to these sources, the modern western habit of excluding and failing to reverence other life, including nonhuman and future life, is contrary to right relationship to God. According to early religious insights that grew out of Afro-Mediterranean soil and water, right relation to God entails right relation to creation. We must contribute to the well-being of those who are and will be loved by God, and God's love includes all creation. No creature, species, race, or gender is excluded.

The philosophy of black power is another important resource for black theological social ethical reflection. The philosophy of black power is defined by an attempt to answer the question, What must we black folk do with the resources that we control in order to contribute to the well-being and empowerment of all the people? The most recent scholarly reflection upon this question includes an attempt to correct what Harold Cruse identifies as the failed tradition of "noneconomic liberalism."[5] Noneconomic liberalism is a social strategy which focuses upon political empowerment without adequate attention to economic empowerment. During the 1980s, Cruse and other black social analysts became increasingly critical of failure to give adequate attention to economic empowerment. We should remain mindful of this criticism when thinking about environmental issues and animal rights.

Social ethical reflection upon contribution to ecological sustainability and animal protection must take account of the fact that pollution and environmental exploitation and oppression of animals and other life are financially profitable. Noneconomic or financially unprofitable environmental animal-protection policies are likely to be no more successful than noneconomic liberalism has been for African-Americans. Given the relentless pursuit of short-term financial profit, significant improvement cannot be achieved until it becomes financially profitable to be ecologically responsible. Like with struggles for human liberation, the quest for liberation of other life requires serious attention to economic matters. Another resource related to the philosophy of black power is the inclusive conception of freedom symbolized by our liberation colors — red, black, green, and gold. Our red-black-green liberation flag was first popularized in the United States by Marcus Garvey (1887–1940) and the Universal Negro Improvement Association.[6] The color red is a symbol for blood, especially blood sacrificed in the struggle for liberty. Black symbolizes people. Green symbolizes land, particularly the motherland of Africa, and, more broadly, the whole earth. During the 1980s, African-Americans in the United States and other black people became increasingly inclined to add a fourth liberation color — gold. Gold is for the wealth and resources stolen from Mother Africa and from the earth as a whole. These colors — red, black, green, gold —

symbolize a conception of freedom and a black liberation agenda which includes concern for the well-being of Mother Earth and all her creatures. Other life and life-forms—including our own future lives, the lives of the beautiful ones not yet born, the earthly ecosystem, and nonhuman lives or creatures inclusive of plants and animals—are important parts of the liberation agenda called for by our black liberation flag and colors.

Our black liberation flag and colors are conceptual resources also in that by inviting our attention to the land and its wealth, they remind us to be attentive to the plight of our farmers. Green is for the land. Gold is for the wealth and resources stolen from the land, most especially from the land of Africa. We Africans in the Americas are part of that stolen wealth. We were stolen from the land of Africa so that we could be forced to work the land that was stolen from red people in the Americas. When we were emancipated from slavery, we were driven from the rural land we had worked and farmed for others, and into the cities. Some few of us were able to stay on the land as landowners and farmers, but, in recent years, the forces of racial oppression and exploitation have joined with the forces of agribusiness and factory farming to drive us from farmland and from farming altogether. In 1910 there were approximately one million minority farmers in the United States. By 1978, there were only 57,000 black farmers in the United States. Between 1910 and 1978, African-American farmers suffered the loss of over nine million acres of land. Given the continuation of these trends, it is estimated that there will be virtually no black farm owners in the United States by the year 2000.[7]

Of course, one of the most basic resources available to us is data from the black experience of suffering and oppression. The witness of our people is that the experience of suffering is such as to entail desire to be liberated from suffering. Insofar as animals suffer, there is no doubt that they experience desire to be free of suffering. There is, then, no good reason for failure to take account of this experience in our social ethical reflection and behavior. Howard Thurman made the point about animals experiencing desire to be free of suffering and oppression by narrating an experience from his youth in Daytona Beach, Florida. Thurman recalled that on one occasion during his childhood, he happened upon a tiny green snake crawling along a dirt path. In the mischievous way that is typical of a boy child, he pressed his bare foot on top of the little snake. Immediately, the little snake began to struggle against this oppression. Young Thurman felt the tremor of the snake's struggle as it vibrated up his leg and through his body. Thurman reasoned that struggle against suffering and oppression is divinely given to the nature of all living creatures, including even little green snakes.[8]

Attention to the cross-generational character of existence and moral obligation; a more holistic vision of life, and a more inclusive understanding of justice; the ancient and antiquitous religions of North Africa, greater North Africa, and the Afro-Mediterranean world; the philosophy of black power, including attention to economic empowerment; the conception of freedom and the inclusive liberation agenda called for by our liberation colors, including attention to the land, especially farmland; and the witness of the black experience of suffering and of other experiences of suffering are all important resources for developing a liberation agenda that includes concern for the well-being of other and future life. The religious and moral reflection of Native American peoples, Korean Minjung theologies, Buddhism, process/neoclassical philosophies, and many other helpful resources are also available. The harvest is plentiful, and there is great need for our labor in these fields and gardens. It is important that black churches and black theology contribute to the growth of more ecologically responsible reflection and behavior. We African-Americans in the United States are not without a measure of responsibility for the global ecological crisis. While it is historically true that through recent generations we have been and continue to be victim of the same Euro-American oppression that has victimized the global environment, nonetheless, it is also true that at this time and in this generation and for our social location in the Euro-American world, many of us are beneficiaries of environmental exploitation. Our piano keys also contain ivory. We also drive cars, eat butchered animal flesh, use animal-tested cosmetics, and otherwise benefit from the misuse and abuse of other and future life.

Moreover, the well-being of earthly creatures and the life-sustaining capacity of the ecosystem are much too important for us to leave entirely to the resources of white people. Given the unfortunate heritage of much western thought, they are not likely to do well without help. Environmental and animal-protection efforts are very much in need of contributions from Native Americans, Latin American campesinos, traditional Africans, and other colored and black peoples. I believe, for example, the Environmental Protection Agency would be a more diligent protector of the environment if it were heavily peopled with Native Americans. Given sufficient economic resources, native South Americans could protect the Amazon rain forests from the destruction that is presently financed by North Atlantic interests. And I am certain that African elephants would be better served if Africans were paid more to protect elephants than they are paid for ivory. For the sake of other life, including elephants, pelicans, buffalo, and humans — black and white and colored, born and yet to be born — and for the sake of right relation to God, all of us are called to help in this important work.

Notes

1. Cain Hope Felder provides another example of ecological concern failing to include the well-being of black and colored humans in an unpublished paper — "Technology, Ecology, and the Eclipse of the Biblical Vision: Theological Reflections on the State of the Environment" — presented at the Fourth Annual Theodore Roosevelt Environment and Conservation Symposium, October 23, 1989. Felder says "It is proper to highlight President Theodore Roosevelt's concern about aspects of the natural environment. . . . Yet, we cannot forget his safaris nor those thousands

of Blacks imported to Panama as cheap labor to build the Panama Canal. Anonymous hundreds of them were killed in the blasting areas, their bodies in pieces buried under the soil, unmarked; while others were crushed under boulders or became victims of malaria. Rarely does anyone dare to mention the lack of human ecology for/of African Americans during his presidency. In the area of moral human ecology, the Roosevelt legacy itself is quite mixed" (pp. 3, 4).

2. See Katie Geneva Cannon, "Surviving the Blight," *Inheriting Our Mothers' Gardens: Feminist Theology in Third World Perspective*, Letty M. Russell, Kwok Pui-lan, Ada Maria Isasi-Diaz, Katie Geneva Cannon, eds. (Philadelphia: Westminster Press, 1988). And see Alice Walker, "In Search of Our Mothers' Gardens," in *Black Theology: A Documentary History, 1966-1979*, Gayraud S. Wilmore and James H. Cone, eds. (Maryknoll, N. Y.: Orbis Books, 1984) (originally published in *MS.*, vol. 2, no. 11, May 1974), and Alice Walker, *In Search of Our Mothers' Gardens: Womanist Prose* (San Diego: Harcourt Brace Jovanovich, 1983).

3. See Ayi Kwei Armah, *The Beautiful Ones Are Not Yet Born* (New York: Collier Books, 1969).

4. Harvey Sindima's "Community of Life: Ecological Theology in African Perspective" appears in *Liberating Life: Contemporary Approaches to Ecological Theology*, edited by Charles Birch, William Eakin, and Jay B. McDaniel (Maryknoll, N.Y.: Orbis Books, 1990), p. 137.

5. See Harold Cruse, *Plural But Equal: Blacks and Minorities in America's Plural Society* (New York: William Morrow, 1987).

6. In March 1921, the Universal Negro Improvement Association (UNIA) issued a "Universal Negro Catechism" prepared by the Reverend George Alexander McGuire (founder of the African Orthodox Church). According to this catechism, red, black, and green were established as the "National Colors of the Negro Race" at the UNIA's First International Negro Convention in New York in August 1920. See Robert Hill, ed., *Marcus Garvey Universal Negro Improvement Association Papers*, vol. 3. (Los Angeles: University of California Press, 1984), p. 319.

7. These statistics come from David M. Graybeal's 1986 film, "From This Valley: On Defending the Family Farm" (Jo Bales Gallagher, executive producer). Drawing upon data from the March 1986 report to Congress by the Office of Technology Assessment, Graybeal reports a national trend toward the increase of large corporate farms and toward decreasing numbers of medium and small family farms. In the U.S. generally, there were 7 million family farms in 1930. By 1986 that had become 2.2 million. The Office of Technology Assessment expects that very large farms will get larger, with only 50,000 of them producing three-fourths of all U.S. agricultural output, while on the other hand, moderate size and smaller farms will decline in number, market share, and net income. The plight of black and minority farmers is a very much more severe instance of this general trend. Graybeal reports that churches are coming to recognize that defense of family farming, including defense of black and minority farming, is an important item on the churchly liberation agenda. Here we are told that: "The churches are concerned by the centralization of coperate control over the national supplies of food and fiber, and by the transformation of agriculture into agribusiness. They are concerned by the pushing of dispossessed farmers into an economy that already has much unemployment. This is especially painful for black and other minority farm families and workers. The churches are concerned about a democracy in which nearly all the land is owned by the white race. They are concerned by tax policies that reward

speculation in farm land by investors interested only in quick gains. . . . In short, the churches are concerned about future generations and the sustainability of a food production system when land, water, and other natural resources are threatened. . . . The churches intend to resist the growth of a new feudalism."

8. Howard Thurman narrated this story on the occasion of his visit to Livingstone College in Salisbury, North Carolina, during the spring of 1978.

Chapter 11

Economics for Animals as Well as People

John B. Cobb, Jr.

I

The humane movement has been around now for a couple of centuries. It is institutionalized in laws and common practice. But the sphere of its success has been limited chiefly to the treatment of pets. Recently it has expressed itself in terms of "animal rights" and begun to seek much wider changes in the treatment of animals. This has aroused far more serious opposition than did the earlier form, both theoretical and practical.

The church and its theologians have treated this whole matter with benign, or not so benign, neglect. In their own estimation they have more important things to do. Until human needs are met, they opine, it is sentimental to concern ourselves with those of animals. In any case, did not God create the animals simply for our use and enjoyment? Are they not exclusively means to our ends?

This anthropocentric attitude led initially to resistance to the environmental movement as well. It seemed to distract from the all-important needs of development and justice. Only as it became clear that what happens to the natural environment does affect human beings — critically so — did the church begin to attend to the natural world.

As the church has been forced to attend to the natural world, it has rediscovered its own doctrine of creation. It finds that this doctrine does not, after all, confer value *only* on human beings. According to the creation story, God saw the world as good even before human beings made their appearance. The church is beginning to acknowledge that the created order is good in itself, that it does *not* exist only for human beings. The health of

John B. Cobb, Jr., is Professor Emeritus from the School of Theology at Claremont and co-director of the Center for Process Studies. His books include *Matters of Life and Death* and *Can Christ Become Good News Again?*, as well as *The Liberation of Life* (with Charles Bird), *For the Common Good* (with Herman Daly) and *Sustainability* (Orbis, 1992).

the biosphere and its many ecosystems has intrinsic importance.

The next step is to ask the question: If the created order is good and therefore deserving of human respect, what about the particular elements within it? Does it matter what these are? As long as the biosphere as a whole is healthy, can the question of its constituent parts be ignored?

This question is in part scientific. If we substitute an agricultural eco-system for a wild one, is anything lost? The answer, we now know, is yes. Wilderness has intrinsic importance. The loss of species matters.

Meanwhile Christians have looked again at their scriptures for guidance. One of the best-known stories provides clear evidence that the writers believed God cared about species and went to great lengths to preserve them against destruction by the flood that was brought on by human sin. It has not been difficult for the church to agree that the rapid extinction of species is an evil to be avoided.

But what finally of the individual members of these species? It has not been hard for Christians to support the humane movement's opposition to cruelty to pets. Most Christian parents have taught their children to treat their pets kindly. If one needs reasons to support one's instinctive dislike for mistreatment in this area, one can argue that it damages human char-acter and is bad for spiritual development. This has been the most common line of argument in Christianity, as in the other "higher" religions. In some, butchers have been treated with contempt, even when the meat they offer for sale is wanted and purchased.

In ways like this Christians and believers in other of the "higher" relig-ions have discouraged cruelty without abandoning their anthropocentrism. Clearly they have refused thus far to consider the rights of the individual animal. And on the whole, they, and especially Christianity, remain silent.

Further, nature does not seem tender with individuals. It aims to pre-serve species by producing far more individuals than it could ever support. The health of the biosphere depends on most of them being killed. Jay McDaniel has pointed to the second pelican chick as a vivid illustration of the ruthlessness toward individuals except as they serve the preservation of the species.

The Noah story seems to place the Bible on the same side. God does not seem to be disturbed about the drowning of most of the members of all the species, innocent though they are of the crimes that brought about the flood. It is the species that matter. Only with human beings, we who are created in the image of God, does God call us individually by name and care for us as personally. Precisely this is the great divide between human beings and animals.

Yet the insistence of the animal rights movement forces Christians to continue to reflect. Nature does sacrifice individuals in overwhelming num-bers to the preservation of the species. Yet this is not the whole story. There are species whose members care for one another as individuals, much as we do. Whalers harpoon a young whale knowing that the others will not leave it to struggle and die alone. This enables them to kill the others at their leisure. Concern by whales for individual whales endangers the survival of whole species. It is not so evident that we should be indifferent to individual whales.

It is certainly true that the biblical emphasis on the importance of individuals is overwhelmingly focused on human beings. Furthermore, Jews and Christians have had their hands full in seeking to gain adequate recognition of human rights and the intrinsic value of individual human beings. If concern for animals distracted from vigilance here, one could oppose it with some justification.

But this is not the only, or the truest, way of viewing matters. Sensitivity to the unnecessary suffering that human beings impose on animals has been characteristic chiefly of people who are also unusually sensitive to the evil of imposing such suffering on other people. Sensitivity of this sort is not a limited good that must be parceled out. It is subject of increase as it is left uninhibited and is freely expressed.

Furthermore, concern for individual animals does find its place in the Bible. According to Jesus, in particular, God's providential care extends even to the individual sparrow. A human being is worth more to God than many sparrows, but this comparison would mean nothing if the individual sparrow were not also of value. Sooner or later Christians will have to recognize that the suffering of individual animals has its importance.

All these changes in the scope of Christian reflection are a gain for Christians. They restore to us the wider horizons of thought and concern that we have lost during the modern period. They make us more biblical and more faithful to Christ.

But will they help the animals? A little. The support of churches will strengthen proposals to protect and extend wilderness. It will also improve the chances for some legislation dealing with livestock, zoos, and laboratories. Life-style changes on the part of serious Christians can reduce the pressure to produce animal products of some types. All of this is important.

But the basic course of events on the planet will not be much affected by church pronouncements and life-style changes on the part of the few. This course is dictated by economic considerations. Only if changes in Christian thinking can affect these economic considerations will Christ truly become good news for animals.

How could this happen? Perhaps the economic theory that underlies economic policies could be changed in ways analogous to the changes that are occurring in Christian thinking. Alternately, perhaps economic goals as defined by current theory could be subordinated to others. The remainder of this paper will consider these two possibilities.

II

One way of looking at contemporary economics is as the result of turning Christian ethics into a science. This, of course, required several steps of simplification. A science requires simple concepts that make measurement possible.

We begin with the Christian teaching of loving others as we love ourselves. That implies that we seek the good of others as of ourselves. The others are, of course, other human beings. Each one counts as we consider what love requires of us. Also, seeking their good involves reducing evil.

Next we must decide how we are to consider the other's good. Here there is a tension in Christianity. Is it for me to decide what is truly good for others, or do I let the others define what is good for themselves? The simplification needed for economics to become a science was to accept only the second option. The way I can express my benevolence toward others is by increasing their goods as they define them.

But how do we know what people consider good? Again, there is a beautifully simple answer. We know by observing what they choose. People use their resources to acquire as much of what they want as they can. If we can increase their resources, we thereby increase their good.

Resources are gained chiefly by labor. Here another great simplification of Christian teaching was required. Labor was understood to be a curse resulting from expulsion from the Garden of Eden. But socially constructive labor was also understood positively as a part of the Christian life. The simplification required in this case was to drop the second part of this teaching. Labor is the price paid in order to be able to acquire goods. In itself it is evil.

A third issue arises. Although we want the good of all, we cannot act so as to benefit all equally at all times. At whose good shall we aim? And if we benefit one but harm another, how shall we judge the overall effects? These concerns have led Christians into complex discussions of justice. No science can be made of all that.

There can be no objective comparison of the goods and evils enjoyed and suffered by different people. We cannot judge whether the happiness experienced by one outweighs the misery felt by another. Hence, if we want a science that leads to implementation, the goal of our benevolence cannot involve such comparisons. Issues of justice must be set aside. The aim should always be to increase the well-being of some without damaging that of any. Only in such cases is our action unequivocally good, and it is the implementation of this unequivocal good at which our science should aim. Translated into the terms of this science, our goal is to increase the ratio of consumption to labor for all.

If the goods available for consumption are not the ones people prefer, then the value of the consumption is less. This can happen if production is controlled by forces other than the expressed preferences of the consumers. For example, centralized planning and bureaucratic control can lead to producing what is wanted less or even not wanted at all. This is wasteful. If producers are free to produce what they can sell most profitably, they will produce what consumers want. Hence the free market leads to the greatest good. When the market is free, increased production is a nearly perfect contribution to the good of consumption. Hence we can restate the goal of benevolence as the increase of the ratio of product to labor. This is what economists mean by productivity.

Much of the science of economics is devoted to showing how productivity can be improved. Economists have shown in great detail, and with convincing theoretical and empirical evidence, that the freedom of markets from interference and the extension of their size lead to improvements in productivity. Further, since this improvement increases the total amount of goods available per person, it tends to benefit all rather than improving the lot of some at the expense of others.

How do animals figure into this scheme of thought? The answer is, not much at all. For the most part they are commodities like any others. Their value is whatever price they bring in the marketplace. There is virtually no separate attention given to them in economic theory.

The application of this theory to agriculture results in factory farming. The goal is to increase productivity, and that means the amount of the animal product desired in relation to the number of hours of human labor invested. The suffering of the animals plays no role in these calculations. The results are now well known.

Economists know that the market cannot be given *total* freedom. For example, a producer should not be free to deceive the consumer, pretending to sell a medicine when what is really offered is poison. Society must set some limits. Society may also demand that the conditions of the workplace be safe and healthful. But these are all extra-economic considerations, and economists, committed to increasing productivity for the sake of all, urge us to keep them to the minimum. Such restrictions on market freedom as have been accepted are always for the sake of human beings in their roles as laborers and consumers. The idea of restricting market freedom for the sake of the commodities themselves cannot arise within this framework of ideas.

What now if we decide that these "commodities" deserve special treatment? We are unlikely to get support from within the community of economists and those policy makers who are socialized in these terms. But if we can maintain a "level playing field," then restrictions on the treatment of animals in factory farming can be tolerated. By a level playing field is meant a situation in which the same rules of the game apply to all players. Each producer can continue to maximize productivity within the restrictions now imposed. A serious problem arises only as the market within which capital and goods move freely is larger than the area within which these rules are imposed. Then the producers within that area cannot compete. Production will move to those areas where it is not restricted. The economy will be damaged and the lot of animals will not be improved.

This latter problem intensifies resistance to restrictions on the treatment of animals in agriculture. Economists want the market to be as large as possible. Hence they resist quotas and tariffs by which local producers, beset by politically imposed restrictions, can compete with other producers not so restricted. Without these restrictions on trade, local producers know that they will be wiped out. Hence their resistance to humane legislation is connected with their economic survival.

My point here is that there is an ineradicable tension between the goals of economics as it now exists and application of concern for animals to the way they are raised for market purposes. It is true that a similar tension exists between the goal of economics and restrictions on the market imposed for the well-being of workers or the protection of the environment. But pointing this out does not help much. As the size of the market expands, all these restrictions are under pressure. Many industries have simply left those areas where restrictions have made their operation less profitable. This is what economic theory dictates they should do. They may move within the country or across national borders.

Today they do not always need to move. The threat of such a move suffices to render labor docile and local governments willing to change the rules or fail to enforce them. As restrictions on international trade decline and as the transnational corporations play an increasing role in the internal economies of all nations, economic survival will require the abandonment of such restrictions more and more. The times are not favorable to protecting animals from ruthless exploitation.

Although by far the most important role of animals in economic theory is as commodities, there is another. In the early days, economists acknowledged that there were three factors of production. In addition to labor and capital, there was land. Land was not, therefore, merely a commodity, but a co-agent with labor and capital in the productive activity.

The idea of land as a separate factor in production is virtually gone from contemporary economics. At most, the productivity of land is subsumed under that of capital. Yet one could argue that with our rising sense of the importance of the land, economics could recapture some of its original vision.

How is this relevant to animals? When economists speak of land they include the entire natural world. On the whole, they pay little attention to the biota, but this is the only place at which they can appear, other than as products of human labor. Could economics be so revised as to include attention to the productive role of animals?

The prospect is not bright. Even in Adam Smith, who still attended to the productivity of the soil, the labor theory of value was applied to farm animals. Their role in reproducing themselves was ignored. The value of a workhorse was the amount of time spent by humans in its care and feeding. The labor of the horse did not count as work.

But we are asking about possible revisions in light of our new recognition that animals are not merely means to human ends but also ends in themselves. Could we go back to first principles and devise a new science of economics based on benevolence to animals as well as to human beings?

This would entail that animal labor be added to human labor as that which is to be minimized and animal consumption added to human consumption as that which is to be maximized. But how would that work out? Would an hour of a hen's labor in producing eggs count equally with an hour of human labor? Would we try to get the hen to consume as much as possible? The result would be that we would try to get the hen to lay still more eggs per day while perhaps force feeding it. Of course, this leads to absurdities in all directions and has nothing to do with animal rights. Our goal is to have chickens free to range and to behave in ways that are natural to them. No conceivable adjustment in economic theory will encourage that. With the possible exception of an occasional chimpanzee, no animal will be able to express its preferences in the human market. It is that market with which economic theory deals.

III

If there is an inherent tension between economics as a science and the improvement of the lot of animals, what are those committed to animal rights to do? There are two possibilities. One is to reject economics as a science and propose a nonscientific approach to economic issues. The other is to subordinate the science of economics to other considerations. I suggest that what is really needed is a combination of these.

If the only motivation for these moves were concern for animals, I would consider the prospects so slight that this discussion would be merely "academic" in the most pejorative sense. But this is not the case. Although radical critique of economics as a science is still in its infancy and is viewed as peripheral from the point of view of the "real world," it does exist. Also, more and more groups are realizing that their goals cannot be attained without the relativization of economic theory. For example, the inherent drive of this theory for the expansion of markets is destructive of the global environment, national sovereignty, the well-being of labor, and human community, as well as animals.

The problem with contemporary economic theory is not its science as such. This *can* be taken as descriptive of what goes on in exchange of goods and services. As a science there is no question of its predictive success in many, many areas. It provides invaluable information about what results will occur from the adoption of particular policies. Even in these respects it is limited and fallible, since features of the situation from which it has abstracted sometimes play an unanticipated role. But that is not a major criticism. To be a science it must abstract, and its abstractions have proved extremely fruitful.

The problem is that it has ordered its research and theory building to an end. This is the end of increasing human consumption. One can argue that as a science this economics merely tells us what policies will produce which results and leaves to others the decision as to which type of results are desired. But that is deceptive. If one approaches an economist and asks what economic policies will result in the improved condition of animals, she is likely to have nothing to say. Economists have not hypothesized a series of diverse ends and examined the policies that would attain them. They have assumed that *the* end is growth of total product, and generations of scholars have studied, with great success, how to attain that. Needless to say, they do not as a group merely provide neutral information. They vigorously support and promote those policies that will lead to greater growth.

We see here a problem with the very organization of knowledge in the modern world. Particular aspects of reality are assigned to particular academic disciplines. In order to get on with the constructing of a science, the practitioners of the discipline must make some simplifying decisions ordered to whatever purpose commends itself to them. There is nothing wrong with that. But this group of practitioners also claims the turf as its own. Of course, there may be disputes, as between Marxists and neo-classical schools. But most of the assumptions, most of the goals, are held in common between them. If one proposes that the economic subject matter be investigated for quite different purposes, one is told that this would not be economics. Yet no one else is recognized as authorized to investigate this material.

This identification of a "science" with research aimed at a particular end would not be so serious a problem except for profound changes that have occurred in the ethos of the North Atlantic nations. Prior to this century this ethos was dominated by religious and political ideologies. Religion dominated down through the seventeenth century. Since then nationalism became triumphant. One lived and died for one's nation as one had earlier lived and died for one's faith.

Nationalism came to its peak in the middle of the twentieth century in what might be viewed as a caricature. Nazism made of German nationalism an absolutistic religion drawing the consequences of its ideology with unstinting consistency. The nationalism of other peoples played a large role in the ultimate defeat of Nazi Germany, but that whole episode spelled the beginning of the decline of nationalism as a spiritual force.

Following on the earlier decline of religion, this decline of nationalism has sometimes been hailed as the end of ideology. Ideology is now replaced by pragmatism. The task is to identify problems and solve them without commitment to any overarching goals.

But it is not quite true that there is no overarching goal. The goal is economic growth. That goal is taken as obvious and simply rational. And indeed it does not involve the call to heroic personal sacrifice that characterized both religion and nationalism in their heyday. On the contrary, one serves the new goal by attending to one's own economic interests. For the first time in history, it is now established that the best way to serve the neighbor is to act in perfect selfishness! One can indeed forget all ideology and go about one's own business of gaining as many of the world's goods as possible at the least cost in labor. The market will take care of the rest.

This nonideological ideology has hardly received a name. I will call it "economism." Christians have not failed to criticize it, but thus far ineffectively. They have complained about its materialism, but they have shared its goal of providing goods for all. They have complained about its selfishness, but since this selfishness leads to the benefit of all, the complaint is difficult to make credible. They have complained also that the market does not implement justice, that it leads to great inequities. And here they have had some success in the political arena. All North Atlantic countries have taken action to mitigate the suffering engendered by the market and to spread the benefits of the increased production it makes possible.

As long as Christians shared with economism the goal of economic growth, they could do little to weaken its hold. They preferred its neutrality with respect to religion to the active opposition of the Communists. They supported its progressive weakening and displacement of nationalism. And they contributed to the educational system and the social ethos that enable economism to dominate.

Economism has also had the acquiescence and support of political leaders. At times their continuing nationalism has led them to resist particular policies that obviously weakened national sovereignty. But on the whole they were persuaded to identify the national interest with growth in Gross National Product, and they accepted the view that this would grow faster as markets became larger.

Thus in the North Atlantic countries, economism has gained the support of the remaining strength of both religious and national feeling. It is now almost undisputed master of the world's most powerful peoples. It is because of this enormous power that this "science" must be so carefully criticized.

Now that it is clear that economic growth is at the expense of the environment and of future human beings, as well as of animals, Christians should be ready to share with others in opposing it. That means declaring our considered opposition to economism as well as to mindless growth of human population. It means insisting that the economy be ordered not to its own expansion but to the well-being of humans and other animals.

IV

Economism succeeded nationalism which succeeded religion as dominant ordering principles in society. If economism is to give way, it must be to something else. Society cannot do without *some* ordering principle. But what might that be?

The most promising candidate today is reverence for the Earth. This is taking many forms. The Gaia hypothesis of James Lovelock has elicited surprising response. Native American spirituality is popular. Some ecologists and environmentalists give themselves sacrificially to saving the planet without any obviously religious expression of their concern. Among Christians there is a renewal of creation spirituality. The picture of the Earth from the moon has become a moving symbol of this new attitude and orientation.

Although almost everyone gives lip service to a concern for the well-being of the planet, and especially its biosphere, thus far this is subordinated to economism. George Bush announced his intention of becoming our environmental president, but he has made it clear that was not to interfere with economism. The result, of course, was a poor environmental record. There is an inherent tension between economism and environmentalism that will not go away by virtue of minor gestures in the direction of the latter. "Planetism," to coin a name for the new ideology, has not yet been able to affect basic policy.

Fortunately, the "yet" in the previous sentence is realistic. As our social and environmental problems get worse, and as the negative consequences of economism become better known, leaders will arise who are truly willing to change course. The opposition will be enormous, and the temptation to sacrifice planetism for modifications of economism will be great. But there is a chance that the choice will become clear and that people in large numbers will choose for planetism.

V

Planetism will not succeed unless it can project the possibility of a viable economy. It must show that although there is a profound tension between economism and planetism, there is no opposition between planetism and meeting the economic needs of all. Otherwise, however much they regret the losses, most people will remain committed to economism. Economism will still come to an end, but it will be a catastrophic one.

For the planetist the goal of the human economy is to meet physical needs with the smallest possible disruption of the larger, natural, economy. Further, the aim is to do so in ways that encourage other human values, especially those associated with human community and a sense of belonging to the larger world. The intention is to accomplish all this in ways that inflict as little suffering as possible on either human beings or other animals.

The assumptions underlying this goal are clearly different from those underlying economism. One assumption here is that human beings are fundamentally communal. That is, their relations to one another are extremely important, more important than consumption of goods beyond a quite minimal level. Economism assumes that individuals are not relational, so that if their consumption is increased their lot is improved, even if their communities are destroyed in the process.

A second assumption is that while human well-being is important, the well-being of the rest of the planet is also important. This follows partly from the interconnectedness of all things, which entails that the well-being of one part contributes to the well-being of others. But the value of the rest of creation is not dependent on its connections with us. It is intrinsic, and planetism holds that human beings should adjust their lives in light of this truth.

A third assumption is that individuals count. Economism already affirms this, too one-sidedly, with respect to human beings. Planetism extends this to all sentient beings. Suffering is an evil. Much of it is unavoidable, and efforts to avoid it are likely to make matters worse. But much suffering inflicted by human beings on other human beings and on other animals is avoidable. It should be avoided. Human beings should meet their physical needs in ways that cause as little suffering as possible on one another and on other animals.

A fourth assumption is that labor is not inherently evil. Certainly much labor is boring, painful, demeaning, and in general, intrinsically unrewarding. Planetism agrees with economism that this should be minimized. As little as possible of such labor should be imposed on animals also. But reducing the hours of labor in general is not the only way of reducing the evil involved in labor. It is also possible to make labor itself more enjoyable and fulfilling. The ideal is to produce the goods we need with as little disruption of the natural economy as possible, and also with as enjoyable human labor as possible. Sometimes more labor-intensive modes of production are both less damaging to the environment and more enjoyable. From an economistic perspective, to shift to such modes would be a backward step. For the planetist, it can be a gain.

That markets are the most efficient means of allocating resources, of adjusting production to consumer preferences, has been demonstrated again and again both theoretically and practically. Planetism will support market economies. But whereas economism seeks to minimize noneconomic restrictions placed on markets and to maximize their size, planetism seeks to minimize their size and to establish rules for each market about the conditions of labor and the impact on the environment. The allocative efficiency of the market is not harmed by these rules as long as they apply equally to all participants. The only "losses" are in productivity and total product, and these are not the goals of planetism. Those who produce under these rules cannot be forced to compete with others who are not so restricted. Each market will be protected from competition to the extent necessary.

Whereas economism leads to making each local area dependent on goods produced elsewhere and capital derived elsewhere, planetism seeks local self-reliance and relative self-sufficiency. There is no harm in trade when this trade is not essential to local survival. The trade is then truly free, and truly free trade will occur only when both partners benefit. But much so-called free trade today is compulsory. Countries trade on terms laid down by others on pain of starvation. Planetism will have none of that.

The aim at self-sufficiency will include the field of energy. A planetary society will price imported energy high so as to provide maximum incentive for the market to engender the urgently needed changes. The first step will be shifting to highly energy-efficient equipment to reduce the need for imported fossil fuels. The second step will be some shift from energy-intensive mass production to labor-intensive handicrafts and small-scale diversified family farming. The third step will be building homes, offices, and even whole cities that meet their energy requirements from direct solar energy alone. The fourth step will be developing new technologies for more efficient transformation of solar energy into electricity. The fifth step will be building cities that do not require use of motor vehicles. These changes will all take time, but reduction in dependence on imported energy can be begun quickly.

Economism has compromised with land-use policies that place some land outside the market. However, even federally owned lands have been exploited for commercial purposes. Planetism will aim at reduced use of the land. Animals will be a major beneficiary of such policies.

Much land now in national forests will be shifted to wilderness, since the extension of wilderness is the single most important contribution human beings can make to animals. Similarly, much land now overgrazed by cattle will be returned to buffalo and deer. Much land now used for crops will revert to pasture. The result will be the reduction of cropland. But this need pose no problem in respect to adequate supplies of food. If livestock are raised almost entirely on grass, far less land will be needed to grow grains. The remaining lands will more than suffice for direct human consumption.

It is clear that the result of these changes will be a reduced production of meat, especially beef. Some of this reduction can be compensated by increased supplies of wild meats, especially buffalo and venison. But a diet for planetism will involve a substantial reduction in red meat.

It will also involve a substantial reduction in chicken. Just as cattle will be raised in pastures, so chickens will be able to live more naturally. Fewer can be raised in this way, and the costs will be higher. Again, a planetist diet will get more of its calories directly from grains, less from meat.

With respect to fish, some increase of consumption may be possible. A planetist economy will move quickly to end the pollution of lakes and rivers, the destruction of wetlands, and the overfishing of the ocean. Some species may recover, and rather large-scale sustainable fisheries may become possible in areas where they have been abandoned.

There will be some increase in the use of animal labor. Small, diversified, labor-intensive family farms will use less fossil fuel and more horses. Horse and cow manure will replace chemical fertilizers. There is, of course, no guarantee that family farmers will treat their livestock well. But if the ethos of planetism grows, they will have inner reasons for doing so. And there will be narrowly economic motivation as well, since animals that are well taken care of produce more and work better. Planetist communities will enact laws supporting the rights of animals to decent treatment.

These brief comments on a planetist economy have had the United States in view. The scenario will be different in other places. Precisely since economies will be local, their problems and responses will be different. But in general they will all aim at a sustainable relationship to their local environment that maintains as much diversity of life there as possible. They will all work against practices that inflict unnecessary suffering on other animals.

VI

I have interpreted planetism in my own way. Other interpretations are possible. This difference comes out with particular clarity in the place accorded animals. At one end of the planetist discussion are those who care only for the health of ecosystems and dismiss interest in the suffering of individual animals as sentimental. At the other end are those who regard all human use of animal products as immoral.

The increase of wilderness is supported by almost all planetists. But from that point the ways part. Against those who are indifferent to the suffering of individual animals, I have proposed the end of factory farming and of cattle feedlots. I am assuming that animals free to live in more natural ways suffer much less. And I am arguing that a planetist economy will adjust in such a way as to impose much less suffering on animals.

But against those who oppose all killing of animals, I am supporting both the hunting of wild animals and the slaughter of domestic ones. I am also supporting the use of animal labor, as long as the animal is well cared for. In other words, I support the right of human beings to use and kill other animals.

This is the part of my own view that has greatest relevance to the economy. Still, for the development of planetism, the more inclusive view of which this is a part is also important. Hence, I want to clarify my position on this point a bit more.

To affirm that human beings have the right to kill individual animals of some species does not entail that we have the right to kill individual animals of *all* species. In my view, the issue of individuality mentioned in Section I, is key. I understand this in two ways.

First, all sentient beings are individuals capable of suffering. Over against human beings, they have a prima facie right to be caused as little suffering as possible. I have drawn conclusions from that about factory farming. I could draw others about the ways animals are killed, and a planetist society would implement laws in this area.

Second, some sentient beings are individuals in another sense. They form deep attachments to one another as individuals, attachments that cannot be replaced readily by others. The absence of a particular individual is missed.

This is the case among the higher apes and some marine mammals. It does not seem to be the case with cattle or chickens. To kill the former would require much more justification than killing the latter.

My proposals also reflect another judgment about animals. I believe that domestication has led to degradation. The domestic animal is inferior to its wild counterpart in the range of capabilities and sensitivities. Where the reduction of domestic animals makes possible an increase in the number of wild ones, there is an overall gain in the richness of the biosphere.

The proposals I have made for returning land to wild animals can be justified without this special argument. Returning abused rangeland to deer and buffalo, if done before desertification has gone too far, will allow eventual recovery of the land's productivity. Also there is food value in wild meat that has been lost over the millennia of domestication. I am confessing that in addition to these reasons, I suspect that the enjoyment of life is greater for the wild animal.

VII

Are there reasons for Christians to support planetism? Not as an absolute. God is greater than the planet, and only God can be an adequate object of devotion. But this is not the real question. Among real options for the future of our society, can Christians find one that more nearly fits their ultimate commitments than planetism? I do not think so.

It is time for Christians to reassert their traditional critique of economism. Economism *is* materialistic in a sense unacceptable to Christians. It affirms the value of consumption at the expense of human relationships. Economism *is* selfish. As long as it could credibly argue that the selfishness it encouraged in individuals served the common good, the criticism carried little conviction.

But now we see that even if it contributes to overall economic expansion, that does not serve the common good. Christians should not pull their punches in the denunciation of the selfishness. And economism *does* ignore justice. The checks and safeguards the Christians have helped impose on it in this respect do not suffice. There is also its injustice to creation and to all the creatures that make it up, as well as to future generations of human beings, to whom it will bequeath an unlivable planet.

It is time for the church wholeheartedly and enthusiastically to call on people to forswear the pursuit of financial gain in favor of committing themselves to building human community, enhancing the whole creation, and reducing the suffering of other creatures. It is time to call for self-giving to the whole as over against the rational self-interest approved by economism. And it is time to call for a justice that is better expressed in the Hebrew term *shalom*, a right relation to the land and all that dwell therein.

The resources and reasons for this shift to planetism are present in the Bible and in Christian tradition. There is growing resonance to the message in the congregations. The shift is already occurring in conciliar and denominational statements. It needs completion through the inclusion of explicit talk of animal well-being and through imaging the world into which the planetist commitment will lead us.

The church is offered at this juncture an opportunity to be a leader in world affairs. As long as it has accepted economism basically and simply protested at peripheral points, it has not been able to lead. Economism has rejected the role of vision and commitment and insisted that all the most important issues are technical ones.

Planetism reverses all this. What is needed above all is vision and commitment. Vision and commitment are central to our whole Christian history. If we can offer these, and we can, we can participate in shaping the planetism of the future. We can be proactive instead of simply adjusting once again to changes made by others.

The question is only whether we have been so beaten down by the dominance first of nationalism and then of economism that we have lost the courage of our own convictions. A leadership struggling for survival in an inhospitable world is not looking for bold new directions. But the Spirit still blows where it listeth, and I believe one of the places in which it is blowing is within the church. Let us hope that the church can yet come alive with the excitement of an historic opportunity.

Chapter 12

Each According to Its Kind

A Defense of Theological Speciesism

Charles Pinches

In the give-and-take about the moral status of animals and the environment, a good deal of criticism has been directed against two "isms": speciesism and anthropocentrism. I take this to be unfortunate, even if entirely understandable. For I am worried that in our appropriate and praiseworthy efforts to correct a long history of human domination over animals, a domination that has been often underwritten and even spearheaded by Christians, we have rushed to "nonspeciesist" and "nonanthropocentric" positions that are both philosophically untenable and theologically ill-founded. So it is that I propose in what follows to defend a brand of speciesism—one that is at least in one sense nonanthropocentric, although I shall eschew the label—that I think is theologically and philosophically acute while at the same time responsive to the important and neglected point that nonhuman animals deserve far better treatment than we humans typically have offered them.

I shall begin by discussing a recent document entitled "Liberating Life: A Report to the World Council of Churches" written by a group of theologians in Annecy, France (henceforth the Annecy report).[1] It is perhaps the strongest public statement issued to date in connection with the Christian Church on the moral implications of Christian theology concerning the treatment of nonhuman animals. As such it intends to be both practical and theological—Christian theological. It begins with a negative assessment

Charles Pinches is Associate Professor of Theology at the University of Scranton, Scranton, PA. Most of his published articles concern some facet of the connection between Christian theological ethics and moral philosophy.

of anthropocentrism and moves beyond to make suggestions about how, alternatively, nonhuman animals as well as other elements of the earth's environment ought to be regarded and treated by humans, whose relationship to them has been transformed by a nonanthropocentric, Christian view of the universe. Like most attempts to impress the moral importance of these concerns upon Christians and others, I take the report's intent to be laudable. Yet I find within it confusions, ones that arise both from a lack of theological care and an uncritical appropriation of the moral rallying cries of the day, particularly those which assume that anthropocentrism and speciesism are necessarily villainous. Uncovering these confusions will be my first task.

Anthropocentrism as the Enemy

There is of late fairly widespread agreement among Americans that we must correct an abusive past in which we have irresponsibly trampled our environment. It is highly debatable as to whether this has been translated into significant corrective action, but the *position* that a correction is necessary is one from which very few dissent. Where the agreement ceases is on the matter of *why* we should do this.

Proponents of significant environmental reform rightly sense that in order to be propelled beyond merely incremental changes in our abusive practices we must reunderstand why the environment should not be abused. Animal liberationists, while not always in agreement with the environmental reformers, argue that this should occur in similar fashion if we hope significantly to alter our practices involving routine abuse to animals. They, like the environmentalists, have often put their proposals for this reunderstanding in terms of the need to go beyond merely anthropocentric concerns about animals. Since the theologian authors of "Liberating Life" wish to stand up for both causes, it is not surprising that they follow the same antianthropocentric path. In their own words, they aim to construct a theology that offers "a view of creation that moves beyond arrogant anthropocentrism and promotes respect for communities of life in their diversity and connectedness to God" (238).

As it usually is understood, an anthropocentric reason for preserving, say, the rain forests exists so long as it can be shown that they contribute to us humans: They produce oxygen for us to breathe or genes we might someday need to cure human disease. But, as a "deep ecologist" might suggest, were it discovered that the oxygen supply or gene pool could be sustained in some other way, the anthropocentric reason would disappear, and we would be left with no clear objection to the cutting of the rain forests. Or, as an animal rights activist might point out, one particular animal, say a rain forest monkey, is not protected by anthropocentric thinking about rain forests, for it is hard to see how the monkey's suffering or premature death could cause any serious damage to any human enterprise. In fact if some particular human wanted to eat the monkey's flesh, so long as this did not disrupt the ecological balance, anthropocentric reasons could just as easily come out on the side of killing the monkey.

Nonanthropocentric reasons, on the other hand, consider the rain forests or the interests of the monkey as valuable in themselves, quite apart from their potential to fulfill and advance human interests. So for the sake of the rain forests or monkeys, the environmentalists and animal liberationists do well to bring them up, or so it seems. Yet this is precisely where I begin having difficulties. Consider the fact that labeling different sorts of appeals for environmental or animal reform either "anthropocentric" or "nonanthropocentric" has the consequence that our moral reasons for some concern are divided starkly into two classes: anthropocentric reasons, having to do with human interests, and nonanthropocentric reasons, having to do with the interests of some nonhuman entity such as a rain forest monkey or a dog.

The following example shows, I believe, a concealed oddity in this. A dog has gotten his collar entangled in my neighbor's bush; he is unable to move his head more than a few inches. I see this and think: "No interest of mine or any other human is directly involved, so I have no anthropocentric reason to untangle him. . . . But on the other hand, perhaps I should nonanthropocentrically consider his interests since, after all, he has them, and they are distinct from mine."

Note that the anthropocentric/nonanthropocentric division requires me to leap from considering my own or my neighbor's "anthropic" interests to what appears a qualitatively different thing, namely the dog's interests. Yet now, how am I to reconnect my anthropic interests to the dog's nonanthropic ones? In effect, the strong anthropocentric/nonanthropocentric distinction leads me to regard the dog's state of well-being, even if I am to honor it, as having nothing to do with my own. This is what seems odd. For shouldn't we rather think that were I the right sort of person, the sight of the dog in such circumstance would bother me? Indeed, I should not be happy myself with him in that condition. That is, I should not see my interests or those of my neighbor as entirely separable from his.

I suspect that to a considerable degree the anthropocentric/nonanthropocentric distinction has its roots in the moral/prudential distinction to be found in the writings of Immanual Kant. On his view, of course, actions are truly moral only in so far as they are done from pure duty, and not from what he calls natural inclination (what would correspond in the present schema to anthropocentric interests). But, contra Kant, shouldn't we rather be the sort of people whose "inclinations" direct us to care for dogs, or for other human beings, or for croplands? We should strive to be, in other words, the sort of person whose happiness, qua *anthropos*, or qua human creature of God, depends upon the well-being of our fellow creatures. If someone says, then, that, so far as his own concerns go, he'd be just as happy to see the dog remain entangled but he'll untangle him, nonetheless, for the dog's sake, he shows a corrupt heart.

Christian theology should be poised to make this point, much more than, say, evolutionary biology. Indeed, it is unfortunate that the authors of the Annecy report often appeal to evolutionary biology as an authority. It may be correct to say, as they do, that "the biological theory of evolution with its ingredients of chance and struggle for existence requires a deeper understanding of divine power" (240). But somewhere we need to be warned that evolutionary biology often carries with it the view that "human interests" can be summed up with the single interest of preservation of the human species, a reduction even more constricting than Kant's. Indeed, one wonders if another engine powering the current emphasis upon the anthropocentric/nonanthropocentric distinction is the style of reflection behind evolutionary biology. Morality, as sociobiologists see it, is reducible to the natural instinct of species survival. Insofar as our human survival is intertwined with the survival of so many other living things, we have sufficient and substantial "moral" (or anthropocentric) reason to preserve them. Yet cases arise, especially those involving individual animals such as dogs and monkeys, where no human species survival interest can be seen. To provide the sociobiologist a reason to care for these creatures, animal liberationists and others have introduced a new class of "nonanthropocentric reasons" which tell us such animals are valuable in themselves, not just for the sake of us or another species.

A Christian theologian might steer the exchange with evolutionary biology in another direction, although no doubt it would put the two on less friendly terms. Anthropocentrism might be described unequivocally as a sin, understood in terms of the human propensity to define and pursue human interests distinct from God and the rest of God's creation. In this form, the "moral reasons" involving species survival offered by sociobiologists would not only be inadequate, they would be built on pernicious assumptions.

In spots the report implies something like the view that anthropocentrism is sin, but it never comes clear on this point — and so never is able to fully realize its implications. For example, the report's key division, "An Ethic for the Liberation of Life," the crucial section on individual animals (which follows two companion sections on ecological communities and biological communities) begins in the following way:

> Section 4 is somewhat different. It does not discuss the benefit to human beings [i.e., anthropocentric concerns] of right treatment of animals. Indeed, it implies that even when respect for animals does not coincide with human benefit it is still required of Christians. Perhaps it is partly for this reason that this topic has been ignored by the World Council of Churches and by most of its member churches up to now. To bring this neglect to focused attention, this section is more

extensive. It rejects anthropocentrism by affirming the integrity of creation with peculiar vividness. (243)

If anthropocentrism is nothing more than sin, then it ought to be rejected from the start, and we do not need any special recourse to a discussion of individual animals to see this. Further, as sin, it ought not to be used, as the report confesses it has just used it, as an argumentative basis of the right treatment of animals, ecological communities or anything else.

The problem rests in how we are to understand "anthropocentric reasons." Are they to be rejected or used? Are they moral? Are they sinful? From the report we get nothing but equivocal answers to these questions. To explain this nagging equivocation, one is tempted by the following genealogy: We inherit from Kant a strong distinction between self-interest and morality. Self-interested considerations in this Kantian scheme become quintessentially nonmoral, morality being concerned with other humans' interests as distinct from our own. With talk of anthropocentrism, we see a duplication of this pattern, yet now extended to the new sphere of nonhuman beings such as rats or chickens, or perhaps to the whole ecosphere. So anthropocentric considerations come to be regarded as parallel to self-interested considerations. As such, the term "anthropocentric" becomes pejorative, like the term "egoistic." Yet the link remains incomplete, for while the association of egoism with the moral notion selfishness is fairly direct, there is no such clear association for anthropocentrism (unless it be to racism, which is sometimes alluded to). Consequently even the nonanthropocentrists, being less clearheaded than Kant, remain equivocal about whether anthropocentric considerations are moral considerations. If a farmer works to preserve farmland for the benefit of future generations of humans who will need to eat its produce, is this to do something moral? Most people would think so. Yet to do so is anthropocentric. (On the other hand, if he preserves it solely to keep its soil content sufficient to insure that he can continue making money off it, we are easily convinced that his action is nonmoral, if not immoral.)

Since nonanthropocentrists such as the report's authors are unsettled about the moral status of anthropocentric reasons, they confuse us all by first giving such reasons for preserving the environment or animal species and then leaving these reasons behind to give new ones that are nonanthropocentric. In the above quotation from the report we see exactly this pattern.

I would suggest that we are far better off abandoning the designation "anthropocentric" (and "nonanthropocentric") altogether. If I begin by convincing myself that morality only involves how I treat others' interests (human *or* nonhuman) and thereby come to understand those interests as entirely distinct from my own, then not only have I severed my own happiness or well-being logically from others, I have shut off the path to my moral education or transformation such that I might learn to become a person who is properly affected by the plight of my fellow creatures, human and nonhuman alike.

The Integrity of Creation and Animal Rights

Theologically a far better way of speaking about the importance of properly regarding and treating the environment and individual animals is in terms of an idea the Annecy report in parts emphasizes: The integrity of creation. The theologian authors take the notion to be imbedded in the biblical stories of creation as well as of Noah. "From these stories we acquire a distinctive understanding of 'the integrity of creation.' *The value of all creatures in and for themselves, for one another, and for God, and their interconnectedness in a diverse whole that has unique value for God, together constitute the integrity of creation*" (239).

To my mind, the report's expression of this important theological idea is far from ideal. Specifically, I wonder why we need to translate Genesis 1 into terms of "value." It carries the unfortunate connotation that members of the created order are, in a sense, repositories into which moral coinage has been poured. We speak, for example, of something "possessing" value, as I possess a pocketknife or capitalists possess capital. So the value I possess is in some basic sense mine, or for me, and the value my neighbor's dog possesses is his, or for him. This is to import notions of ownership that better reflect modern western than ancient Hebraic thought. To rephrase the idea in more biblical terms: Creation, both in its whole, its parts, and in the relation of its parts to one another, is good, for it is the work of a good God who stands in relation to it and delights in it.

These objections aside, whatever its form of expression, by emphasizing "the integrity of creation" the report has seized upon a promising theological idea. Indeed it is nicely used as the authors of the report explain why Christians ought to care for ecological communities and biological species. They point out, for example, our need to overcome a human tendency to see the wilderness or some species of animal as adversary, which "attitude of conquest should give way to reverence toward the integrity of these parts of creation" (246).

However, again the report is less vigilant than one might hope. Indeed, when the report turns specifically to address the matter of how individual animals should be treated, thinking stressing the integrity of creation seems to disappear. It is replaced, as we shall see, by a far less theologically integrated and, ultimately, far less philosophically coherent alternative.

The new terms adopted by the report are evident in the following quotation, when it discusses the specter of "sport" hunting, specifically of the African elephant and the black rhino.

Like the previous examples, these further ones have a common denominator: A creature having intrinsic value is reduced to one having only instrumental value—an object of mere scientific curiosity, a trophy, or a source of illegal profit.

The ethic of the liberation of life is a call to Christian action. In particular, how animals are treated is not "someone else's worry," it is a matter of individual and collective responsibility. Christians are called to act respectfully towards "these, the least of our brothers and sisters." This is not a simple question of kindness, however laudable that virtue is. It is an issue of strict justice. (248-49)

This is powerful language about justice and intrinsic value. Yet we are left to wonder how it fits with the integrity of creation. If we say that the treatment of individual animals is a matter of strict justice, does this mean that the treatment of croplands is not? If elephants have intrinsic value, with what is this being contrasted that has merely instrumental value? Marine communities?

I believe the report has here replaced its "integrity of creation" theology with thinking most characteristic of the animal rights movement. While comparatively young, this movement has been with us long enough to have developed certain patterns in its literature, as well as a language, both which are detectable in this subsection of the report. To begin, it is usually asserted that nonhuman animals are being mistreated by humans, a patent truth. The mistreatment is often identified as a violation of animal rights, or of the animal's intrinsic value. Second, there is a classification of the human uses animals are being put to: as food, as entertainment, in research, etc. Third, various specific instances of mistreatment are cited, often in rapid succession. We might hear about cattle, chickens and mink in the same paragraph. In this section the report follows such a pattern.

Suppose upon reading this report or some other graphic description of human mistreatment of nonhuman animals, I become distressed about the suffering of the black rhinos who are being hunted for their horns or about the calves being raised and slaughtered for veal? How am I to understand my concern? On the pattern suggested by the animal rights advocate's analysis, I am to understand it in the same way as my concern that minks are confined or that pigs are castrated or that humans are underpaid and overworked. Indeed, my concern for a particular rhino or calf is not for it qua rhino or calf but qua sentient being. This is made even plainer by the fact that nowhere in the animal rights literature does one hear talk of human mistreatment of "nonsentient" spiders or salamanders.

I mean to suggest that rights appeals typically abandon a whole range of fairly fine but significant distinctions, replacing them with one enormous distinction that cannot possibly bear the weight it is asked to bear. Distinctions between, for instance, pigs and goats and mink are abandoned and that between pigs, goats, mink, etc. and, say, clams (not as clams but as nonsentient) grows to fill their places. Goats, pigs and mink are said to have "independent interests" and, therefore, to be rights bearers—something clams (and oaks and broccoli plants) are not.

This is quite like the rights strategy generally applied to people. That x is a homosexual is considered irrelevant to his moral status; insofar as he is a person, he is entitled to our respect, he is a rights bearer. So Tom Regan, an animal rights proponent, simply extends the large class of creatures worthy of respect (formerly persons) to include all nonhuman animals who can be sensibly understood to have independent interests. Consequently, for him what matters when considering any given nonhuman animal as a possible rights bearer is not whether he or she is a goat or a pig or a mink, it is rather whether he or she has interests or is sentient.[2] Species peculiarities, in other words, are strictly irrelevant, in the same way that whether someone is a homosexual is irrelevant to whether or not he should be granted basic human rights.

This last fact helps explain why animals rights literature, which I consider this section in the Annecy report to represent, is no respecter of animal species but rather mixes the woes of all of them (at least those who are sentient) indiscriminately together. Beyond that, the logic of rights thinking makes clear the meaning of the new language regarding value, and once again changes—although nicely clarifies—the language of nonanthropocentrism. Rights advocates would have us credit the intrinsic value of sentient animals—which value they have as rights bearers—as distinct from instrumental value, which is all nonrights bearers can have. And so we should embrace nonanthropocentrism—now conceived as the view that there are other rights bearers besides humans—over anthropocentrism, the view that only humans bear rights and have intrinsic value.

Wolves, Rights, and Theological Speciesism

As we have noted, the Annecy report attempts to address both human abuses of the environment and mistreatment of nonhuman animals. This is less common than one might think; indeed, often the two concerns are not only separate but at odds. The fact that both environmental holists (or deep ecologists) and animal rights advocates view themselves as nonanthropocentrists by no means establishes a connection between them. Animal rights advocates take themselves to be nonanthropocentrists in the sense that they understand the class of moral "patients" (i.e., rights bearers to whom direct duties are owed) to extend beyond members of the human species including also certain nonhuman animals. Environmental holists, on the other hand, see nonanthropocentrism as not so much an extension of what were formerly human rights to a new yet limited class of nonhumans but rather as a reorienting of our thinking to fix upon what is good for the whole biosphere or geosphere rather than what is good for one particular part such as the human race, a particular human, or a particular nonhuman animal. So Tom Regan has characterized this latter position as a sort of "environmental fascism"[3] which entails the view that causing the suffering of animals is not wrong when the suffering does not detract from the good of the whole geosphere.

It should be noted that environmental holism is one possible way to understand the report's phrase, "the integrity of creation." Indeed, when in an earlier section it says explicitly that "the universe appears to us as God's 'body' " (241) it comes dangerously close to taking up this option. This sort of understanding, however, is unwarranted in the light of the Bible. There God is portrayed as caring for separate parts of creation, not because they are part of Godself or they fill a niche, but because they are good and delightful in themselves. In the first account of creation in Genesis we read:

> Then God said, "Let the water teem with an abundance of living creatures, and on the earth let birds fly beneath the dome of the sky." And so it happened God created the great sea monsters and all kinds of swimming creatures with which the water teems, and all kinds of winged birds. God saw how good it was, and God blessed them, saying, "Be fertile, multiply and fill the water of the seas; and let birds multiply on the earth." Evening came, and morning followed—the fifth day. Then God said, "Let the earth bring forth all kinds of living creatures: cattle, creeping things, and wild animals of all kinds." And so it happened: God made all kinds of cattle and all kinds of creeping things of the earth. God saw how good it was. Then God said: "Let us make man in our own image, after our likeness. Let them have dominion over the fish of the sea, the birds of the air, and the cattle, and over all the wild animals and all the creatures that crawl on the ground." (Genesis 1:20-24)

In this seminal passage, various kinds of creatures are mentioned, and emphasis is placed upon the multiplicity of the kinds, implying not only that it was God's idea but that God delighted in each kind in its uniqueness and diversity. The integrity of creation, therefore, is not best understood just in terms of the completeness of the whole or the intrinsic value of some parts over against the instrumental value of others, but rather as the goodness of each of the parts (to use the language of the report) "in and for themselves, for one another and for God" (239).

Let us dub this view—the view that each part of creation is good in and for itself as well as for others and God—"theological speciesism." It demands further display, which I shall attempt to offer in the following pages. To begin, suppose we first consider not more from the Bible or about God but the current plight of the wolves, cattle and ranchers of Minnesota.

Minnesota has instituted a program whose purpose is to revive and stabilize the grey wolf population in certain of its regions where wolves once thrived, but were either driven out or significantly reduced in number by past generations of humans. The program necessarily involves the cohabitation of wolves and cattle on the same land. Unfortunately, sometimes the wolves kill a cow. When this happens, the forest ranger in whose district the kill occurred sets traps by the fresh carcass, eventually killing the wolf or wolves who return to feed upon it. He does this because the ranchers involved in the program must be assured that the specific wolves who threaten their cattle will be eliminated. If they are not, the farmers will take the killing on themselves, resulting in the death of many more wolves than the few involved in the death of the cow.

One wonders, of course, if it might not be possible to revise the program so as not to kill the wolves, or not to trap them. Or perhaps the ranchers ought to learn to endure the loss of a cow or two for the sake of the wolves. But let us for the moment set these points aside. What is crucial about this case for our purposes is to see that situations exist in which the preservation and continued vitality of a habitat or species depends upon the suffering or death of a particular member of that species or habitat.

I am assuming we share a fairly strong if not transparent conviction that it is a good thing that grey wolves are being reintroduced into their former habitat in Minnesota.[4] Yet as I shall develop the point, an animal rights position can neither support nor explain this. For as I have already suggested, animal rights positions are simply blind to species distinctions. An animal rights defender may argue that we owe it to a particular wolf not to cause it suffering, or even that we owe her freedom to pursue her desires or instincts with minimal human intervention, but we do not owe wolves anything as a species.[5] We have no reason to wish that the wolf population increase any more than that the cattle population increase. We may, perhaps, be obliged to procure for a given wolf a mate (if we can) with whom she can live and propagate, for she may have a decipherable "interest" in doing this, but of course individual cattle and individual rabbits seem to have the same interest at least as strongly, and so there is no reason why we should prefer and privilege any particular wolf's interest in propagation or companionship over their interests. Most especially, on the rights view we have no reason to reintroduce wolves into this particular section of Minnesota. Perhaps earlier our grandparents had a responsibility not to deprive a particular wolf of her peculiar Minnesota habitat, for she no doubt had a decipherable interest in living there. But no such wolves existed before the reintroduction program began; they had all died off or adapted to a new environment elsewhere. Indeed, if our grandparents had such a responsibility, we may have the same in reverse, for the lives of individual wolves surely are disrupted when captured elsewhere and transported by humans to a new habitat, as reintroduction programs often involve.

The animal rights defender simply has no way to understand our concern for wolves qua wolves, that is, our concern that wolves as a species be preserved, even if this involves the possible sacrifice of some of their number. Indeed, adding in the cattle who surely, as much as wolves, have a right not to be killed and the additional rights of wolves not to be captured and transported to a new habitat, animal rights advocates may be compelled in this case and many others to stand up *against* this and many other reintroduction programs.

The environmental holist does no better. He can acknowledge species distinctions but cannot privilege any one species as worthy of preservation in itself. If wolves perform some necessary and irreplaceable function in the ongoing biological life on earth or in the universe, a reason exists for their maintenance and preservation. But if, like a particular individual animal, they perform no such function or their function can be just as well performed by another species, no clear reason for any moral concern about this exists.

In contrast to both the rights and holist positions, the theological speciesist will affirm that wolves are themselves a good part of God's good creation. God wishes them to be fertile and multiply; God delights in their variety and (presumably) laments when they no longer walk the earth or, more particularly, the forests of Minnesota. The array of creatures in Minnesota and elsewhere is a good, and each of these various creatures is good as unique and various.[6]

No doubt to the speciesist the question will be put: Why treat *species* as the privileged unit of this variety?

Let us think of a species designation less as a scientific label (although it is importantly that), more as a name that sets varieties of creatures apart from one another as essentially different, not just as they seem to us or one another, but as they are. The force of this can be best appreciated by referring again to Genesis, the second account of creation, where we find Adam naming the animals (Genesis 2: 19-20). Consider what sorts of names he might have given the various animals we call wolves, cats and monkeys. He might have organized them exclusively according to categories of use for humans. For example, As are good to eat, Bs are dangerous, Cs are thick furred and therefore good for coats and so on. On such a system of classification, there would be no barking dog in distress, entangled in the mulberry bush behind my neighbor's house, there would rather be only a "noisy house-watch" or perhaps a "whining pet."

This dog example illustrates that in fact a good number of our descriptions are assembled in this way: "noisy," "whining," and "pet" are terms which essentially organize sounds and living beings in relation to how we humans use or are affected by them.[7] (One might call these anthropocentric designations—and as such open a way better to understand a moral-theological nonanthropocentrism. Theological speciesism is in this sense nonanthropocentric.) Species terms resist this absorption into human functional terms. We have no temptation to say my cat is a good finch or even a good dog. A dog is a dog if entangled in my neighbor's bush or roaming in a pack on the Galapagos Islands. *Dog*, then, should remind me that I should not make any particular dog a mere pet. It emphasizes that he *qua* dog is different from me, essentially. No other designations do this so well.

Specious Views of Speciesism

The above defense of species designations carries the implication that any system of ethics which leads to the abandonment of species distinctions or even relegates them to the unimportant has not helped us or members of nonhuman species much in the long run. This applies both to animal rights advocates and environmental holists, as I have suggested. It applies all the more to a recurring diatribe that has as its specific end the abandonment of species distinctions as in any way morally relevant. I refer to the attack of some against "speciesism." The term, in fact, was coined by Richard Ryder in *Animals, Men and Morals* and used by Peter Singer in his seminal review article "Animal Liberation." (My reuse of it in this essay is a continuation of this discussion from a quite different point of view. I hope the term can be restored after Singer's plundering.) As the latter defines it, speciesism is "the belief that we are entitled to treat members of other species in a way in which it would be wrong to treat members of our own species."[8]

For Singer, speciesism is directly analogous to racism. Indeed, as the term has come to be used by animal liberationists, it is meant to be pejorative in the same way "racism" is. In defending theological speciesism, I run the calculated risk of appearing to defend something parallel to theological racism, which of course I do not mean to do.

What prevents the correlation between racism and speciesism? In the first place, from the fact that wolves are significantly different from cattle (on speciesism) it does not follow that they are worth more (or less) than cattle. Rather, we should treat wolves as wolf-creatures of God and cattle as cattle-creatures. Applied to race, the correlative position would not entail, therefore, racial superiority or inferiority, just difference. This is akin to the separate but equal view propounded in American jurisprudence for a time. This view was, of course, racist, but contingently so, rather than necessarily. What made it racist was simply that it rested upon false (perniciously false) beliefs about blacks. For example, nineteenth-century white American slaveholders once believed simultaneously that it was not wrong to "keep" a black man while deeply wrong to "enslave" a white man. (The meaning of "keep" and "enslave" depend on other descriptions with which they are combined by their user, so in this description they must be kept apart.) In a parallel way, many of us believe it is not wrong to keep a dog, while enslaving any human is reprehensible.

The reason, of course, that it is wrong for the members of one race of humans to "keep" those of another while it is not wrong for humans to "keep" dogs is simply that dogs are quite different from humans such that keeping a dog does not violate his dogness while, as we say, keeping a human clearly violates his humanness.[9]

I take this point to be plain enough; it is by no means beyond debate, however. That is, one of the benefits of speciesism is that it is open to empirical observation of the sort which helped unseat racism in some minds in the past century. Claims about crucial differences between one and the other species — ones allegedly based in some set of natural facts — might turn out to be, like the so-called facts upon which racism is based, simply false.

An argument along these lines might proceed in two quite different ways. On the one hand one might argue that the differences between dogs and humans are quite insignificant. A given dog is, in the crucial respects, as like a given human as any other human, such that enslaving one or the other comes to the same thing. Or, on the other hand, one might argue that keeping a human violates his humanness *and* keeping a dog violates his dogness, perhaps in a quite different way. Both could be said to be wrong, but different accounts of why — one involving how we ought to regard and treat humans and another involving how we ought to regard and treat dogs — would be called for in each case.

Theological speciesism may appear better disposed to the second sort of argument than the first. Nonetheless, there is no reason why it cannot countenance the first sort. Indeed, it should. If it does not, it is open to Singer's charges that species designations are arbitrary ways of asserting privilege.[10]

In this regard, it is essential that a certain fluidity remain in any species-based classificatory scheme. (The necessity of this is made all the more plain by species evolution.) I have emphasized the point that species designations such as "frog" are not framed exclusively according to categories of human usefulness, as are other designations such as "pet." Yet there are other nonspecies designations, such as "quadruped," that are not clearly framed according to human patterns of use. It is therefore fair to ask why some similarities are overlooked and others emphasized in a given species classification such that, for example, four-footed frogs and four-footed horses are understood to be quite radically different animals.

I do not think it is foolish to say that we should attend in our species classifications to those characteristics that are important to the animals themselves. Species in this way are best thought of as communities of association. At the simplest level, this involves sexual activity or reproduction. In many species it includes much more: wolves establishing a social order, bears marking territory against intrusion from other bears, or even perch swimming with perch. One might say that species associations display to those who closely observe them a given animal's self-description and perhaps even reveal a sort of self-knowledge that humans, as caretakers of God's variety, must credit. A bear knows herself to be a bear in a way she does not know herself as a quadruped, and she signals the significance of the former description by her patterns of life.

Accepted biological species classifications generally correspond to these self-descriptions. Initially we all simply depend on biologists to explain what is known about the further characteristics of a given group of interbreeders.[11] Biological classification, however, will also have limits, particularly at a trans-species level. For if we wish to credit animal self-descriptions, and these involve more than interbreeding or genetic makeup (which I believe it should), we may be mistaken to distinguish so sharply between mammalian dolphins and the tuna with whom they often swim, or between white rhinos and the red-billed oxpeckers with whom they routinely cooperate.

Species designations, then, are best understood (ideally) as both fixed and fluid. Fixed in the sense that it is according to the species category that subsequent judgments about how a particular species member ought to be treated, and fluid in the sense that the community of living things the designation covers — and therefore the meaning of the designation itself — might change and vary, either as we humans come better to hear the self-description other living things are proffering or as that description itself changes and evolves.

Returning once again to the Genesis account, we find it said that God created "cattle and creeping things and beasts of the earth according to their kinds" (1:24). This is not, evidently, an exhaustive taxonomy. We are given no reason in the text to think that it is based upon full knowledge of "kinds" or that they will not change and vary. Rather the simple notion seems to be that God creates according to kinds, and this is significant.

In conjunction, perhaps we should understand the predication in the subsequent verses in Genesis of one of those kinds — namely humans — as being made "in the image of God" (1:26) partly in terms of the human capacity to identify, know and delight in the multitude and variety of kinds God created. In the second story of creation, Adam is given the task of naming the animals, not according to their use for him, but as he, being in God's image, can see them in and for themselves. When we name and study species, we continue Adam's work.

Essential to the correct exercise of this naming function is that humans recognize that it is not their own creation they study and classify but God's. As I have suggested, misnaming animals in terms of our own needs and desires is a form of sinfulness of which we are told in Genesis 3. It is nothing less than an attempt to rob God of God's creation, claiming it entirely as our own, as made in our own fallen image. This, of course, is just what we have done, for humans have grossly failed not only correctly to name the diversity of kinds but also to protect and preserve them. The dominion over creation offered humans in Genesis 1:28 can be well understood in terms of this unique human role as caretaker of diversity. Sinful humanity, on the other hand, has turned from the task to become the great destroyer of diversity, dominating rather than exercising dominion, entirely subjecting other living things to its whims. Creation therefore, as Paul says, "awaits with eager expectation the revelation of the children of God; for creation was made subject to futility, not of its own accord but because of the one who subjected it, in hope that creation itself would be set free from slavery to corruption and share in the glorious freedom of the children of God" (Romans 8:20-21). While it is God who shall bring us to the day in which all of creation is set free, it is both the privilege and responsibility of humans to participate so far as they are able in the present work of redemption as well as to wait, together with others of God's creatures, for its completion.

Some Corollaries

I have identified in previous pages the position I call theological spe-ciesism. I have sought to make plain its general disposition as well as the arguments from which it arises. Yet no doubt its implications remain some-what sketchy. The following five corollaries represent an initial attempt to fill them in.

Assessment of what treatment of a given individual animal is morally good or bad must follow from an analysis of what we know or can learn about the species to which it belongs.

In any analysis of wolves, let us say, one characteristic will be readily apparent: Wolves feel pain and seek to avoid it. It will follow that, *ceteris paribus*, we ought to avoid causing pain to any particular wolf. Yet closer observation reveals much more about wolves: they have habitual patterns of social interaction with other wolves, they characteristically howl on cer-tain occasions, and so on. Once having discovered these features, the con-sistent theological speciesist will honor them, she will work as she is able to insure that a particular wolf is freed, even encouraged, to behave in these ways. (Sentience, therefore, turns out to be one of a number of features of a given animal that humans must consider when seeking to treat it well. It has no special, privileged status.)

While species must be the primary category under which our moral assess-ment is made, other larger or smaller categories, such as ecological communities or subspecies, are appropriately the objects of our moral concern.

Privileging species designations is a way to remind us that a vast variety of types of creatures exist who are substantially different from ourselves. As such they have a peculiar integrity and independence from us that we, who are given the special task of preserving and enhancing the diversity of God's creation, are bound to acknowledge. This independence and integrity occurs, however, in other forms than merely species variety. Red wolves are different from grey wolves, and the differences are to be preserved. Wetlands, in which a vast number of animal and plant species thrive sym-biotically, are biological units different from, say, grasslands, and so, *ceteris paribus*, a given wetland area ought to be preserved.[12]

Determining how one should regard and treat a member of a given species of plant is not in principle different from determining how a member of a given animal species should be treated.

This is a benefit that follows from the Annecy report's emphasis upon the integrity of creation. Concerns for animals (including humans), for plants and even, say, for mountains, need not be held at odds as they are by utilitarians or rights theorists who make so strong a distinction between sentient and nonsentient life forms. Ironically, this cannot but lead to more and greater real conflicts for the theological speciesist, for we cannot dismiss our concern for mountains or nonsentient animals as falling outside morality. It is, however, the predetermination or the limitation of such conflicts against which we must remain vigilant, not their proliferation.

Special considerations are appropriately extended to members of a species whose existence is threatened.

Individual members of an endangered species represent their entire species; with their loss we lose more than the sum of their individual lives. Therefore protecting these few lives especially carefully is a human duty. Ironically this might sometimes entail individual sacrifice on their part, perhaps long periods of confinement or sometimes painful and invasive human medical attention. No doubt limits will need to be observed, but by itself it does not appear wrong to ask a particular animal to make such sacrifices, for he is an "individual" not by himself but within his species.

The creation of new species, as well as the genetic manipulation or the domestication of significant numbers of a given species — practices humans have engaged in for millennia, but of late more directly and forcefully — must come under our closest moral scrutiny.

Domestication is best understood as a human bending of the species characteristics of a given animal to serve human ends. A possible implication, therefore, of the arguments presented is that domestication is in all cases wrong. This conclusion does not follow directly, for one might well argue that some species are by nature more amenable to domestication than others, and so to domesticate members of them is appropriate, quite in keeping with who they are.

Yet if we add to domestication what invariably follows, human control of breeding, we see that humans actually mean to some degree permanently to change the species, not just, as one might say, borrow some of its members for a time. The modern domesticated turkey is an example of this process extended over time, and run afoul, for the modification of the domestic turkey has led to the creation of a category of creature that has no other clear place at all in God's creation but to be consumed by humans at Thanksgiving. (There is the deepest irony in this. For if the idea of Thanksgiving is to recall that God has provided us with the great bounty of creation from which we take thankfully, not only thankfully to God but to that plant or animal which has given up its life so that we may have life, then by eating domesticated turkey at Thanksgiving we do nothing more than thank ourselves, who have fashioned a new world in our own fallen image.)

So domestication must always have limits, limits that could also apply to genetic manipulation in other contexts, and perhaps even to our own human co-creative activities. Two of these limits must be: (1) That any domesticated animals always be acknowledged as no mere extension of the human species. Dogs must be dogs first and pets second. Cows must be cows first and givers of milk or of "beef" second, if indeed ever at all.[13] (2) That humans who domesticate always keep in mind that they have invited a stranger into their community, to whom they now owe hospitality. This in a way includes the concerns in (1), but extends beyond it. For we humans do not and should not see one another solely under the description "fellow human," but as individuals with peculiarities that are worthy of respect and honor, peculiarities which by definition are not species wide. In like manner, in inviting a specific animal to share our life, we are bound to regard her or him not just as "dog" but as *this dog*, and to interact with her or him accordingly. This point is perhaps best illustrated by the fact that we name our pets. Its implications are carried further by advancing the seemingly modest proposal that no farmer have more cows (or chickens, or goats—although perhaps not catfish) than she can name, or at least identify without having to look at a tag or leg band. If this follows from the theological speciesism advanced in this paper, it can no doubt join with the advocates of animal rights or of "nonspeciesism" in calling for a significant revision in our practices involving nonhuman animals.

Notes

1. The text of the report appears in Appendix B of this volume. Page citation will henceforth be included in the text.

2. Tom Regan's *The Case for Animal Rights* (Berkeley: U of California Press, 1983) is the most substantial work written to date in defense of animal rights. He is adamant that acknowledging that animals have rights does not affect the status of human rights at all. Animal rights in fact are the logical extension of human rights. See, for example, pp. 294-297. On the questions of what it is about (some) animals that makes them rights bearers, Regan has generally settled on the fact that they have "interests." In other contexts he has emphasized the connected characteristic of sentience, and has even more recently spoken of right-bearing animals as having independent "stories."

3. See ibid , p 362.

4. I may be hasty in making this assumption in this particular case, for obviously there is disagreement among humans on the wolf reestablishment programs. Indeed, it has gotten national media attention. (See the cover story of *Newsweek*, August 12, 1991.) I do not think, however, that I am wrong to assume that species preservation programs generally enjoy broad support. Yet very seldom are the reasons for species preservation investigated. When they are, I would suggest, we will find their strongest roots in something like the speciesism I am developing, and not at all in rights thinking or utilitarianism. This general point is the one I hope to

make plain by discussing the specific example of wolves in Minnesota.

5. As Regan puts it plainly, "Species are not individuals, and the rights view does not recognize the moral rights of species to anything, including survival." *The Case for Animal Rights*, p. 359.

6. Augustine in places makes creative use of the language of the Priestly account of creation in Genesis: that each thing which God created was "good" and all things together were "very good" (Genesis 1:31). He takes it to affirm the goodness of each of the parts separately and together. See, for example, *The Confessions*, Book VII, Chap. 13.

7. "House-watch," the only term manufactured in this sample, is quite close to "watchdog," a word we might use in our purely anthropocentric description were it sensible, and it very nearly is, to say "my cat has turned out to be an excellent watchdog."

8. Richard Purtill, *Moral Dilemmas* (Belmont, CA: Wadsworth, 1985), p. 372. Reprinted from *The New York Review of Books*, April 5, 1973.

9. Singer no doubt would respond that *some* humans (e.g. those with mental handicaps or fetuses) are comparable to some dogs in crucial respects — intelligence, for example. For this point to have force, however, individualism such as the kind behind rights thinking must be presumed. It is just this individualism I have been denying in arguing for speciesism. In short, the response begs the question.

10. Singer and other anti-speciesists, I think, have failed to see the significant differences between rats and humans and have, further, limited their vision (principally by embracing a moral theory — in Singer's case, utilitarianism) so that they cannot see the significant differences between, say, wolves and cattle. On the other hand, like the abolitionists of the previous century, they have challenged us all to remove genuine blindnesses about animals. For example, Descartes was blind to the suffering of animals because of a prior belief about human souls and the like. We owe a debt to the anti-speciesists for challenging this dominant Cartesian view.

11. As students of the biological world, animal and plant biologists are to some degree the keepers of species designations. They teach us where to begin as we think about these classifications, which is not to say, as I imply here, that their biological expertise should always carry the day. As keepers of species distinctions, they have important observational and classificatory work to do that cannot be reduced to, say, biochemistry. The scientific community's propensity to reduce one natural science to another (e.g., biology to chemistry) is another example of the attitude that wishes to reduce many distinctions to one.

12. This logic applies in like manner to communities of humans who have evolved into culturally diverse units. *Ceteris paribus*, we are better off if the Amish way of life in Pennsylvania is kept intact or the Eskimos continue to pass on to their children the traditions of their ancestors. Particularly this latter example poses difficulties, for it could be that the preservation of an Eskimo way of life will threaten a given species of whale, or involve cruel practices toward particular animals. These are simply conflicts, similar in nature to the conflicts involved in the case of the wolves of Minnesota. They should not surprise us; nor should we attempt to avoid them. Rather we should attempt to avoid ways of thinking about ethics, such as the utilitarianism from which anti-speciesism derives, which deny conflicts or attempt to resolve them in principle rather than to require close attention to particular cases.

13. I leave open the question of vegetarianism. I am not one, although it would

seem to me that the logic of the position I am developing is not incompatible with vegetarianism. One would need to say, merely, that no animal species member is well treated under that species description by being killed and eaten. The continuity I have maintained between plant and animal species makes this a position that would need defense, for the good treatment of broccoli, which involved killing and eating, would need to be distinguished from the good treatment of shrimp. Or else (depending on the variety of vegetarian) the good treatment of these both—which would include killing and eating—would need to be distinguished from the good treatment of rabbits who could not be killed and eaten. In any case, what is clearly excluded by the view is modern factory farming that turns all animal species it touches into one thing: meat.

Chapter 13

Christianity and the Oppression of Animals

Tom Regan

The Politics of Animal Rights

Recently, I was privileged to share the platform with America's most eminent contemporary theologian, John Cobb. The occasion was the annual Vosburgh Lectures at Drew University's School of Theology. Our respective contributions addressed the Christian church's response to animal rights, broadly conceived. Cobb, who was first to speak, began by making reference to the historically important Annecy document, which is reproduced in this volume (Appendix B). Entitled "Liberating Life: A Report to the World Council of Churches" (hereafter the Annecy Report), this document, as Cobb duly noted, has had a paradoxical history. On the one hand, animal rights advocates from throughout the world have greeted it with thunderous applause, and understandably so. In view of the Annecy Report's strong condemnation of buying fur and its recommendation to "avoid meat and animal products that have been produced on factory farms," for example, partisans of animal rights believed that they were witnessing encouraging signs that the Christian church was beginning to rouse itself from its dogmatic slumbers regarding nonhuman animals. On the other hand, however, there is no evidence that the Annecy Report's section on "Respect for Individual Animals" or its practical recommendations concerning what Christians can do to advance the cause of animal liberation have had any influence whatsoever on subsequent WCC thinking or WCC programs. It is not as if the Annecy Report's contents have been publicly considered, debated, and rejected on their merits; it is, rather, that they have been publicly ignored.

John Cobb offered a number of possible explanations for the WCC's

---

Philosopher **Tom Regan** is University Alumni Distinguished Professor at North Carolina State University. Among his more than twenty books are *The Case for Animal Rights* (1983), *The Three Generations: Reflections on the Coming Revolution* (1991), and *Matters of Life and Death*, third edition (1992).

deafening silence. One was the oft-heard claim that "there are many other, more important issues than animal rights," another, the possible WCC fear of being publicly associated with "animal rights fanatics." And there were other, more substantive possible explanations that Cobb enumerated (for example, that Christian thought is more systemic, less individualized when it comes to its understanding of nonhuman animals). When the time came for my presentation, it was my unhappy duty to offer an explanation of a very different kind.

In January of 1991, in Phoenix, Arizona, the American Farm Bureau held its annual conference. A highlight of the conference was a session on the animal rights movement. Among the featured speakers were United States Representative Vin Weber (R-MN) and Steve Copperud, president of the North American Feed Industry Association. Someone asked Mr. Copperud a general question about religion and animal rights and, in the course of giving his answer, he referred explicitly to the Annecy Report. Here, in part, is what he said (the quotation that follows is excerpted from a transcription of an audiotape of Mr. Copperud's remarks).

> Just so you all know, we spent three months convincing the World Council of Churches, to drop out of its coming encyclical [sic], a flat-out statement condemning factory farming in the Western hemisphere ... [The leadership of the WCC] admitted ... that they had never looked at it [that is, factory farming], that they didn't know what factory farming meant ... They have since dumped it [that is, the condemnation of factory farming].

If Copperud is right, then the leadership of the WCC was moved to "dump" the Annecy Report's sections on factory farming not for substantive theological reasons, but because representatives of the North American Feed Industry Association "spent three months convincing [them] to drop" it. While, in short, the authors of the Annecy Report slept, naively assuming that their report would be judged on its merits, representatives of the North American Feed Industry Association, a special-interest group if there ever was one, were busy lobbying in favor of their economic interests in factory farming. Speaking only for myself, as a contributor to the Annecy Report, I find the behavior of the leadership of the WCC, *if* what Copperud says is true, shameful beyond measure, not because the leadership decided to dump the sections on factory farming in particular and all but buried the Annecy Report in general, but because WCC leaders evidently did not have the decency to invite Annecy participants to give their side of the story.

If the North American Feed Industry Association's special-interest lobbying of the WCC was an isolated case, one might view it as an unfortunate aberration. But it is not an isolated case. It is part of a pattern of the *politicization* of animal rights by powerful economic and political forces that have a vested interest in business as usual when it comes to human exploitation of nonhuman animals, whether on the farm, at the lab, or in the wild. Nor is the Christian church beyond politics in this regard. Witness the following excerpts from a November 17, 1990, presentation addressed to a Vatican conference by United States Secretary of Health and Human Services, Louis Sullivan.

> In the 1990s, animal rights extremists constitute a clear and present danger to developing knowledge that is directed to the betterment of human health. In equating to animals rights traditionally reserved for humans these activists pose a threat not only to research but to the vitality of the human spirit.[1]

What is significant about Secretary Sullivan's remarks goes beyond the fact that they were addressed to a conference organized by the Roman Catholic Church; the *content* of his remarks is no less important. In Secretary Sullivan's view, there are *extremists* in our midst—*animal rights* extremists. And if we ask who these people are, Secretary Sullivan has an answer. These are the people who "equate" human and animal rights. What Secretary Sullivan fails to mention—and one can only conjecture about his motives for failing to do so—is that *no one fits his description*. For there is no one, even among the most "radical" advocates of animal rights, who believes that the rights of humans and other animals are in every respect equal. Like others, Secretary Sullivan might delight in pillorying the idea of animal rights by asking us to image that pigs and cows should have the right to vote, for example, but this would only prove how much he and others wish to distort rather than to address this idea.

"Extremists" is a favored word in the lexicon of those who oppose animal rights. Others include "fanatics," "misanthropes," "monomaniacs" and— by far the favorite—"terrorists." Animal rights advocates are also "misinformed," "emotional," "antiscience," "anti-intellectual," and "anti-rational." Lest one think that only people in low places would engage in such pejorative rhetoric, consider just these three examples. The first comes from the 1988 "Animal Research Action Plan" of the American Medical Association. Among its recommendations: "The animal activist movement must be shown to be not only antiscience but also (a) responsible for violent and illegal acts that endanger life and property, and (b) a threat to the public's freedom of choice." A second example comes from the pen of Frederick K. Goodwin, who heads the United States government's Alcohol, Drug Abuse, and Mental Health Association. He writes: "Stripping away the facile, pathetically misinformed, and/or dishonest arguments against animal research reveals a philosophy based on the moral equivalence of humans and other sentient animals." And, lastly for present purposes, United States Representative Vin Weber, founder of the Congressional Animal Welfare Caucus, in an invitation to a fund-raising event featuring Secretary Louis Sullivan, has this to say: "It is my pleasure to invite you to meet a national leader in the fight to counteract the mindless emotionalism and violent tactics of the animal rights movement."

And so it goes. As these few examples illustrate, the AMA's Action Plan is well underway. No matter that truth is the first casualty. If Secretary Sullivan can tell his Catholic audience that animal rights advocates "equate" human and animal rights, Frederick Goodwin surely can rage against "the facile, pathetically misinformed, and/or dishonest arguments" these partisans use, and Congressman Weber can fiercely denounce their "mindless emotionalism." And the public? Well, the public can be none the wiser. In the face of this willful, deliberate, and well-crafted "pro-active" strategy, whose goal is to protect vested interests in business as usual when it comes to animal exploitation, respect for truth is more honored in the breach than in the observance. *Everybody* knows, for example, that animal rights "terrorists" are pouring blood on people who wear fur coats in New York City. And everybody thinks this shows just how "extreme," how "fanatical" these Bambi-loving "terrorists" really are. The fact that *there has not been a single recorded instance* of such vandalism in New York, a fact confirmed by New York City police and (reluctantly) conceded by representatives of the fur industry, shows just how successful special-interest groups are in manipulating the media and, with this, in molding public opinion.

The fate of the Annecy Report, then, is just one chapter in a larger political story, a story with a recurring plot: Do what needs to be done to protect vested interests in animal exploitation. If this means misrepresenting the ideas of those who challenge these interests, or demeaning their character, or insulting their intelligence, or spreading false rumors, then so be it. Thus the real tragedy of the fate of the Annecy Report lies, not in the fact that it was not incorporated into subsequent WCC deliberations and programs, but (assuming Mr. Copperud is correct) in the fact that "the leadership" of the WCC was a victim in a small but important chapter of this larger political story, as was the good-faith trust of the authors of the Annecy Report. Unless or until the WCC and other representatives of Christianity realize that they are not immune to the politics of pejoration, there is no hope that an informed, compassionate Christian response to the issue of animal rights will be forthcoming.

The Philosophy of Animal Rights

In addition to matters political, there are substantive moral and theological questions that must be addressed. What are the grounds, and how strong are they, for attributing rights to nonhuman animals? Which animals, if any, have rights, and what rights do they have? More fundamentally, what does it mean to speak of someone's "rights"? And how, if at all, can an informed Christian theology accommodate the rights of animals? I have addressed these questions at length elsewhere. What I offer here is a summary of my position, and a very condensed summary, at that.[2]

Suppose we start with the question, "What rights do nonhuman animals have?" And suppose we limit our discussion of this question to just one right, namely, the right to be treated with respect. This is a right I believe we recognize in the case of human beings. What it amounts to is this: Human beings are not to be treated *merely as a means* to someone else's ends, whether this someone else is another individual human being or some larger collection of humans (for example, the state). Other ways of expressing this same point are: (1) that my moral status in the world is not reducible to my being yours or anyone else's resource, and (2) that my moral status in the world is not reducible to any potential instrumental value I might have for you or anyone else. I have my own life to live, and this life is of value to me apart from any possible utility I might be to you. In this sense, one might speak of human beings as having "inherent worth" or "intrinsic value," in contrast to a pencil or a nail file, for example. Thus, to use deceit or coercion against me, for example, in the name of furthering your ends, is to fail to treat me with respect. It is to treat me as if I am morally on a par with a pencil or nail file. And because this kind of treatment — respectful treatment — is something I am owed, not out of kindness but as a matter of strict justice, it is a kind of treatment I can claim as my right. It is something to which I am entitled simply because I am the human person I am; it is not a right I have to earn.

The preceding helps answer the question, "What does it mean to speak of someone's rights?" Fundamentally, rights are valid claims that limit the freedom of moral agents. If I have a right to be treated with respect, then you must — morally, you must — limit your freedom in how you treat me. Morally, you are not at liberty to lie to me merely because you will benefit, nor can you physically assault me or force me to run your risks for you, for this same reason.

Thus, to speak of animal rights is first and foremost to say that there are *morally valid limits* on how we may treat nonhuman animals. Moreover, these rights are not something these animals, any more than you or I, must earn; in this sense, animal rights are natural rights. What is more, if other animals share with us a right to be treated with respect, then they, too, are not to be treated merely as means to our ends, nor is their moral status in the world reducible to their usefulness relative to our purposes, needs or interests. Those nonhuman animals, then, if any, whose value is not merely instrumental, may, like us, be viewed as having inherent worth or intrinsic value.

Which nonhuman animals, if any, have this kind of value and share with us the right to be treated with respect? The answer I have offered in general is the following. Some nonhuman animals not only are in the world, they are aware of the world: They hear, taste, smell and feel the physical reality we jointly cohabit. Moreover, these animals also have various cognitive capacities (they can learn, remember, and anticipate what takes place in the world as they experience it); they have a variety of desires, preferences, wants and needs, and are able to act in pursuit or avoidance of these desires, etc.; like us they can experience pleasure and pain, surprise and anxiety, and a fairly generous family of emotional states; and, for our purposes, finally, these various psychological capacities are not disparate, they are unified in the sense that, for example, this dog Spot, who remembers where his ball is, is the same dog Spot who wants to go for a walk. On my view, then, there is a psychologically unified life that is this dog Spot's life story, or, to put the same point differently,[3] in addition to having a biology, Spot also has a *biography*. Like us, Spot is a somebody in the world, not a something.

Where one draws the line vis-à-vis animals' possession of the right to be treated with respect, in my view, thus turns on where, as we move through the phylogenetic scale, the basis for attributing this biographical presence grows weaker and weaker. Of course, no one knows with certainty where this line should be drawn; the best we can do is to make our best effort to render our best judgment. Because we have abundant empirical evidence for believing that *human* biographical presence in the world has a material basis (depends, that is, on an intact, functioning central nervous system), we have a reasonable guide on which to rest our line-drawing decision: The more like us other animals are, in terms of their relevant physical make-up, the stronger are the grounds for viewing them as biographical beings; the less like us, the weaker are the grounds. Using this basis, the case for attributing a biographical presence in the world to species of birds and mammals is very strong indeed, as is the case for denying this kind of presence to oats, peas, beans and barley, for example. If, in response to this judgment, someone says (and someone always says), "But what about fish? Oysters? Clams? Bees? Ants? Other insects?," then I believe the honest answer is, "It's not altogether clear what one should say. There is some evidence for, and some against. These are hard cases." But (and this is what is crucial) our uncertainty about some cases does not entail that we are uncertain about all cases. The plain fact of the matter is, wherever one draws the line, pigs and cows, coyotes and dolphins, mice and rabbits, sparrows and eagles, wrens and robins are on our (that is to say, the biographical) side of it. And it is with what we know, not with what we are uncertain, that the future of our moral thinking and our moral life should seek direction.

That direction in practice calls for massive social change. Nonhuman animals are raised to be eaten by us, are shot for sport and trapped for purposes of fashion by us, are used as laboratory models and tools by us, are trained to perform and are exhibited in zoos by us, because we view them as our resources. The philosophy of animal rights calls for the abolition, not the humane reform, of any and all such practices. As such, the philosophy of animal rights mounts a categorical moral assault on those vested economic and professional interests for which the likes of Steve Copperud, Louis Sullivan, Frederick Goodwin, and Congressman Vin Weber speak. This philosophy, like any other, may be mistaken. But whether it is or not must surely be decided on the basis of a careful examination of the arguments that are marshalled in its favor. Respect for reason, respect for science, respect for intelligence demand nothing less. Sadly, as the opening section of this paper documents, just such respect is demonstrably lacking on the part of those public officials who oppose those who accept the philosophy of animal rights. One can only hope that those who speak for the Christian faith will not add their voices to the choir of pejoration or that, in the wake of special-interest lobbying, these same voices will not be silenced.

Theological Speciesism

Minds far more versed than mine have addressed the question of the Christian faith's position vis-à-vis the moral status of nonhuman animals. Most have reached conclusions that differ from those reached by the philosophy of animal rights. A small minority have reached the same conclusions.[4] If we had reason to suppose that truth could be determined by taking a vote, the truth in this case would be clear. But, of course, we must all agree that truth is not purchased by the coin of majority opinion. It remains possible, therefore, that, as has been true in other cases, so in this one: The minority Christian view may be the correct one. How might one attempt to show that it is? A detailed response to this question is beyond my abilities. All that I can offer — and on this occasion even this will be sketchily drawn — are the broad outlines of a larger landscape of ideas.[5]

One challenge asserts itself immediately. The philosophy of animal rights takes individual animals seriously. Arguably, the locus of value for an informed Christian theology is *species* and, allied with this, the diversity of life, not the individual. Following Charles Pinches,[6] we might term this "theological speciesism," a view he evidently favors over animal rights. Commenting on Genesis 1:20-24, Pinches writes that "in this seminal passage, various kinds of creatures are mentioned, and emphasis is placed upon the multiplicity of the kinds, implying not only that this multiplicity was God's idea but that God delighted in each kind in its uniqueness and diversity."[7] Moreover, later in this same essay, where he directs his comments to the idea that human beings are given dominion over creation, he writes that "the dominion over creation offered humans in Genesis 1:28 can be well understood in terms of the unique human role as caretaker of *diversity*."[8] Thus, because the philosophy of animal rights[9] does not recognize the rights of species as such, and in view of the importance of species diversity, according to Pinches, in an informed Christian theology, it would seem that the two ideas — the philosophy of animal rights on the one hand,

and Christian theology on the other—are necessarily at odds with each other. One would have thought, however, that the insistence on this kind of conflict is greatly exaggerated. From a practical point of view, the philosophy of animal rights is not in principle at odds with protecting the diversity of life. On the contrary, because this philosophy implies that animals in the wild have a right to be treated with respect (and thus, for example, that they are not to be killed in the name of sport or trapped in pursuit of fashion), this philosophy is committed to retaining and reclaiming wildlife habitat. Will anyone suggest that, in view of this commitment, the philosophy of animal rights is therefore at odds with the biblical view that humans have a unique role as caretakers of diversity? It is difficult to imagine how such a judgment could be supported.

Pinches cites the case of the grey wolves' reintroduction into their former range in Minnesota as something of a test case. He favors their reintroduction and believes that most people would concur. "An animal rights position," he insists, "can neither support nor explain this."[10] Why not? Because "animal rights positions are simply blind to species distinctions . . . (According to such positions) we do not owe wolves anything as a species. We have no more reason to wish that the wolf population increase any more than that the cattle population increase."[11] Now, there may be some thinker whose views about animal rights Pinches is disputing, but it is unclear who this thinker might be. For one thing, animal rights thinkers do not think it would be a good idea that "the cattle population increase." Just the opposite: There should be greatly fewer cattle in the world, according to this philosophy, and their raison d'être should not be that humans might consume them.

But what about grey wolves? Should there be more of them? The animal rights position is supportive of this outcome. If we give back to these animals the natural habitat we have taken from them—and this is something we fail to do if we imagine, as Pinches seems to, that commercial cattle ranchers can "share" the habitat with these wild animals—then, in the natural course of events, there will be more grey wolves, and the individual animals ranging over the woods and hills of Montana will have been treated with the respect they are due, according to the philosophy of animal rights. In short, the attempt to undermine this philosophy by attempting to show that it is at odds with wildlife restoration policies, such as the case at hand, misfire.

The Theology of Animal Rights

There are, of course, more fundamental issues that need to be addressed. Even if it is false—Pinches's protestations to the contrary notwithstanding—that the philosophy of animal rights, because of its emphasis on the inherent value of individual animals, "can neither support nor explain" wildlife restoration efforts, we need to ask whether this emphasis upon individual wolves, or cows for that matter, is at odds with the biblical message. By my own (confessedly inexpert) lights, I do not think the biblical message is as unambiguous as Pinches, for example, would have us assume. What are we to make of Genesis 1:29, for example, where God is said to provide primal humans with a diet of "all plants that bear seed everywhere upon the earth, and every tree bearing fruit which yields seed"? To infer that God permits us to eat *species* of trees bearing seeds, for example, is absurd; for no one can eat a species of anything. Rather, we are given permission to eat individual plants that fit this description. In other words, although our authorized diet in paradise is spelled out in general terms, we are to understand that we do not consume generalities, only particulars. And the particulars we are permitted to consume, as food, are nuts, berries and other fruits; particular cows, sheep, hogs, chickens and the like are conspicuous for their absence. Permission to eat them is not forthcoming at this point in the biblical story.

Consider, further, for example, the eschatological vision of Isaiah, which in part reads as follows:

> The wolf shall dwell with the lamb,
> and the leopard shall lie down with the kid,
> and the calf and the lion and the fatling together,
> and a little child shall lead them.
> The cow and the bear shall feed;
> their young shall lie down together;
> and the lion shall eat straw like the ox. . . .
> They shall not hurt or destroy
> in all my holy mountain. . . . (Isaiah 11:6-9)

In this prophecy of future time, we are to understand that not only do humans live in peace with the other animals, and so do not eat them, even the other animals do not prey on one another for nourishment. (Like the cow, even the lion eats straw.) Again, moreover, since whoever eats, eats individuals, not species, both the earlier creation saga in Genesis and the prophetic vision of Isaiah speak with one voice: Individual animals matter, not just species or their balance and diversity. By way of a final example: When, in the New Testament, Jesus testifies that "not a sparrow falls" that God is not mindful of that creature, only a Byzantine theology would infer that God's love extends only to species, not to individuals.

Thus do I for one find the imputation, to God, of a theology that exempts individual animals from moral standing and extends this only to species and their diversity, biblically impoverished. I do not say that the Bible contains no passages that might support this view; in fact, the passage Pinches cites, Genesis 1:20-24, arguably is one of them. My more modest point is different—namely, that other passages no less clearly reflect a divine concern for the individual—this or that particular flesh-and-blood creature. For it was, after all, individual animals, not species, that Jesus is reputed to have set free in his protest against the money changers.

But even if it is true, as I believe it is, that some passages in the Bible support the view that individual animals are not ours to eat or in other ways to make use of for our purposes, we are obliged to ask whether all other life forms have a lesser kind of value. Again, Pinches correctly insists upon the necessity of raising this question when he writes that "if we say that the treatment of individual animals is a matter of strict justice, does this mean that the treatment of croplands is not? If elephants have intrinsic value, with what is this being contrasted that has merely instrumental value?"[12] How, within the constellation of values recognized by the philosophy of animal rights, might one respond to these important questions?

To begin with, there is nothing in this philosophy that requires that values come in two kinds only—*either* intrinsic *or* instrumental. Any number of other kinds of values, including certain virtuous character traits, as well as aesthetic and spiritual values, for example, can consistently be recognized by this philosophy. Moreover, even within the category of instrumental values, it is important to realize that this philosophy can insist upon strict limitations on human freedom. Aside from the possible aesthetic and other sorts of value they may possess, the philosophy of animal rights will recognize the instrumental value of croplands. But in categorizing croplands as having instrumental value, one does not imply that they may be used in any way one pleases.

Croplands have instrumental value relative to the legitimate human purpose of raising food, but they have this value not only relative to present but also to future generations of human beings. Moreover, how croplands are treated also impacts upon both the diversity and sustainability of the larger nonhuman ecosystem of which they are a part and the nonhuman animals who make their home within these ecosystems. Today's dominant agricultural approach to raising crops (chemically intensive, monocultural agriculture) can be faulted on all these grounds. It is not a sustainable form of agriculture and thus imperils the interests of future generations of human beings. It causes enormous damage to ecosystems as a whole; and it is highly detrimental to individual land and aquatic animals who, by being subjected to chemical runoff and other harms, suffer and die.[13]

Thus, even croplands must be treated appropriately (that is, in ways that are consistent with the legitimate human good they serve), according to the animal rights position, which is why it may be misleading to say that they "have merely instrumental value." For in saying this, it is easy to infer that it does not matter how they are treated, an inference which, for the reasons just given, is simply mistaken. More generally, to say that something has instrumental value, viewed against the backdrop of the philosophy of animal rights, does not mean that we are at liberty to treat it in any way we please. If, in view of these observations, someone wants to insist that "appropriate use" should be viewed as a matter of "strict justice," one need have no quarrel, just so long as it is recognized that the logic of what is owed (as a matter of strict justice) to what has instrumental value, relative to legitimate human purposes, differs in important ways from what is owed (as a matter of strict justice) to those individuals whose value is noninstrumental. On this view, in short, croplands may be used for the legitimate human purpose of raising food, provided they are treated appropriately, whereas cows and hogs may not be used for this purpose, howsoever humane their treatment.

Suppose I am right (a large assumption, to be sure). Then the distinction between the bearers of intrinsic (or inherent) value and the bearers of instrumental value has both a philosophical and a theological basis. More-over — and importantly, for present purposes — the former category is not reserved for humans only. Those other animals who, like humans, were created on the sixth day also possess noninstrumental value and, as such, are to be treated respectfully (not merely appropriately) relative to the pursuit of legitimate human ends. This is, as I have indicated, the message I for one glean from the biblical message about primal and eschatological time. As such, we humans who, as Pinches would agree, are the divinely appointed caretakers of the Earth, have a choice either to journey back to Eden or to journey forward toward the realization of Isaiah's vision. How-ever we view the journey, whether as traveling backward toward a lost paradise or forward toward a promised one, an essential step along the way is to stop treating the other animals as if they are our resources. And this means, in part, that we stop eating them, as distasteful as that might be.

Animal Rights and Human Virtues

Whether argued for philosophically or theologically, how nonhuman ani-mals are treated *is* a matter of strict justice. It is not human kindness, not human generosity, not a tender human heart, not any human interest that is the basis of respectful treatment. It is justice, understood as treating others as they are due. Morally, we are obliged to treat nonhuman animals as they deserve to be treated, whether we like them or not and whether or not we view our own happiness as tied to their well-being. Because of this emphasis on justice, someone might infer that animal rights advocates are committed to driving a sharp wedge deeply between the respectful treat-ment of animals, on the one hand, and human happiness, on the other. Pinches offers the example of a dog who has gotten his collar entangled in a neighbor's bush. In the rights' view, it seems, it is only the dog's, not any human interest, that is at stake. Pinches finds this unacceptable. In his view, he would not "regard the dog's state of well-being . . . as having nothing to do with my own." "[S]houldn't we rather think," he asks, "that were I the right sort of person, the sight of the dog in such circumstances would bother me? Indeed, I should not be happy myself with him in that condition. That is, I should not see my 'interests' or those of my neighbor as entirely separable from his. . . . [Instead] I should strive to be . . . the sort of person whose happiness, qua *anthropos*, or qua human creature of God, depends upon the well-being of our fellow creatures."[14]

To the extent that Pinches believes that this constitutes an objection to the philosophy or theology of animal rights,[15] he is mistaken. There is nothing in the animal rights position that precludes our seeing the connection between acting on behalf of the interests of a nonhuman animal and acting to promote human interests. If we assume that Pinches's neighbor cares for his dog's well-being, then it would be in his neighbor's interests, not simply his neighbor's dog's, to release the animal. Moreover, if Pinches is the "right sort of person," one whose own happiness depends upon "the well-being of our fellow creatures," then freeing the dog will be something that is tied to Pinches's own happiness. All this may be granted. The problem is, not everyone is "the right sort of person." Pinches's neighbor, for example, might care precious little for his dog. The dog in fact may be entangled by the bush because of his neighbor's willful neglect. Are we then not to free the dog? Or suppose that, not Pinches but some other neighbor, who is not the "right sort of person," sees the dog and is unmoved by the animal's plight. This neighbor, in other words, does not see that his happiness "depends upon" the dog's. Are we then to conclude that this person has no obligation to free the animal? It is implausible to imagine that the answer to either of these questions would be in the affirmative. And this is crucial. It illustrates an important general truth—namely, that the basis of the obligation to free the dog is independent of what does and does not satisfy human interests.

Having said this, however, it is important that the animal rights position not be misunderstood. One need have no quarrel with Pinches's understanding of what is involved in being the "right sort of person." Indeed, it is perfectly consistent with the animal rights position that one evolve into a person who takes satisfaction in treating other animals as they deserve to be treated and who sees the pain and suffering and the needless death of other animals as something that diminishes his or her own happiness. In other words, the "right sort of person" is one whose well-being, as a person, is connected with the well-being of all who have a well-being. It is not simply "every man's death" that diminishes such a person; such a person is diminished by the needless suffering and death of nonhuman animals and the inappropriate treatment of all that sustains life on this planet. The "right sort of person," one might say, rejoices in doing the right thing and is pained by the wrongful treatment of any member of the life community. This—which is a truer view of the wholeness of the animal rights position regarding moral development and motivation—is a far cry from one that, according to Pinches, would "shut off the path to (one's own) moral education or transformation such that I might learn to become a person who is properly affected by the plight of my fellow creatures, human and non-human alike."[16] If I am right, Pinches has got it altogether wrong.

Concluding Practical Postscript

My remarks on this occasion have been narrowly focused. I have not attempted to comment upon, let alone to defend, the Annecy Report in its entirety. Nor have I even addressed all parts of its section on our treatment of individual nonhuman animals. In addition to summarizing some of my views and alerting readers to the politicization of animal rights, I have been mainly concerned with responding to some (but not all) of the criticisms lodged by Charles Pinches. Pinches at one point faults the authors of the Annecy Report for "a lack of theological care and an uncritical appropriation of the moral rallying cries of the day . . ."[17] One of those cries, I assume, is "animal rights," and though I would be the first to admit that a more careful theological basis than the one I have proffered is needed, the burden of supplying one must understandably pass to more qualified hands than my own.

One final practical point. Pinches acknowledges that he is not a vegetarian, although, as he says, "the logic of the position [he is] developing is not incompatible with vegetarianism."[18] "In any case," he goes on to add, "what is clearly excluded by [his] view is modern factory farming that turns all animal species it touches into one thing: meat."[19] This is an important point of practical agreement, notwithstanding the apparent theoretical disagreements that separate us, especially in view of the fact that virtually *all* "meat" is produced by factory farms. I, for one, cannot help believing that the well-being of Pinches's "right sort of person" would be diminished by the grotesque suffering and needless death of these animals, if and when such persons as these become familiar with factory farming methods. In this respect, then, the authors of the Annecy Report would have welcomed Pinches's presence in the open public debate about the report's condemnation of factory farming which, thanks to the political zeal of special-interest lobbying, the WCC apparently lacked the courage or wisdom to organize.

Notes

1. Quoted in the April 1991 newsletter of the International Primate Protection League.

2. See, in particular, Tom Regan, *The Case for Animal Rights.* Berkeley: University of California Press, 1983.

3. I owe this way of expressing this point to James Rachels.

4. For representative selections from partisans of both sides, see A. Linzey and T. Regan (eds.), *Animals and Christianity: A Book of Readings.* New York: Crossroad, 1988.

5. See also my "Christianity and the Rights of Animals: The Challenge and the Promise," in C. Birch, W. Eakin and J. McDaniel (eds.), *Liberating Life: Contemporary Approaches to Ecological Theology*. Maryknoll, N. Y.: Orbis Books, 1990.

6. See Charles Pinches, "Each According to Its Kind: A Defense of Theological Speciesism," in this volume, pp. 187-205.

7. Ibid., p. 195.

8. Ibid., p. 200, emphasis added.

9. Pinches consistently misrepresents my ideas, interpreting me as holding that rights are correlated with interests. Although this is a common and important analysis of rights, it is not mine. See my *The Case for Animal Rights*.

10. Pinches, p. 196.

11. Ibid.

12. Ibid., p. 193.

13. Perhaps the best introduction to these matters is John Robbins, *Diet for a New America*. New York: Stillpoint Press, 1989.

14. Pinches, p. 189.

15. Pinches often lodges his objections against those who are anti-speciesist or anti-anthropocentrists. Thus the target of his criticisms includes, even as it goes beyond, advocates of animal rights.

16. Pinches, p. 191f.

17. Ibid., p. 188.

18. Ibid., p. 205n13.

19. Ibid., p. 205.

Appendix A

The State of the Animals

Human Impact on Wild and Domestic Animals

Richard M. Clugston

Human beings first began to significantly alter the natural world some 6,000 years ago with the development of agriculture and urban centers. They tamed and bred animals, clear-cut forests, dammed rivers, built cities, and plowed the soil. While these activities often were very destructive to local ecosystems, only recently has the human presence begun to significantly threaten the life systems of the planet as a whole.

The human population is growing explosively. At the beginning of the century, it was less than 2 billion. It is 5.3 billion now, and will grow to some 10 billion early next century. In addition to our explosive growth in numbers, we humans are developing and applying more "effective" technologies for exploiting natural resources, including animals. The development of genetic engineering, DDT, dioxin and plutonium; the mass production of automobiles, televisions and countless other consumer goods; the expansion of the suburbs; and the development of high-tech weaponry—all these technological developments make the human presence much more destructive of the earth and its creatures than ever before in history.

This essay describes the current state of the animals. It reports on the impact of the human presence on wild and domesticated animals. It looks first at the extinction rate and number of threatened mammal and bird species in selected countries, illustrating the loss of animals by estimated

Richard M. Clugston is the Executive Director of the Center of Respect for Life and Environment in Washington, D.C. The center is a division of the Humane Society of the United States.

221

population declines in the cases of a few large mammals and migratory birds. The sources of these threats are explored—from the destruction of wild habitat to pollution and pesticides. The state of domesticated animals is then reviewed, focusing on the numbers and conditions facing farm and laboratory animals and also those kept as companions.

While no comprehensive information exists on the numbers of animals on our planet or on the specific condition facing them, the information that does exist can be combined to suggest a general picture. This is one of a massive assault on the animal world—resulting in an accelerating extinction of animal species, the degradation of habitats, rapid decline in populations, and the increased confinement and manipulation of animals.

The principal purpose of this essay is to sketch in some of the details of this appalling picture. Yet it is assumed that readers will be concerned to work to change it so far as they are able. Such change requires that our life-styles, policies, and institutions embody humaneness and sustainability. So the essay concludes with a brief summary of five steps we must take individually and collectively to protect animals and the earth.

The Death of Life: Threats to Wildlife

Life is remarkably diverse. The animal kingdom contains some 1,032,000 described species. It consists of sponges, jellyfish, worms, mollusks, starfish, insects and other arthropods, and the vertebrates. Roughly three-quarters of all species in the animal kingdom are insects. The majority of nonvertebrate species are still unknown—credible estimates are that we have only discovered between 4 percent and 20 percent of existing species. Approximately 42,000 known species of vertebrates exist, containing 4,000 species of mammals; 9,000 species of birds; 6,000 species of reptiles; 4,000 species of amphibians; and 19,000 species of fish (Wilson, 1988).

This great diversity of life-forms is being rapidly diminished by the explosive growth of human population coupled with increasing consumption and invasive technologies. Major attention has focused on dramatic species extinction rates particularly due to the destruction of tropical rain forests. Scientific experts vary somewhat in their assessment of current and future extinction rates, but the general consensus is that "by the end of this century, our planet could lose anywhere from 29% to 50% of its species" (Lugo, in Wilson 1988, 58). Over the past decade, the extinction rate has increased from one species a day to one each hour. This is an extinction rate some 1,000 to 10,000 times as great as would be occurring without humans. From 500,000 to several million of currently existing species are likely to perish by the year 2000.

Threatened Species of Mammals and Birds

Extinction is the final act in a slow process of weakening and decline. For each species pronounced dead today, the populations of other species are currently declining, often rapidly. While information does not exist for many countries, the following table gives a conservative glimpse of the current numbers of threatened species. These numbers are based on World Conservation Union Classifications, which break threatened species into five categories:

- Endangered. Taxa in danger of extinction and whose survival is unlikely if the causal factors continue operating.
- Vulnerable. Taxa believed likely to move into the Endangered category in the near future if the causal factors continue operating.
- Rare. Taxa with world populations that are not at present Endangered or Vulnerable, but are at risk.
- Indeterminate. Taxa known to be Endangered, Vulnerable, or Rare but where there is not enough information to say which of the three categories is appropriate.
- Insufficiently Known. Taxa that are suspected but not definitely known to belong to any of the above categories.

The number of threatened species listed for most countries includes species that are endangered, vulnerable, rare, indeterminate, and insufficiently known, but excludes introduced species. The total number of species includes introductions. The data on mammals excludes cetaceans (whales and porpoises) (World Resources Institute 1990-91, 20) (see p. 224).

Europe has the largest numbers and percentages of threatened species, reflecting both its population density and the advanced state of industrial development. There is little undisturbed habitat remaining. In European countries where data is available, from one-fourth to one-half of bird and mammal species are threatened. In the Americas, about 10 percent of the mammal species are threatened, with a smaller percentage of bird species. As development proceeds and population increases in Africa and South America, these numbers and percentages will continue to increase.

Illustrative Cases of Population Decline

The following information on large mammals and neotropical migratory birds illustrates some cases of population decline. Over the past twenty years, the elephant population in Africa has declined from 3 million to 700,000. White rhinos have gone from 1,500 to 12. Asian tigers have dropped from 100,000 in 1940 to a low of 4,000 in 1970. With protection, their numbers have increased to about 7,500 today (Middleton 1989, 33 and 37).

Whale populations are between 3 percent and 25 percent of what they were before whaling became industrialized. Though these whale species are protected, illegal poaching continues, as does the continued degradation of the ocean habitat.

More than 100 species of vireos, warblers, flycatchers and thrushes win-

	Mammals		Birds	
	Known Species	*Number Threatened*	*Known Species*	*Number Threatened*
Africa				
Algeria	97	15	X	4
Cameroon	297	18	848	16
Cote d'Ivoire	232	23	756	6
Morocco	108	13	X	3
Nigeria	274	57	831	8
Zaire	409	24	1086	27
Americas				
Argentina	255	26	927	18
Brazil	394	42	1567	35
Colombia	358	25	1665	28
Mexico	439	32	961	123
United States	466	49	1090	79
Asia				
India	341	29	1178	135
Japan	186	4	632	35
Philippines	96	7	541	2
Europe				
Austria	83	38	201	121
France	113	59	342	136
Netherlands	60	39	257	85
U.S.S.R.	357	78	765	80
Australia	320	43	700	23

Sources: World Conservation Monitoring Centre; Organization for Economic Co-operation and Development; and United Nations Economic and Social Commission for Asia and the Pacific. Table from World Resources Institute 1990-91, 302-03.

ter in the tropics of Central and South America, flying north to nest and breed. Populations of these songbirds are generally perceived to be in sharp decline. For example, in Rock Creek Park, a fairly undisturbed woodland reserve in the District of Columbia, "from 1948 to 1983, the migrant songbird breeding population plunged by more than 70 percent. At least three songbird species vanished. Ovenbirds and red-eyed vireos declined by 94 percent and 79 percent respectively" (*New York Times*, June 6, 1988, C1).

In a comprehensive study of nearctic avian migrants in the Neotropics, a United States Fish and Wildlife study listed the following species as already reduced to near extinction or likely to show serious decline within the next decade: Bachman's Warbler, Golden-cheeked Warbler, Whooping

Crane, Eskimo Curlew, Buffbreasted Sandpiper, Roseate Tern, Sooty Tern, Gull-billed Tern, Least Tern, and the Kirkland's Warbler. (U.S. Fish and Wildlife Service, *Neartic Avian Migrants in the Neotropics*, July 1983, 90-92).

Research and public attention focus primarily on those animal species which seem most sentient, and whose loss is most apparent. But the largest loss of species will be in the tiny creatures that inhabit the soil and tropical treetops. As Paul Erlich comments:

> Many of the less cuddly, less spectacular organisms that *Homo sapiens* are wiping out are more important to the human future than are most of the publicized endangered species. People need plants and insects more than they need leopards and whales (which is not to denegrate the value of the latter two). [Also], the loss of genetically distinct populations within species is, at the moment, at least as important a problem as the loss of entire species. Once a species is reduced to a remnant, its ability to benefit humanity ordinarily declines greatly, and its total extinction in the relatively near future becomes much more likely. By the time an organism is recognized as endangered, it is often too late to save it. (in Wilson 1988, 21-22)

Sources of Decline in Wildlife Populations

In some cases extinction is a direct result of killing by humans — such as the passenger pigeon, or in all likelihood, the white rhino. However, the major threat is not such a focused assault, but the unintended consequence of habitat loss and degradation. The previously mentioned study of declining neartic avian migrants listed the following reasons for population declines (not in order of their importance): direct disturbances by humans, e.g., hunting, disruption of breeding colonies, etc.; preferred habitat decreasing; small population size; restricted range; and vulnerable stopover points where large segments of population concentrate (United States Fish and Wildlife Service, July 1983).

In reviewing the seventy-eight case studies of endangered species in the

Whale Populations

Species	Pre-Exploitation Numbers	Present Numbers
Blue	200,000+	5-10,000
Bowhead	65,000	8,000
Fin	500,000+	120,000
Humpback	125,000+	12,000+
Right	50,000	3,000
Sei	250,000+	50,000

Source: James D. Darling, "Whales — An Era of Discovery," *National Geographic*, December 1988, 891.

Red Data books and a recent endangered species report of the U.S. Government Accounting Office, Tony Povilitis identified a number of specific threats. In order of the frequency in which they were reported for the species, these specific threats were:

1. Land development for urban, commercial, industrial, or recreational purposes
2. Land conversion for agriculture
3. Changes in natural communities through livestock grazing, control of natural fire, etc.
4. Pollution and pesticides
5. Water development, such as reservoir construction and stream channelization
6. Predator and pest control
7. Hunting, poaching, and collecting (in the case of insects and plants)
8. Vehicle collisions
9. Direct human disturbance of roosting and nesting areas

For a greater appreciation of the nature of these threats, they are elaborated below.

Land development and conversion. Forests are cleared for timber, fuel, or to make room for human habitation and enterprise. Wetlands are drained for agricultural, industrial or residential use. Grasslands are plowed up. For example, in the United States, "between 1945 and 1975, an area of farmland about the size of Nebraska was covered with asphalt" (Carson, 81). The expansion of suburbs and shopping malls, the increasing levels of consumption and waste, and the requirements of the automobile for roads, freeways and parking lots have resulted in this rapid land conversion following World War II.

The following chart (see p. 227) lists habitat loss for three major habitat types (forests, grasslands and wetlands) for selected countries.

Although this data is somewhat sketchy, it illustrates the amount of original habitat lost in various countries. The United States lost from 98 percent to 100 percent of its original prairies while retaining 74 percent of its forests. India and Senegal have lost about 80 percent of their original habitats. Population and development pressures are causing countries to use more and more of what remains. Habitat loss is accelerating.

Having adequate habitat in a particular country does not guarantee the survival of a species. Many species roam or migrate across large geographic areas, or depend for their survival on species that move about. The loss of vulnerable stopover points (such as nesting areas) or other critical habitat areas thus can imperil species even though there may be a respectable percentage of remaining habitat in a particular country.

Change in natural communities through the management and use of natural areas. Many undeveloped public lands are grazed extensively by

Habitat Types (areas in sq. Km)

	All Forests		Savanna/ Grasslands		Wetlands/ Marsh	
	Current sq. Km	% lost	Current sq. Km	% lost	Current sq. Km	% lost
Africa						
Botswana	112,926	62	122,470	53	23,310	10
Cameroon	184,678	59	3,760	72	160	80
Ethiopia	55,700	86	274,685	61	0	0
Kenya	22,738	71	276,816	43	0	0
Senegal	25,200	82	11,200	80	15	X
Zaire	832,540	57	54,050	30	2,150	50
Americas						
Mexico	384,608	66	X	X	32,640	X
U. S.	2,994,780	26	30,000	100	870,000	54
Argentina	360,000	50	1,300	X	61,699	X
Asia						
India	499,285	78	0	0	9,408	79
Myanmar	241,305	64	12,025	74	490	98
Pakistan	7,635	86	0	0	3,200	74
Europe						
Greece	80,940	70	X	X	865	X
Italy	X	X	X	X	30,000	94
U.S.S.R.	375,730	38	X	X	28,732	X

Source: World Conservation Union and others in *World Resources Institute* 1990-91, 306-07.

livestock. In the United States, ranchers are given permits to graze their cattle and sheep in Forest Service and Bureau of Land Management areas. While there is considerable debate over the extent of overgrazing and the damage it causes, at the least overgrazing causes degradation of land through erosion and the displacement or death of wild grazing and predatory species, which are killed as pests. Overgrazing has contributed to the desertification in many parts of the world, including 10 percent of the United States. Increasing land available for cattle ranching is causing much tropical deforestation. "In Amazonia, tax incentives and subsidies led to the establishment of 469 cattle ranches that were responsible for 30 percent of Amazonia's deforestation" (Fox 1990, 25). Providing food and water for the world's 4 billion livestock and 9 billion chickens results in the rapid conversion of habitat into pasture and farmland and the diversion of streams and depletion of aquifers to provide large amounts of water, particularly for intensive animal agriculture. This also disrupts natural communities.

Pesticides and pollution. Rachel Carson's *Silent Spring* was a warning of the destruction, particularly of songbirds, caused by pesticides (at that time the major culprit was DDT). Pesticide use continues to rise worldwide with destructive effect. For example, "[i]n the Paris basin (of France) chemical pesticides have caused a 70 percent reduction in the 800 species of animals, of which only 5 percent are harmful to cereal crops" (Middleton 1989, 7).

Rivers, lakes, and groundwater are contaminated by pesticide and fertilizer runoff, industrial wastes and sewage. Many of the world's great rivers, such as the Ganges, Rhine, Seine, Thames, and Mississippi, have drastically reduced fish species. Cadmium, a heavy metal, is dangerous to humans and animals in very small doses, producing neurological damage. It is present in many rivers, such as the Elbe in Germany, the Rimac in Peru, and the Missouri River in the United States, in concentrations 20–60 times the maximum concentration set by the World Health Organization. The Vistula River in Poland is so polluted that the stretch of it running through Krakow is totally devoid of biological life (Middleton 1989, 30-31).

About 5 million tons of oil are spilled into the oceans each year, imperiling many animals. Animals are caught in slicks and drown or die from exposure. In addition, this oil disperses widely and is lethal for fish larvae and plankton, thus reducing the base of the food chain (Mauritz la Riviere 1989, 89).

The combined effects of various forms of pollution are thought to have weakened the immune systems of seals of the North Sea, which experienced a massive die-off in 1989. Fish and shellfish in many coastal and fresh waters often show concentrations of various contaminants as well as lesions and other damage attributable to pollution. Governments in developed countries frequently recommended that individuals limit their intake of seafood due to the health risk it poses.

Water development. The U. S. Army Corps of Engineers (and its equivalents in other countries) alter natural waterways. Rivers are dammed, flooding large areas and endangering species (such as the snail darter). Environmental groups oppose current efforts in Brazil, Quebec, India, China and the American West to build large dams whose purpose, ironically, is to produce nonpolluting electricity. In addition, many streams are diverted, dammed up, or used as sewage systems, resulting in extensive damage to the ecosystems that once existed in and around them.

Sport hunting, predator control and poaching. Approximately 200 million mammals and birds are shot and killed each year in the United States by sport hunters. According to the U. S. Fish and Wildlife Service for the 1988-89 season this included: 28 million bobwhite quail; 20 million ringneck pheasants; 5 million ducks; 21,000 black bears; 2,200 brown and grizzly bears; 250,000 coyotes; 1,500 mountain lions; and 1,000 wolves. In addition, some 100 million animals are trapped worldwide each year for fur. In the United States, some 17 million target animals (beavers, lynx, fox, mink, raccoons, muskrats) are trapped with an additional 2–8 million "trash" animals, including dogs, cats, raptors, and livestock (Sleeper 1990, 25).

The U. S. Animal Damage Control program also shot, poisoned, burned, drowned or gassed 4.6 million birds; 9,000 beaver; 76,000 coyotes; 5,000 raccoons; 300 black bears; and 200 mountain lions, to name a few. These animals were destroyed at a cost to taxpayers of $29.4 million to protect agricultural interests—particularly wool growers—from undesirable losses (Sleeper 1990, 25).

Many animals are captured (legally and illegally) from the wild for pets, research, or zoos. The following quote from an HSUS pamphlet on the "Wild Bird Trade" illustrates one example of trade in wild animals:

Each year, millions of birds are snatched out of the wild to supply the cage-bird business. Because grossly inhumane capture techniques, injuries, inadequate care, and shock cause an appalling number of deaths, supplying worldwide imports of seven and a half million birds actually necessitates the capture of 30 million birds. One method of capture involves trapping the birds with leg snares from which they dangle helplessly for indefinite periods. Those that survive capture are highly stressed and may die as a result of the immense cruelties of shipment; hundreds of birds are often packed in tiny crates meant for two or three dozen and are left for days with no food or water. Fighting often erupts and many birds are maimed or killed. Sometimes, every bird in a shipment of three or four thousand will be dead on arrival. Poor conditions and disease outbreaks in quarantine also kill many birds. Of the 913,653 birds the U. S. imported in 1984, only 741,921 survived the rigors of transport and quarantine. Many of them would die later, in the pet shop or in their owners' homes. Parrots and other birds pair for life and thus suffer even further from the loss of their mates. The birds endure these horrors at the hands of the legal trade, to say nothing of what goes on in the illegal trade. Both are pushing many species to the brink of extinction. (HSUS, "Wild Bird Trade" n.d.)

Other threats. An often overlooked threat to species comes from the introduction of exotic species into the native habitat. Often exotic species are at a competitive advantage and, over time, displace the indigenous species. Nineteen percent of all endangered, vulnerable and rare species of vertebrates are threatened by exotic species which are displacing them from their natural habitat.

Another source of destruction is war (and the preparation for war). For example, over the years of the Iran-Iraq War, the marsh ecology of southern Iraq was badly disrupted, as was that of the gulf. Due largely to oil spills from damaged wells, all fishing was suspended, and the populations of dugong (a manateelike mammal) were greatly reduced. The U.S. Gulf War resulted in massive ecological warfare in Iraq's torching of the oil fields and dumping of oil into the gulf. In the Vietnam War, 14 million tons of high explosives were used by the United States, as well as 100,000 tons of chemical agents, such as Agent Orange. This produced significant environmental damage. The Pacific region, in which most above ground nuclear test explosions occurred, shows the highest rate of species extinction in the world (Barnaby 1988, 102-03).

The State of Domesticated Animals

It is not only wild animals who suffer in their shrinking and degraded natural habitat. Domestic animals are being increasingly confined and manipulated. Human beings, in their efforts to remake the earth to be more secure and bountiful, have selected and bred certain animal species for food, labor, entertainment, companionship and scientific research. Natural ecosystems have been replaced by human-shaped ecosystems. Cows, pigs, chickens, horses, dogs, cats, and mice have been bred for traits desirable for food production, work, show and research. Intensive confinement systems are increasingly replacing free roaming in pastures or pens as the habitat for farm animals. Now genetic engineering and biotechnology promise to increase the human capacity to produce animals with desired traits. This section will consider the current state of various domesticated animals.

Farm Animals

Worldwide there are approximately 4 billion livestock, including 1.3 billion cattle, and more than 9 billion chickens and other fowl. In developing countries animals not only provide food, but much of the labor. In the United States in 1988, there were 100 million cattle and calves; 19 million dairy cows; 55 million hogs; 11 million sheep and lambs; and 239 million laying hens. In addition, 5.15 billion broiler chickens were slaughtered (1988 USDA figures).

The conditions in which food animals are raised, transported and slaughtered vary considerably. In the United States, increasing numbers of livestock and poultry are raised in confinement. Virtually all these 239 million laying hens live their entire lives packed in small cages. They cannot turn around or stretch their wings. They never see the sunshine or peck at the ground. Calves are also confined to produce white or milk-fed veal. They are separated from their mothers, often within days of birth, and placed into crates where they too cannot turn around. They are fed formula and become anemic. Their muscles atrophy from lack of movement, thus producing tender, white veal. Hogs are increasingly raised in confinement and cattle concentrated in feedlots to enhance economies of scale. These creatures, while inclined to roam about foraging for food, caring for their young, interacting with their kind, are jammed together in tiny spaces, with little opportunity to move about to see the light of day. Being so crowded and otherwise distressed, they are susceptible to many diseases which are controlled through the extensive use of antibiotics. To increase their yield, these animals are often given hormones and fed highly processed mixtures. All too often they suffer unnecessarily from thirst, exposure and improper handling in transport and slaughter.

Laboratory Animals

Every year 17 to 22 million animals are used in research and testing in United States laboratories. The animals used include (in decreasing order of use) mice, rats, guinea pigs, rabbits, hamsters, dogs, primates, cats, and a variety of other animals.

Data collected by USDA/APHIS showed the breakdown (for 1983) to be: 7,913,000 mice; 3,269,000 rats; 521,000 guinea pigs; 509,000 rabbits; 454,000 hamsters; 182,000 dogs; 59,000 primates; 55,000 cats; 100,000 to 500,000 birds; 100,000 to 500,000 amphibians; and 2.5 to 4.5 million fish. (Alternatives to Animal Use in Research, Testing and Education, OTA Report, Washington, D.C., 1986, 64). In addition, animals are used extensively in laboratory exercises and demonstrations at the secondary, postsecondary, and graduate levels of education. A 1983–84 study conducted by the Association of American Medical Colleges determined that approximately 54,000 animals were used in medical and veterinary education in the United States (Association of American Medical Colleges, "Use of Animals in Undergraduate and Graduate Medical Education," Washington, D.C., 1985).

The most common areas of use include:

• Research (medical, biological, psychological, and military)
• Safety testing (cosmetics, household products, industrial chemicals, drugs, and other substances)
• Education (dissection and other activities)

Laboratory procedures often involve infecting, poisoning, burning, shocking, injecting, or subjecting animals to painful or deadly experiments. Many animals are housed alone in small, barren cages (HSUS Laboratory Animals Fact Sheet, 1988).

Companion Animals

The most positive images of loving and beneficial human behavior toward animals involve our relationship with our "pets." Cats, dogs, horses are our companions with whom we play and work and for whom we worry and grieve. Individual owners of pets often vary in their treatment, from great concern to neglect or abuse. The pet industry also varies from puppy mills and the wild bird trade to more responsible pet store management. A few facts are sobering:

• More than 7,000 puppies and kittens are born every day in the United States. Only one out of five will end up for their entire lifetime in a

responsible home. Most end up scavenging for food, living a shortened
life, or dying alone through some misfortune.

• Some 8 million dogs and cats are euthanized in animal shelters in the
United States each year, reflecting the extent to which pet populations
are out of control.

• In puppy mills dozens of dogs may be crammed together in pens and
cages, usually wire, completely exposed to heat and cold, the blazing
sun, and the freezing rain and snow. Their excrement lies everywhere,
contaminating food and water bowls. One estimate is that there are
5,000 puppy mills in the six midwestern states targeted by the HSUS
boycott, breeding approximately 500,000 puppies annually (HSUS
Close-Up Report, March 1991).

The millions of other animals that are sold for pets, from fish to gerbils
to exotic species, also often fare poorly.

Animals for Entertainment and Recreation

Rodeos, zoos, dog and horse racing, dog and cock fighting, circuses, fairs
and many other forms of entertainment use animals. Here too the conditions vary considerably. Many, particularly rodeos and bull, dog and cock
fighting, inflict major suffering on animals purely for entertainment. Others,
even the more responsible circuses and zoos, confine wild animals and,
particularly in the case of circuses, train these animals through pain and
deprivation to perform in ways that are very unnatural.

Summary

The human impact upon animals is devastating. It is true that numerous
wild animals still carry out their lives without disruption by humans, and
some animals may even acquire symbiotic benefits through their association
with people. But for the vast majority of animals — both wild and domestic —
the human presence is destructive and restrictive, destroying or poisoning
their habitat, reducing their numbers, confining and manipulating them in
ways that thwart their instinctual expression, to say nothing of the many
cases of deliberately inflicted pain and deprivation. The scope of this assault
is immense, from habitat destruction and poisoning to the confinement and
manipulation of billions of farm and experimental animals.

The devastation will continue. Rates of species extinction, habitat
destruction and contamination, and animal confinement will no doubt rise
as the human population doubles again next century. And if market economies are successful in bringing the developing countries and eastern
Europe the high-consumption life-styles typical of the American Dream,
we can only expect that these destructive trends will grow worse, even with
significant efforts to be more ecologically responsible. (Paul Erlich esti-

mates that the average American child will cause 200 to 1000 times more harm to the environment than a child living in a poor third world country.) Enabling more and more to own cars, suburban houses, televisions expanding consumption for an expanding population accelerates the destruction of habitat and the confinement and manipulation of the animals which remain. As the essay by John B. Cobb, Jr., in this volume makes clear, our economy and politics encourage this exploitation of animal life. In the predominantly human-centered worldview, animals and the earth are regarded as property and raw materials devoid of sentience.

Epilogue: What Can We Do?

My task has been to describe the state of animals in our world today. But given this deplorable state, it is impossible to conclude without pointing in a direction which promises the best opportunity for living in a respectful, if not reverential, way with animals and nature, while still meeting the basic (nontrivial) needs of all human beings.

The suffering and annihilation of the animal kingdom is the direct result of our short-term exploitative relationship to life. We, the fortunate few in the developed world, have made it a priority to increase the goods, services, conveniences, and opportunities to own and consume. Yet as fortunate as we are, we still want more money and the latest, nicest, most exciting consumer goods. We have built a vast capital- and energy-intensive infrastructure based on the wholesale exploitation of animals and the rest of nature. Rapid economic growth has been our central social priority. But the American Dream is turning out to be a nightmare for the earth and for animals—for it has been based on modes of domination, production and consumption which are profoundly short-sighted and destructive.

Our central task is to shift the bottom line of our culture from exploitation to sustainability. This requires that we recognize how our dominant values and economic system encourage the abuse of the earth, people, and animals, and undermine local self-reliance, diversity and community.

This last decade of the twentieth century is a period of fundamental crisis in which we must work out a more respectful and nurturing relationship, not only with the poor, oppressed and disenfranchised of the earth, but also with the earth itself—its processes and its creatures. Our life-styles and communities, as well as our politics and economics, theologies and cosmologies will need to become more ecological, humane and sustainable. Developing this new relationship to life involves taking the following five steps:

1. *Awakening our deep ecological sensibilities and ethics.* This involves a perceptual and value shift in which we appreciate the depth of life and feeling that exists in each being and in the processes and balance

of nature. These sensibilities move us to act to enhance the quality of
life for all sentient beings.

2. *Developing a critical understanding of the personal and social structures
   that promote exploitation or sustainability.* Our personal choices, social
   policies and institutional structures contribute variably to the liberation and fulfillment or oppression and desecration of life. Seeing
   clearly, for example, how pesticides, factory farming, or suburban
   sprawl contribute to the suffering of animals and the diminishing of
   life strengthen our resolve to reform self and society.

3. *Making a significant personal effort to modify our life-styles and consumer
   habits to live more lightly and compassionately on the earth.* This involves
   changing our assumptions, diets, modes of transportation and shelter,
   and our general purchasing patterns—both to minimize harm to life
   and the environment and to support enterprises that are not only
   economically viable but socially just, humane and ecologically sound.

4. *Cooperating with others to build more human and sustainable communities.* We can't do it alone—we must work with our neighbors and co-
   workers to fashion a local community able to provide its own food,
   energy and services, and to handle its own waste in an ecologically
   sound fashion, all in the context of a rich, unique culturally and biot-
   ically diverse region.

5. *Engaging in political action and advocacy to shift institutional priorities
   and social policies toward humaneness and sustainability.* Clearly our
   legal, economic, political and value structures often favor centralization, short-term economic gains, and the exploitation of natural
   resources, animals and many people. Images, incentives and regula-
   tions must be reformed to encourage humaneness and sustainability.

If enough of us take these steps, we can protect habitat and create a
society that leaves more space for wild animals and does not inflict such
suffering upon those animals it domesticates.

Appendix B

Liberating Life

A Report to the World Council of Churches

Introduction: The Historical Context

The theme of the 1991 General Assembly at Canberra is "Come Holy Spirit, Renew the Whole Creation." There are many ways in which creation needs renewal. It needs renewal from the debilitating poverty, repression, and violence under which hundreds of millions of people now suffer. It needs renewal from the shrinking of its forests, the loss of its topsoil, the pollution of its atmosphere, and the contamination of its waters. It needs renewal from the abuse of individual animals in factory farms and scientific laboratories. It needs renewal from war and the threat of nuclear war. This

This appendix is the text of "Liberating Life: A Report to the World Council of Churches." It was composed by a group of fourteen thinkers meeting at the behest of the WCC in Annecy, France, in September of 1988, among them Jay McDaniel, John Cobb, and Tom Regan, whose essays appear in this volume. Indeed, Tom Regan's essay opens with a description of what has (possibly) become of the report since its submission to the WCC. Both he and Charles Pinches refer to passages from it throughout their essays. We include it here not only to aid in the understanding of their two essays but also because it represents a significant attempt by a recognized Christian body to speak theologically and practically to questions concerning the moral treatment of animals.

This report was produced at a consultation sponsored by the World Council of Churches held at Annecy, France, in September 1988. Fourteen theologians attended, representing different theological traditions and coming from different parts of the world. As is apparent from the introduction to the report, liberation theologies and non-Western theologies played a prominent role in discussion. All participants, including those from North America and Europe, came to realize that the theme of liberation can itself be a promising stimulus toward modes of Christian thought that free people, the earth, and other creatures from various forms of exploitations.

The Annecy report is not an official report *of* the World Council of Churches. Rather it is a report *to* the World Council of Churches *by* people brought together by the World Council for the purpose of deliberating upon the integrity of creation. The report appears here in the form produced at Annecy, although Charles Birch and Jay McDaniel have added a few additional paragraphs and sentences. The additional material is bracketed.

renewal depends on us as empowered by God, the Holy Spirit, who works in and through the whole creation.

Indeed, life, in all its forms, cries out for liberation, for freedom. People across the earth are fighting for liberation from the pain of oppression due to poverty, gender, race, handicapping conditions, and many other causes. Liberation needs to be extended to animals, plants, and to the very earth itself, which sustains all life. Thus "the liberation of life," which is the theme for this report, extends the worldwide plea for peace and justice to all creatures, whom we humans need in order to exist, but of equal importance, who are valuable in and for themselves and to God.

Exploitation of People and Destruction of Other Forms of Life Are Inseparable
Consider South Africa. In 1988 the Afrikaner minority celebrated the 150th anniversary of the white man's "trek" into "the North," which was described in the Piet Relief Manifesto as "a beautiful country teeming with game" of every kind. In fact it was a beautiful country, where grass grew as tall as humans and silver streams cascaded down to the oceans on either side. In spite of internecine conflict, humans lived together in community with nature, and children innocently played with crystals later identified as precious diamonds. The indigenous people felt the presence of what they called *Modimo*, the Source and Presence of life, which penetrates through plants, humans and other animals, dark caverns and tall mountains. With "industrialization" and "development" this land has now been divided and fenced into farms, and its surface scarred and scratched to make a few people rich and powerful. It has been disemboweled at points and left agape in a quest for minerals, coal, gold, diamonds, and uranium for nuclear power. For sport alone, animals are hunted as trophies and some species have been rendered extinct. In less than two centuries a land of pristine splendor has become a repository of human heartlessness, a victim of "progress" and "civilization." As if this were not enough, this relentless onslaught has spilled over to human beings themselves. By means of Land Acts, native reserves were created and then developed into tribal homelands, human movement restricted by influx control, homes and family life disrupted to serve the interests of industry and commerce.

Or consider Korea. For four thousand years the Korean peninsula and the island just south of it, Cheju, had been a homogenous community of people united with the land. People spoke of their home as "the land of morning calm." In 1910 the Japanese colonized Korea, after which Korean women were recruited into the military, then forced to be prostitutes. Over two hundred thousand women died of sexual abuse. Then, immediately after the liberation from Japanese rule in 1945, the United States and the Soviet Union divided the peninsula. The Korean people were not consulted. Family members were separated against their will, and eighty thousand of the three hundred thousand Cheju islanders who protested the division of the peninsula were killed by Korean soldiers under the Far East command of the United States. Most of the victims were male. Now the island is famous for three things, strong winds, volcanic rocks, and its many women. Indeed, Cheju has become a center of international sex tourism. There are houses of prostitution with three to five hundred women in each. Meanwhile, polluting industries have been exported to the southern parts of the peninsula. Not only the land, air, and water have been harmed. Not long ago tens of thousands of people mourned the death of a fifteen-year-old boy who died of toxic poisoning as a result of working for only six months in a mercury-producing factory. A once united land has become a land of violence, division, and exploitation.

In each of these and myriad other situations, integral communities of people, animals, plants, and land have been neglected and destroyed. [This is not to say that the communities existed in a state of perfection prior to the arrival of foreign powers. They did not. As with all communities, they were mixtures of good and evil. It is to say, however, that the good they had achieved—in terms of satisfying relations between humans, between humans and other animals, and between humans and the earth—has been dramatically disrupted by the arrival of foreign powers, bringing with them science, technology, and nonindigenous concepts of "development."

Increasingly we realize that "development" promoted by advances in science and technology has been a two-edged sword. It has freed human life from much superstition and has opened a Pandora's box of goods and services to enrich life. But with these obvious benefits have come setbacks and destruction. With every passing day the potential of science and technology for bringing swift and widespread benefits to humanity is matched by its potential for ever swifter and more widespread damage and destruction to life and the environment.]

In many cases in the past the foreign powers offering "development" came from the West. They were accompanied by inadequate Christian perspectives—what Korean Minjung theologians call "division theologies"—which themselves become a source of community disintegration. The disintegration of these communities as a result of this assault by foreign powers, sometimes with the collaboration of indigenous elites, has had tragic consequences.

What characterizes a "division theology"? In its neglect and disdain for living communities, it has at least two features. The first is an arrogant approach to nature. The land and its creatures are objectified as mere tools for human use. The value of plants, animals, and land in their own right—as expressions of the Source and dynamic Presence of life itself, called *Modimo* by some Africans, and *Hanulnim* in Korea—is forgotten. Moreover, those who see nonhuman life in this way also often see human life in a similar manner. People become objects. The second feature of "division theology" is that it is male-centered. This way of thinking subordinates nature to human exploitation, the poor and destitute to the privileged and powerful, and women to control by men.

In response to the massive destruction of all forms of life, a theology that serves the liberation of life is needed. Such a theology must offer a view of creation that moves beyond arrogant anthropocentrism and promotes respect for communities of life in their diversity and connectedness to God. Moreover, the needed theology should welcome contributions from many voices, from those who have been heard, and especially from those who have not. Finally, and perhaps paradoxically, this new theological vision must promise to liberate those who, often unwittingly, are parties to oppression. Just as it liberates the victimized, humans and other living beings, a theology for the liberation of life can liberate people of privilege and power from their complacency and isolation. A theology that so serves the liberation of life is a theology of justice, peace, and respect for the integrity of creation.

A Theology for the Liberation of Life

As just said, the current destruction of living communities demands conversion to new thinking and commitment, a theology for the liberation of life. Informed by the biblical witness, the insights of science, and our experience of the interdependence of life, this theology needs to address the brokenness of our world and its intricate web of life with a new statement of the healing words of Christian faith.

The Biblical Witness

Christian visions of the world and of salvation are profoundly shaped by the biblical story of creation. For many generations in the West, this story was read primarily in human-centered terms; human beings were created in the image of God, commanded to be fruitful and multiply, given dominion over the rest of creation, only to disobey God and fall. This one-sided interpretation led to reading the remainder of the Bible as the story of human salvation alone. It also supported exploitative attitudes and practices in relation to the remainder of creation and the destruction of the habitat of many species.

As the disastrous consequences of this exploitation, both for the rest of creation and for humanity as a whole, have become manifest, Christians have reread the creation story. We have found that it locates the story of humanity in a much wider context, as a cosmic one. Before and apart from the creation of human beings, God sees that the animals are good. When humanity is added creation as a whole is very good. The command to human beings to be fruitful and to multiply does not nullify the identical command to animals. The image of God with its associated dominion is not for exploitation of animals but for responsible care. The plants that are good in themselves are given to both animals and human beings for their food. This is the integrity of creation in its ideal form.

According to the biblical stories, human sin disrupts this integral creation. As a consequence, there emerges competition and war between farmers and pastoralists. Injustice and strife proceed so far that God repents having created the world. Nevertheless, God saves the Noah family from the deluge, and at God's command this human family exercises its rightful dominion in saving all animal species from a watery death. When the waters recede God makes a covenant with the animals. From this vision of creation and human sin there follows a longing for inclusive salvation. The whole creation praises God, but this whole creation also groans in travail. As human sin has caused the subjection of all creation to futility, so the liberation of all life can come about only through the liberation of humanity from its bondage to Mammon.

The ideas expressed in the creation and Noah stories and the consequent vision of universal salvation have profound relevance today. All creatures have value in themselves as well as for one another and for God. Each, therefore, claims respect from human beings. The whole creation in all its rich complexity has a special value that is diminished when forests are turned into grasslands and grasslands are turned into deserts. The Noah story highlights God's concern for the preservation of species.

From these stories we acquire a distinctive understanding of "the integrity of creation." *The value of all creatures in and for themselves, for one another, and for God, and their interconnectedness in a diverse whole that has unique value for God, together constitute the integrity of creation.*

As human beings who participate in this creation we have a unique responsibility to respect its integrity, but in fact we have violated it in many ways. Indeed, our violence against one another and against the rest of creation threatens the continuation of life on the planet. It is now our opportunity and our duty, by God's grace, to be restored to peace and justice both in our relations to one another and in our relations with the rest of creation. As long as human beings order their lives to short-sighted economic gain or increased wealth, there will be no end to violence, oppression, or to the exploitation of the other creatures. Only a society ordered to the regeneration of the earth will attain peace and justice. Only in such a world is the integrity of creation respected and achieved.

Within the message of Jesus we find a profound deepening of the importance of our treatment of one another and especially of the weak and oppressed. "Truly, I say to you as you did it to one of the least of these my brothers and sisters, you did it to me" (Mt 25:40). Primarily this refers to our treatment of human beings, but on the lips of the Jesus who speaks of God's care for the grass of the field and the fallen sparrow, these too are included among "the least of these." In the hunger of millions of children, in the loneliness and humiliation of the homeless, in the wretchedness of the raped, in the suffering of the tortured, and also in the pain of myriads of animals used for human gain without regard to their own worth, Christ is crucified anew (Eph 1:10).

The Contributions of Science

The contributions of the sciences are also an essential part of a theology for the liberation of life. When they avoid the assumptions of scientism and materialism, they open up the mystery of the cosmos in a most impressive way. Indeed, while in one sense science diminishes the area of the unknown, in another sense it leads us deeper into incomprehensible mystery. Recent discoveries in physics, biology, and other sciences tell us the story of an evolving universe that needs to be put side by side with our religious narrative. According to recent astrophysics, the universe originated in an event known as the Big Bang. During the first few moments of our world's infancy its fundamental pre-atomic physical features acquired numerical values that would eventually allow for the origin and evolution of living, sentient, and thinking beings. The stellar production of elements that make up cells and organisms required a universe of sufficient breadth and temporal duration to make life possible. The specific physical properties, the immense size, and the age of the universe are intimately related to the existence of life.

The biological theory of evolution with its ingredients of chance and struggle for existence requires a deeper understanding of divine power. God is not a magician but one who lovingly invites the created world to participate in the unfolding of the cosmic story. Evolutionary thinking compels us to acknowledge more explicitly than ever before the continuity of the whole network of life with the universe as such. The evolutionary cosmic epic contributes to a deeper understanding of the universe as our origin and our home. We are made of the same stuff as the stars. Our existence is deeply embedded in the existence of the universe itself.

Of course, there are senses in which human life is unique. Our unique qualities lie, not in an ontological discontinuity between us and the rest of nature, but rather in the remarkable degrees to which we can realize certain evolutionary capacities. We humans are unique in the range of our sensibilities, in our degree of freedom, in our capacities to understand the world, and in our control of the world through cultural evolution. These capacities are themselves developments out of, rather than apart from, the evolutionary process.

As these remarks concerning evolution suggest, an ongoing dialogue between science and theology is indispensable for addressing environmental issues. Such a conversation will help science to understand its task in the service of the whole creation. And it will also enable theology to remain in contact with the real world and thus be faithful to the earth. The world of the sciences, including the social sciences, is of special significance for demonstrating the intricate interrelatedness and interdependence of the biosphere, human community, and the cosmic totality. Without constant attention to the latest developments in the sciences, Christian theology will become irrelevant to those who strive to preserve peace, justice, and the integrity of creation. For theology to do less than come to terms with our present scientific understanding, for it to accept outmoded assumptions about reality from a different time, seems blatantly wrong-headed, even allowing for the qualification that science is an evolving and fallible enterprise.

Imaging the New Sensibility

A contemporary reading of Scripture suggests an interrelatedness of all creatures within the earth and with God. Likewise, the story of the universe emerging from the sciences indicates that all that exists is part of everything else. How should Christians image this sensibility when speaking of God and of world? Whenever human beings attempt to speak about God, we do so in the language of our own time, our various cultures, and from familiar and important relationships. In biblical times, this language was of God as king and lord, but also of God as creator, father, mother, healer, and liberator. As we think about the way to express the relationship of God to the world in our time, we realize that metaphors such as king and lord limit God's activity to the human sphere; moreover, these metaphors suggest that God is external to the world and distant from it.

The creation narrative of our time, the awesome story of the beginning of the universe some ten billion years ago, evolving into our incredibly complex and intricate cosmos in which "everything that is" is interrelated, suggests the need for different symbolic language. Instead of a king relating to his realm, we picture God as the creator who "bodies forth" all that is, who creates not as a potter or an artist does, but more as a mother. That is to say, the universe, including our earth and all its creatures and plants, "lives and moves and has its being" in God (cf. Acts 17:28), though God is beyond and more than the universe. Organic images seem most appropriate for expressing both the immanence of God in and to the entire creation as well as God's transcendence of it. In the light of the incarnation, the whole universe appears to us as God's "body." Just as we transcend our bodies, so also the divine spirit transcends the body of the universe. And, just as we are affected by what happens to our body, so also God is affected by what happens in the world. The sufferings and joys of people and other creatures are shared by God.

When we express the relationship between God and the world (or universe) in organic images, several things become clearer. First, all of us, humans and other living creatures, live together within this body—we are part of each other and can in no way exist separately. Second, unlike the king-realm image which is hierarchical and dualistic and encourages human beings to adopt similar postures toward other members of their own species as well as toward other species, the organic symbolism underscores the inherent worth of all the different parts of the body, different species as well as individuals within those species. Third, while the body metaphor has been used since the time of Paul to express Christ, the Church (1 Corinthians 12:12-26), extending it to the cosmos (we are all members of the body of God, the universe) places us in intimate relations with all our fellow human beings as well as with all other forms of life. We not only empathize with all who are oppressed and suffer—victims of war and injustice, both humans and other living creatures—but we also feel responsibility for helping to bring about peace and justice to the suffering members of God's "body." God's glory and God's closeness are expressed in this image. We stand in awe of the One upon whom this universe depends, whether we view it through a telescope in which its vastness enthralls and terrifies us or through a microscope in which the intricate patterns of the veins of a leaf amaze us. And at a molecular level of life, the complex and beautiful structure of the DNA molecule that can exist in an indefinite variety of forms gives us a sense of awe and wonder. We also, each of us, are part of this universe, this body, in which God is present to us. We feel God's presence here in our world as we touch one another, love and serve one another, that is, all the others that make up the fabric of existence.

Our scripture speaks of the cosmic Christ (Colossians 1), the presence of God in the cosmos, God's embodiment, God's "incarnation." In this image of divine embodiment, we have a helpful way of talking about creation that is biblical, consonant with contemporary science, and experientially illuminating. The universe, everything that is, each and every living thing and the ecosystem that supports all things, is bound together, intrinsically and inextricably, with its creator. Within this bond, the oppression of life is common history, the liberation of life is our common responsibility and our common hope.

An Ethic for the Liberation of Life

An ethic for the liberation of life calls for seeing the whole of creation in its integrity and therefore demands respect of every creature. Human respect for fellow creatures properly emphasizes individual members of the human community itself. Peace among nations and justice both within and between them are crucial. But this human community is part of a larger community of creatures whose health is essential for the well-being of human beings. An ethic for the liberation of life involves concern for this larger community not only because of its importance to human beings but also for the sake of its other members.

An ethic for the liberation of life would involve treating all of these topics in detail. Fortunately, the issues of peace and justice have been treated throughout the history of the World Council of Churches and vigorous discussion is continuing. Accordingly, section 1 is a brief statement pointing toward this larger discussion. Section 2 is a slightly longer statement building on earlier discussions of a sustainable society. Section 3 notes very briefly the special importance of drastically reducing the extinction of species caused by human actions. These three sections are not unrelated. When any of these levels of the discussion is pressed, the others appear.

Although reflection about peace and justice begins with human relations, relations with other creatures are extricably involved. The health of the ecosystem is essential for animals and human beings alike, and violence against ecosystems involves the oppression of human beings and the decimation of species. The need to preserve species is for the sake of the creatures themselves and at the same time for the sake of human purposes.

Section 4 is somewhat different. It does not discuss the benefit to human beings of right treatment of animals. Indeed, it implies that even when respect for animals does not coincide with human benefit it is still required of Christians. Perhaps it is partly for this reason that this topic has been ignored by the World Council of Churches and by most of its member churches up to now. To bring this neglect to focused attention, this section is more extensive. It rejects anthropocentrism by affirming the integrity of creation with peculiar vividness. The themes that unite this fourth section to the others are two: first, that the integrity of creation requires human beings to abandon domination and exploitation as a style of relating both to one another and to the rest of creation, and, second, that respect for the integrity of creation calls upon us to expand our conviviality, that we live with other creatures in peace and justice.

Peace and Justice

Much of the discussion of peace and justice has dealt with their interrelatedness: There is no peace without justice, no justice without peace. This means that the mere absence of war between the superpowers, essential as that is, is not peace, and that an egalitarianism enforced by violence is not justice. An ethic for the liberation of life expands on these familiar ideas. For there is no true peace when the wider community of life is violated, and there is no justice when its animal members are not respected.

The quest for peace between nations aims to end the enormous expenditures and preparations especially for war by the superpowers and their allies. These expenditures not only add to the threat of military destruction but also rob the earth of resources that could be used to meet pressing human needs and contribute to global pollution. In the United States the endless preparation for war gives grossly unjust power to the military-industrial-university complex. Even unaligned nations are drawn into arms races that distort their economies. The emphasis on arms often leads to military dominance of their governments and the oppression of their people.

Respect for the Integrity of the Ecological Community

The integrity of the ecological community is threatened when plants and animals are used exclusively as objects without due consideration for the long-term sustainability of the ecological community.

With the exception of minerals and petro-chemical products, modern civilization depends entirely upon products from four ecological systems: croplands, pastures, forests, and fisheries. Yet in most if not all countries today, each of these ecological systems shows symptoms of being over-stressed. In the case of forests and fisheries, the stress is so great that global production itself is declining.

Below are some selected examples of ecological communities that are under threat. They are a few of any number of examples that might be chosen. In each of these examples ecological communities are used for food and other products. There is a conflict between the present self-interest of some people, the present public interests of many people, the interests of posterity, and the interests, present and future, of nonhuman nature itself. No one of these interests can become dominant without another suffering.

[The conception of the sustainable community is one that is helpful here. It envisions a management of ecological communities such that they continue to exist indefinitely into the future. This does not necessarily mean that they persist without change, but that such changes as do occur are within the limits that permit sustainability of the community as a whole. The sorts of changes in the Sahel regions of Africa in the last decade, for example, were such as to result in desertification and irreversible destruction of the ecological community that had persisted for numerous biological generations. These sorts of changes are unsustainable; what is needed are modes of human interaction with the rest of nature that are sustainable.]

Modern Agriculture — Croplands and Grasslands. Agricultural practices over the millennia have often proved unsustainable. Whole civilizations have collapsed when they exhausted the soils that supported them. Half the land that was available when farming began is now unstable. The pace at which desertification proceeds has greatly accelerated with capital-intensive agriculture in the past fifty years as much sustainable family farming has been replaced by corporate agriculture. This has driven millions of people off the land and into urban slums especially in the United States and in many third world countries. The laborers who replace the family farmers often suffer from the chemicals that also cause the soil to deteriorate. Nations formerly capable of feeding themselves are now dependent upon imported food. For example, in parts of Brazil, mono-cultures of sugar cane have replaced the staple crops of rice and beans that formerly contributed to a staple diet.

One major cause of the unsustainability of modern agriculture, which is chemically intensive, energy intensive and mono-cultural, is the deterioration of soil structures. This in turn is caused by the intensive use of chemical fertilizers and pesticides, which deplete the soil of microorganisms that normally maintain soil structure. Another cause is rising water tables in irrigation areas with consequent salination of the soil. When the plants no longer cover the soil from these and other causes, wind often blows away much of the top soil. The violence of much industrialized agriculture to the life-support system is at the same time violence against the poor. It violates the integrity of creation.

Forestry. Tropical rain forests are now disappearing at the rate of one football field every second, mostly in Latin America and South East Asia. These forests sustain the greatest diversity of plants and animals known in any terrestrial habitat. The destruction of habitats is the main cause of extinction on earth today. Hence the destruction of rain forests is the main cause of the extinction of species in our own time. When the forests are cleared, soil erosion sets in and in many places the soil becomes useless. In other places attempts are made to replace the forest with farms, often with disastrous results. The chances of the forests returning are remote. So when the rain forest is gone, it is gone forever. The tragedy of the ecological community is paralleled time and time again by human tragedy. This is particularly so when the forests have been the home and livelihood of indigenous peoples. As in unsustainable agriculture, we find unsustainability of the ecological community due to human interference by one group of people leads to misery and tragedy for others.

Marine Communities. Much could be said about disrespect for the integrity of marine communities. A few examples will have to suffice. The major oceanic fisheries around the world have declining yields (for example, the anchovy fisheries off the coast of Peru and a number of fisheries in the North Atlantic). Two main causes of these declines seem to be over-fishing and pollution. In both cases we have good guidelines for preventing such interferences with the natural communities so that they may be sustained. But the implementation of such practices seem to be exceedingly difficult. Very often the people who suffer most are the poor who are dependent upon such fish as they can catch or buy cheaply. The greed and mismanagement of the few leads to the suffering of the many.

The recent deaths of seals in the North Sea and Baltic Sea illustrate a trail of interconnections that lead to ecological disaster. It seems that toxic wastes in the sea, resulting from industrial pollution, may cause an immune deficiency in the seals. This renders them susceptible to a virus or viruses to which they are normally immune. In a healthy environment seals do not succumb to such viruses. A greater respect for the health of their environment might well have avoided the death of the seals.

Experience tells us that if we look after nature, nature looks after us. That is a prudential reason for not turning ecologically sustainable communities into unsustainable ones. But an ethic for the liberation of life goes only part of the way if it ends there. It should be extended to the well-being of individual organisms. This is the subject of section 4.

The Maintenance of Biological Diversity

Throughout the history of life numerous species have become extinct. Human activity from early times has increased the rate of extinction. With the vast growth of human population and economic activity in this century the rate of extinction has accelerated.

There are many reasons to be concerned. Much of potential value to human beings is lost. Innumerable creatures that should be respected are being destroyed instead. The rich diversity of plant and animal life which, according to Genesis, God saw to be, in community with human beings, "very good," is being simplified. The life of God is impoverished.

Although attention is often focused on efforts to protect some endangered species, such as the California condor, by quite artificial means, the major cause of extinction is destruction of habitat. In general, habitat has been wilderness, and the human pressure on wilderness has greatly reduced it on every continent. The lessening of this pressure is a matter of moral urgency. Instead of viewing wilderness as empty or undeveloped, we must learn to see it as full of life, often far richer and more diverse than what we call "occupied" or "developed" land. Wilderness is usually able to sustain a vast diversity of life for tens of thousands of years, whereas "development" often leads to great reduction of this diversity and sometimes to the inability to sustain even that for extended periods. The attitude of conquest should give way to reverence toward the integrity of these parts of creation.

Respect for Individual Animals

The biblical and theological messages about the value of animals speak with one voice: Animals do not exist for the sake of the unbridled pursuit of human avarice and greed. And yet the increasingly powerful transnational corporations prefer that people not know, or not care, about the pain and death literally billions of animals are made to suffer every year in the name of corporate mass-production and consumer over-consumption. Some examples follow.

Cosmetics and Household Products. Many areas of the world have an abundance of toothpastes, colognes, after-shaves, deodorants, perfumes, powders, blushes, detergents, oven and window cleaners, furniture and floor polishes, and other cosmetics and household products. This is well-known. What is not well-known is that these items routinely are tested on animals in a variety of painful ways, including acute eye-irritance tests as well as so-called "lethal dose" tests, in which animals are force-fed a deodorant or floor polish, for example, until a specific number die. When we purchase the products of the major cosmetic and household products' corporations, we support massive animal pain and death—all of which is unnecessary. For there are alternatives. Attractive cosmetics and effective household products that are both safe and economical, that have *not* been tested on animals, already exist and are available, and others would be if enough consumers demanded them.

Fashion. Mass-production and over-consumption encourage ignorance and indifference in the name of fashion. Nowhere is this more evident than in the case of fur products (coats, capes, gloves, and the like). Fur-bearing animals trapped in the wild inevitably suffer slow, agonizing deaths, while those raised on "modern" fur-farms live in unnatural conditions that severely limit their ability to move, groom, form social units, and engage in other patterns of behavior that are natural to their kind. When we purchase the products of commercial furriers, we support massive animal pain and death — all of which is unnecessary. For there are alternatives. Many attractive coats, capes, gloves, and the like, which are not directly linked to the commercial exploitation of animals, already exist and are available, and others would be if enough consumers demanded them.

Food. Increasingly, the family farm is being replaced by national and often multi-national interests, business ventures void of any roots in the land or bonds to the animals they raise. The goal of mass-production is to raise the largest number of animals in the shortest time with the least investment. The "good shepherd" has given way to the corporate factory.

Corporate animal agriculture relies on what are called "close-confinement" or "intensive rearing" methods. The animals are taken off the land and raised permanently indoors. There is no sunlight, no fresh air, often not even room enough to turn around. In many cases six to eight laying hens are packed in a wire-mesh metal cage three-quarters of the size of a page of daily newspaper. For up to five years, many breeding sows are confined to stalls barely larger than their bodies. Veal calves (typically male calves born to dairy herds) routinely are taken from their mothers at birth and raised in permanent isolation. Increasingly even dairy cattle are being taken off the land and raised indoors.

Because of the massive numbers of farm animals raised for slaughter (upwards of 4 billion annually, just in the United States), huge amounts of grains are used as feed. More than 90 percent of the oats, corn, rye, barley, and sorghum crops grown in the United States, for example, are fed to animals, and this use of food is enormously wasteful. Every pound of complete protein produced by beef cattle requires eight to nine pounds of complete vegetable protein, while every pound of complete protein supplied by hogs requires four to five pounds of complete vegetable protein. When more protein is being used to produce less, it is no exaggeration to say that we have a protein production system running in reverse.

On the corporate factory that is today's animal farm, virtually every natural form of behavior is thwarted, from preening and dust bathing in chickens to nursing and gamboling in veal calves. When we purchase the products of corporate factory farming, we support massive animal deprivation and death — all of which is unnecessary. For alternatives exist. People can choose to purchase the products of the remaining small-scale family farms or explore a dietary life-style free from all direct commercial connections with the suffering death of animals.

Entertainment. Many different animals are used for commercial purposes in entertainment. The forms of entertainment include circuses, stage and aquatic shows, rodeos, bullfights, and organized cock and dog fights. In whatever form, the animals are treated as mere means to human ends. Sometimes (as in the case of bull and bronco busting in rodeos) the animals are caused more than incidental pain. Sometimes (in the case of the housing and transportation of circus and other "performing" animals) the animals are subjected to severe and often protracted deprivation. Sometimes (as in the case of animals who perform "tricks" in stage and aquatic shows) the animals are rewarded for their ability to mimic human behavior (for example, by balancing themselves on balls or jumping through hoops). And sometimes (as in the case of bull, cock, and dog fights) some of the animals are killed and all are made to endure acute suffering.

When we patronize these forms of entertainment, we support those commercial interests that reduce the value of animals to the status of the purely instrumental, often at the cost of great pain (and sometimes even death) for the animals themselves—and all of this is unnecessary. For alternatives exist. We do not have to train, exploit, outwit, or outmuscle animals, or to support those who make a profit from doing so, in order to take pleasure in their presence or their beauty. Benign forms of recreation involving animals exist. For some people this may involve photography, scuba, and other forms of ocean diving, or the viewing of any one of the thousands of films about wildlife. For all people this can involve becoming attentive to and appreciative of many forms of animal life that live in community with us, wherever we live.

Education. A traditional rite-of-passage for children and adolescents in the affluent world is compulsory dissection of animals. Those students who resist or refuse for reasons of conscience routinely are ridiculed or punished for their moral sensitivity. Often they stand alone, abandoned even by their parents, ostracized by their peers. And yet this exercise in scholastic coercion is totally unnecessary. For alternatives exist. These include detailed drawings of animal anatomy and physiology, state-of-the art videos of relevant dissections, and even computer programs that enable students to "dissect" a frog, for example, on a screen rather than dissect a once living organism. When we support an educational system that callously punishes young people for being concerned about the integrity and value of animals, we tacitly support not only the unnecessary pain and death of countless numbers of animals but also the moral damage done to our children.

The examples given above are only that: examples. There are many other ways in which people fail to show minimal respect for animals as creatures of God. These include instances of wasteful, needlessly duplicative, and poorly executed scientific use of animals, the "sport" of hunting, and the killing of members of rare and endangered species, such as the African elephant and the black rhino. Like the previous examples, these further ones have a common denominator: A creature having intrinsic value is reduced to one having only instrumental value—as an object of mere scientific curiosity, a trophy, or a source of illegal profit.

The ethic of the liberation of life is a call to Christian action. In particular, how animals are treated is not "someone else's worry," it is a matter of our individual and collective responsibility. Christians are called to act respectfully towards "these, the least of our brothers and sisters." This is not a simple question of kindness, however laudable that virtue is. *It is an issue of strict justice.* In all our dealings with animals, whether direct or indirect, the ethic for the liberation of life requires that *we render unto animals what they are due, as creatures with an independent integrity and value.* Precisely because they cannot speak for themselves or act purposively to free themselves from the shackles of their enslavement, the Christian duty to speak and act for them is the greater, not the lesser.

In facing this new challenge—this challenge to liberate all life, the animals included—Christians should aspire to two ideals:

1. Seek knowledge.
2. Act justly.

The first ideal enjoins us to break the habit of ignorance when it comes to how animals are being treated. It bids us to ferret out truth, to make the invisible visible, to make the obscure clear. The second ideal bids us to make our own life a living expression of justice towards God's creation, to bring peace to our own lives even as we work to bring peace to the world. Indeed, we are unlikely to succeed in doing the latter if we fail in doing the former. There is little hope, that is, that we can change the world if we cannot even change ourselves: in the choice of the cosmetics and household products we use, the clothes we wear, the food we eat, and the entertainment we patronize. The ethic for the liberation of life begins at home.

Much else remains to be considered. Laws and institutions that permit or encourage the oppression of animals need to be identified and changed. The truth about the ways animals are oppressed needs to be made known, beginning in the church itself. Our children need to be sustained in their natural empathy with and compassion for animals, and this means that certain traditional practices in their education, including in particular compulsory dissection, will have to be altered. Clearly, the struggle to liberate life is not for the faint of heart.

Yet just as clearly it is a struggle no thoughtful Christian can avoid. When St. Paul says that "the whole creation has been groaning in travail together until now," he speaks to our time and our circumstances. For the animals have been groaning, though we have heard them not. We hear them now. They cry for justice. We cannot fail to answer.

CONCLUSION

The theme of this report is "the liberation of life." Increasingly during this century Christians have come to understand the gospel, the Good

News, in terms of freedom, both freedom *from* oppression and freedom *for* life with God and others. Too often, however, this freedom has been limited to human beings, excluding most other creatures as well as the earth. This freedom *cannot* be so limited because if we destroy other species and the ecosystem, human beings cannot live. This freedom *should not* be so limited because other creatures, both species and individuals, deserve to live in and for themselves and for God. Therefore, we call on Christians as well as other people of good will to work toward the liberation of life, *all* life.

RECOMMENDATIONS

1. There is a real need to bring together persons of diverse emphasis and perspective from Latin American liberation theologies, feminist theologies, black theologies, ecological theologies, Minjung theologies, and African theology, those committed to animal rights, those struggling to free Christianity from its anti-Jewish tendencies and those involved in dialogue with persons of other living faiths.

The aim would be to go beyond the still somewhat fragmentary and divisive works of such thinkers to a consensual theological statement that would not be a specialized theology geared to particular issues, but a fresh statement of the heart of Christian faith for the whole community of believers.

We therefore request JPIC ("Justice, Peace, and Integrity of Creation") to organize such a meeting for the further development of Christian theology that expresses the convictions of persons concerned for justice, peace, and the integrity of creation.

2. We recommend that JPIC and the sub-unit on Church and Society of the World Council of Churches co-sponsor a series of conferences designed to envision in concrete terms what social, economic, agricultural, and industrial structures and practices would make possible ecologically sustainable modes of development and progress which take account of human respect for the integrity of creation, peace, and justice. Such conferences should include persons representing points of view similar to those identified in recommendation 1. Those willing to think in new categories from such areas as political theory, sociology, anthropology, economics, agriculture, climatology, and oceanography should also be included.

3. We commend the sub-unit on Church and Society for its work in bringing together theologians and scientists for informative and critical dialogue. In the light of our description of the role of the sciences in the theology for the liberation of life, we recommend that these conferences continue.

4. In view of the ecologically unsustainable practices of modern agriculture and forestry we recommend to JPIC that these issues be priorities on the agenda of JPIC.

5. Seminary education is woefully lacking in basic courses in ecology and/ or perspectives in science and religion. It is certainly not necessary for divinity students to have in-depth understanding of scientific procedures. What is imperative is a basic, even minimal, perspective of how contemporary science depicts reality. Many men and women preparing for the ordained ministry hold a Newtonian, individualistic, substantialist view of reality. It is this understanding that they attempt to correlate with Christian faith, resulting in an individualistic, otherworldly theology of salvation. We recommend to the sub-units of Theology and Education of the World Council of Churches that member churches of the WCC counsel their seminaries to require coursework in the contemporary scientific "picture" of reality, a picture that underscores the interdependence and interrelatedness of all reality. Such a view could profoundly influence how church leaders preach and teach in regard to the relationship of human beings to the environment.

6. In view of the widespread maltreatment of animals throughout the world and in view of the intrinsic value of individual animals to themselves and to God we recommend that Church and Society take appropriate steps to: (a) encourage the churches and their members to acquire knowledge about how animals are being treated and in what ways this treatment departs from respect for the intrinsic value to themselves and of animals as creatures of God and how abuses could be minimized through legislation and other means; (b) encourage members of the Christian community to act according to such guidelines as the following:

i. Avoid cosmetics and household products that have been cruelly tested on animals. Instead, buy cruelty-free items.

ii. Avoid clothing and other aspects of fashion that have a history of cruelty to animals, products of the fur industry in particular. Instead, purchase clothes that are cruelty-free.

iii. Avoid meat and animal products that have been produced on factory farms. Instead, purchase meats and animal products from sources where animals have been treated with respect, or abstain from these products altogether.

iv. Avoid patronizing forms of entertainment that treat animals as mere means to human ends. Instead, seek benign forms of entertainment, ones that nurture a sense of the wonder of God's creation and reawaken that duty of conviviality we can discharge by living respectfully in community with all life, the animals included.

7. We recommend that Church and Society encourage the member churches of the World Council of Churches to involve Christians in environmental causes and to cooperate with organizations which defend ecological communities at regional and parish levels.

8. We recommend that Church and Society sponsor a series of courses for church leaders on the emergent theme of our consultation: the liberation of life. In such courses church leaders from different parts of the world, selected by a subcommittee of the sub-unit in consultation with any addi-

tional sponsors, could be introduced to the environmental crises of our time, to problems of animal abuse, and to theological perspectives emerging out of the JPIC process, such as those proposed in this report, which encourage a constructive response to such issues.

Bibliography

Adams, Carol. 1990. *The Sexual Politics of Meat: A Feminst-Vegetarian Critical Theory.* New York: Continuum.

———. 1991. "Ecofeminism and the Eating of Animals. *Hypatia* 6(1).

Akers, Keith. 1983. *A Vegetarian Sourcebook: The Nutrition, Ecology, and Ethics of a Natural Foods Diet.* New York: G. P. Putnam's Sons.

Anderson, Bernard. 1984a. "Creation in the Bible." In *Cry of the Environment: Rebuilding the Christian Tradition.* Santa Fe: Bear and Company, pp. 19-44.

———. 1984b. "Creation and the Noachic Covenant." In *Cry of the Environment: Rebuilding the Christian Tradition.* Santa Fe: Bear and Company, pp. 45-61.

———. 1984c. "Creation and Ecology." In *Creation in the Old Testament.* Philadelphia: Fortress Press, pp. 252-71.

Ayi Kwei Armah. 1969. *The Beautiful Ones Are Not Yet Born.* New York: Collier Books.

Barnaby, Frank, ed. 1988. *The Gaia Peace Atlas.* London: Doubleday.

Barnard, Neal. 1990. "The Evolution of the Human Diet." *The Power of Your Plate.* Summertown, Tenn.: Book Publishing Co.

Barr, James. 1972. "Man and Nature—The Ecological Controversy and the Old Testament." *Bulletin of the John Rylands University Library of Manchester:* 9-32.

Barth, Karl. 1960. "Creation as Justification." *Church Dogmatics,* vol. 3(1). Edinburgh: T & T Clark.

Bentley, Sarah R. 1989. *For Better or Worse: The Challenge of the Battered Women's Movement to Christian Social Ethics.* Union Theological Seminary doctoral dissertation.

Berry, Thomas. 1988. *The Dream of the Earth.* San Francisco: Sierra Club Books.

Birch, Charles, William Eakin, and Jay B. McDaniel, eds. 1990. *Liberating Life: Contemporary Approaches to Ecological Theology.* Maryknoll, N.Y.: Orbis Books.

Bleich, David J. 1989. *Contemporary Halakhic Problems.* New York: KTAV.

Brody, Jane. 1981. *Jane Brody's Nutrition Book.* New York: W. W. Norton & Co.

———. 1990. "Huge Study Indicts Fat and Meat." *New York Times,* May 8.

Brueggemann, Walter. 1977. *The Land: Place as Gift. Promise and Challenge in Biblical Faith.* Philadelphia: Fortress Press.

———. 1978. *The Prophetic Imagination.* Philadelphia: Fortress Press.

Byrnes, J. 1976. "Raising Pigs by the Calendar at Maplewood Farm." *Hog Farm Management,* September.

Callicott, J. Baird. 1988. "Animal Liberation and Environmental Ethics: Back Together Again." *Between the Species* 4 (Summer): 167.

———. 1989. *In Defense of the Land Ethic: Essays in Environmental Philosophy.* Albany, N.Y.: SUNY Press.

Carson, Walter H., ed. N.d. *Citizen's Guide to Sustainable Development.* Washington, D.C.: Global Tomorrow Coalition.

Cheney, Jim. 1987. "Eco-Feminism and Deep Ecology." *Environmental Ethics* 9:2 (Summer): 115-45.

Clark, Stephen R. L. 1977. *The Moral Status of Animals.* Oxford: The Clarendon Press.

———. 1982. *The Nature of the Beast: Are Animals Moral?* Oxford: Oxford University Press.

Clarke, P. A. B., and Andrew Linzey, eds. 1990. *Political Theory and Animal Rights.* London and Winchester, Mass.: Pluto Press.

Cleave, T. L., G. D. Campbell, N. S. Painter. 1969. *Diabetes, Coronary Thrombosis and the Saccharine Disease.* 2d ed. Bristol, England: John Wright & Sons.

Clift, Elayne. 1990. "Advocate Battles for Safety in Mines and Poultry Plants." *New Directions for Women* (May/June), p. 3.

Cobb, John. 1990. *Matters of Life and Death.* Louisville, Ky.: Westminster/John Knox Press.

Cohen, Alfred S. 1981. "Vegetarianism from a Jewish Perspective." *The Journal of Halacha and Contemporary Society* 1(2): 38-63.

Collard, Andre, with Joyce Contrucci. 1989. *Rape of the Wild: Man's Violence Against Animals and the Earth.* Bloomington, Ind.: Indiana University Press.

Collingwood, R. G. 1960, 1981. *The Idea of Nature.* London: Oxford University Press.

Comstock, Gary, ed. 1987. *Is There a Moral Obligation to Save the Family Farm?* Ames, Ia.: Iowa State University Press.

Daly, Lois. 1990. "Ecofeminism, Reverence for Life, and Feminist Theological Ethics." In Birch, et al. *Liberating Life: Contemporary Approaches to Ecological Theology.* Maryknoll, N.Y.: Orbis Books.

Darling, James D. 1988. "Whales—An Era of Discovery." *National Geographic* (December), pp. 872-909.

Dawkins, Marian Stamp. 1980. *Animal Suffering: The Science of Animal Welfare.* London and New York: Chapman and Hall.

De Araujó, Virginia. 1982. "The Friend." *Sinister Wisdom* 20: 17.

Dijksterhuis, E. J. 1961. *The Mechanization of the World Picture.* Trans. C. Dikshoorn. Oxford: Clarendon Press.

DuBois, Page. 1982. *Centaurs and Amazons: Women and the Pre-History of the Great Chain of Being.* Ann Arbor, Mich.: University of Michigan Press.

Ehrlich, Paul, and Anne Ehrlich. 1989. *Extinction: The Causes and Consequences of the Disappearance of Species.* New York: Random House.

Feinberg, Joel. 1974. "The Rights of Animals and Unborn Generations." In William T. Blackstone, ed. *Philosophy and Environmental Crisis.* Athens, Ga.: University of Georgia Press.

———. 1980. *Rights, Justice and the Bonds of Liberty.* Princeton, N.J.: Princeton University Press.

Fiorenza, Elisabeth Schüssler. 1984. *In Memory of Her: A Feminist Theological Reconstruction of Christian Origins.* New York: Crossroad.

Fox, Michael W. 1984. *Farm Animals: Husbandry, Behavior, and Veterinary Practice (Viewpoints of a Critic).* Baltimore: University Park Press.

———. 1990. "The Cattle Threat." *HSUS News* (Fall), pp. 14-17.

Frey, R. G. 1980. *Interests and Rights: The Case Against Animals.* Oxford: Clarendon Press.

Fund for Animals. 1990. "Animal Agriculture Fact Sheet #2. Factory Farming: Misery on the Menu."

Gaffney, James. 1990. "Animals and Ethics: A Catholic Blind Spot." *America* 163 (October 27), pp. 297-99.

Gewirth, Alan. 1978. *Reason and Morality*. Chicago: University of Chicago Press.

Griffin, Donald R. 1984. *Animal Thinking*. Cambridge, Mass.: Harvard University Press.

Gustafson, James. 1981. *Ethics from a Theocentric Perspective*. Chicago: University of Chicago Press.

Hafez, S. E. 1969. *The Behaviour of Domestic Animals*. Baltimore: Williams and Wilkins.

Harrison, Beverly. 1985. *Making the Connections: Essays in Feminist Social Ethics*. Carol S. Robb, ed. Boston: Beacon Press.

Harrison, Ruth. 1964. *Animal Machines*. London: Ballantine Books.

Hauerwas, Stanley. 1981. *A Community of Character: Toward a Constructive Christian Social Ethic*. Notre Dame, Ind.: University of Notre Dame Press.

———. 1983. *The Peaceable Kingdom*. Notre Dame, Ind.: University of Notre Dame Press.

Haught, John. 1986. *What is God?* New York: Paulist Press.

Hedgepeth, William. 1978. *The Hog Book*. New York: Doubleday.

Hinde, Robert A. 1982. *Ethology: Its Nature and Relations With Other Sciences*. New York: Oxford University Press.

Hoagland, Sarah Lucia. 1988. *Lesbian Ethics: Toward New Values*. Palo Alto, Calif.: Institute for Lesbian Studies.

Humane Farming Association. 1989. "Scrambled Priorities." *Watchdog* (Spring), pp. 3-5.

Humane Society of the United States. n.d. "Dogfighting—Why It Must Be a Felony."

———. 1988. "Laboratory Animals Fact Sheet."

———. 1991a. "Close-Up Report: Puppy Mills Exposed." March.

———. 1991b. "Just One Litter: Facts About Spaying or Neutering Your Pet."

Hur, Robin. 1985. "Six Inches from Starvation: How and Why America's Topsoil Is Disappearing." *Vegetarian Times* (March), pp. 45-47.

Hur, Robin, and David Fields. 1984. "Are High-fat Diets Killing Our Forests?" *Vegetarian Times* (February), pp. 22-24.

———. 1985a. "America's Appetite for Meat Is Ruining Our Water." *Vegetarian Times* (January), pp. 16-18.

———. 1985b. "How Meat Robs America of its Energy." *Vegetarian Times* (April), pp. 24-27.

Inge, W. R. 1926. "The Rights of Animals." *Lay Thoughts of a Dean*. New York and London: The Knickerbocker Press.

Jonas, Hans. 1966. *The Phenomenon of Life*. Chicago: University of Chicago Press.

Jung, L. Shannon. 1986. "Autonomy as Justice: Spatiality and the Revelation of Otherness." *The Journal of Religious Ethics* 14:1 (Spring): 157-83.

———. 1987. "Ethics, Agriculture, and the Material Universe." *The Annual of the Society of Christian Ethics 1986*. Washington, D.C.: Georgetown University Press, pp. 219-50.

———. 1988. "Feminism and Spatiality: The Recovery of a Hidden Dimension." *Journal of Feminist Studies in Religion* 4:1 (Spring): 55-71.

———. 1990. "The Recovery of the Land: Agribusiness and Creation-Centered Stewardship." In Rowland A. Sherrill, ed. *Religion and the Life of the Nation: American Recoveries.* Urbana, Ill.: University of Illinois Press, pp. 109-27.

Kant, Immanuel. 1949. *Foundations of the Metaphysics of Morals.* Trans. Lewis White Beck. Indianapolis, Ind.: Bobbs-Merrill.

Kaufman, Gordon D. 1972. "A Problem for Theology: The Concept of Nature." *Harvard Theological Review* 65 (July): 337-66.

Kellogg, Kathy and Bob. 1985. *Raising Pigs Successfully.* Charlotte, Vt.: Williamson Publishing.

Kevles, Bettyann. 1990. "Meat, Morality and Masculinity." *The Women's Review of Books* (May), pp. 11-12.

Kheel, Marti. 1988. "Animal Liberation and Environmental Ethics: Can Ecofeminism Bridge the Gap?" Paper given at the Western Political Science Association, San Francisco, March 10-12.

Kohler, Wolfgang. 1927, 1976. *The Mentality of Apes.* Trans. Ella Winter. New York: Liveright Publishing Co.

Kook, Abraham Isaac. "Fragments of Light: A View as to the Reasons for the Commandments." In *Abraham Isaac Kook: The Lights of Penitence, The Moral Principles, Lights of Holiness. Essays, Letters and Poems.* Trans. Ben Zion Bokser. New York: Paulist Press.

Krebs, A. V. 1990. *Heading Toward the Last Roundup: The Big Three's Prime Cut.* Des Moines, Ia.: PrairieFire Rural Action.

Krizmanic, Judy. 1990a. "Is a Burger Worth It?" *Vegetarian Times* 152 (April), pp. 20-21.

———. 1990b. "Why Cutting Out Meat Can Cool Down the Earth." *Vegetarian Times* 152 (April), pp. 18-19.

Lappé, Francis Moore. 1971, 1982. *Diet for a Small Planet.* New York: Ballantine.

Leakey, Richard E. 1981. *The Making of Mankind.* New York: E. P. Dutton.

Lewis, Andrea. 1990. "Looking at the Total Picture: A Conversation with Health Activist Beverly Smith." In Evelyn C. White, ed. *The Black Women's Health Book: Speaking for Ourselves.* Seattle: The Seal Press, pp. 172-81.

Linden, Eugene. 1981. *Apes, Men and Language.* New York: Penguin Books.

Linzey, Andrew. 1987. *Christianity and the Rights of Animals.* New York: Crossroad.

Linzey, Andrew, and Tom Regan. 1986. *Animal Sacrifices: Religious Perspective on the Use of Animals in Science.* Philadelphia: Temple University Press.

———. 1988a. *Animals and Christianity: A Book of Readings.* New York: Crossroad.

———. 1988b. *The Song of Creation: An Anthology of Poems in Praise of Animals.* London: Marshall Pickering.

Lorenz, Konrad Z. 1981. *The Foundations of Ethology: The Principal Ideas and Discoveries in Animal Behaviour.* Trans. Konrad Z. Lorenz and Robert Warren Kickert. New York: Simon and Schuster.

Mauritz la Riviere, J. W. 1989. "Threats to the World's Water." *Scientific American* (September), pp. 80-94.

McDaniel, Jay. 1988. "Land Ethics, Animal Rights, and Process Theology." *Process Studies* 17:2 (Summer): 88-94.

———. 1989. *Of God and Pelicans: A Theology of Reverence for Life.* Louisville: Westminster/John Knox Press.

———. 1990. *Earth, Sky, Gods, and Mortals: Developing an Ecological Spirituality.* Mystic, Conn.: Twenty-Third Publications.

McFague, Sallie. 1987. *Models of God: Theology for an Ecological, Nuclear Age.* Philadelphia: Fortress Press.

Macquarrie, John. 1970. "Rethinking Natural Law." *Three Issues in Ethics.* London: SCM Press.

Martin, M. Kay, and Barbara Voorhies. 1975. *Female of the Species.* New York: Columbia University Press.

Mason, Jim, and Peter Singer. 1980. *Animal Factories.* New York: Crown.

Middleton, Nick. 1989. *Atlas of Environmental Issues.* Oxford: Facts on File.

Midgley, Mary. 1978. *Beast and Man: The Roots of Human Nature.* Ithaca, N.Y.: Cornell University Press.

———. 1983. *Animals and Why They Matter.* Athens, Ga.: University of Georgia Press.

Merchant, Carolyn. 1983. *The Death of Nature: Women, Ecology and the Scientific Revolution.* San Francisco: Harper and Row.

Obis, Paul. 1990. "From the Editor." *Vegetarian Times* (July), p. 4.

O'Neill, Molly. 1990. "The Cow's Role in Life Is Called into Question by a Crowded Planet." *New York Times* (May 6), Section 4, pp. 1, 4.

Phillips, Anthony. 1983. *Lower than the Angels: Questions Raised by Genesis 1-11.* The Bible Reading Fellowship.

Pimental, David. 1975. "Energy and Land Constraints in Food Protein Production." *Science* 190 (November 21), pp. 754-61.

———. 1976. "Land Degradation: Effects on Food and Energy Resources." *Science* 194 (October 8), pp. 149-55.

Povilitis, Tony. 1990. "Where Will Wildlife Live?" *HSUS News* (Spring), pp. 8-13.

Rappole, John H., et al. 1983. *Nearctic Avian-Migrants in the Neotropics.* Washington, D.C.: U.S. Department of the Interior, Fish and Wildlife Service.

Regan, Tom. 1983. *The Case for Animal Rights.* Berkeley, Calif.: University of California Press.

Rimbach, James, 1988. "All Creation Groans: Alive Upon the Face of the Earth." In Granberg-Michaelson, ed. *Ecology and Life.* Waco, Tex.: Word Books.

Robbins, John. 1989. *Diet for a New America.* New York: Stillpoint Press.

Rollin, Bernard E. 1990. *The Unheeded Cry: Animal Consciousness! Animal Pain and Science.* Oxford: Oxford University Press.

Rosenfield, Leonora. 1968. *From Beast-Machine to Man-Machine: Animal Soul in French Letters From Descartes to La Mettrie.* New York: Octagon Books.

Ruether, Rosemary Radford. 1975. *New Woman, New Earth.* New York: Seabury Press.

———. 1983. *Sexism and God-Talk: Toward a Feminist Theology.* Boston: Beacon Press.

Russell, Letty M., Kwok Pui-lan, Ada Maria Isasi-Diaz, Katie Geneva Cannon, eds. 1988. *Inheriting Our Mothers' Gardens: Feminist Theology in Third World Perspective.* Philadelphia: Westminster Press.

Santmire, H. Paul. 1985. *The Travail of Nature.* Philadelphia: Fortress Press.

Sequoia, Anna. 1990. *67 Ways to Save the Animals.* New York: HarperCollins.

Serpell, James. 1986. *In the Company of Animals: A Study of Human-Animal Relationships.* London: Basil Blackwell.

Shepard, Paul. 1982. *Nature and Madness.* San Francisco, Calif.: Sierra Club Books.

Simpson, Cuthbert, and Walter Russell Bowie. 1952. *The Interpreter's Bible (Genesis).* New York and Nashville: Abingdon Press.

Singer, Peter. 1975. *Animal Liberation.* New York: Avon Books.

———. 1985. *In Defense of Animals.* New York: Basil Blackwell.

Sleeper, Barbara. 1990. "Animals and the Earth—Sport Hunting." *Animals* (March/April), p. 25.

Soler, Jean. 1979. "The Dietary Prohibitions of the Hebrews." *The New York Review of Books* (June 14), pp. 24-30.

Sorrell, Roger D. 1988. *St. Francis of Assisi and Nature: Tradition and Innovation in Western Christian Attitudes toward the Environment.* New York: Oxford University Press.

Stanton, Elizabeth Cady. (1898), 1974. *The Woman's Bible: Part I.* New York: European Publishing Co.; Seattle: Coalition Task Force on Women and Religion.

Stephens, Martin L. 1986. *Alternatives to Current Uses of Animals in Research, Safety Testing, and Education: A Layman's Guide.* Washington, D.C.: The Humane Society of the United States.

Tannenbaum, Jerrold, and Andrew N. Rowan. 1985. "Rethinking the Morality of Animal Research." *Hastings Center Report* 15(5) (October), pp. 32-43.

Tanner, Nancy Makepeace. 1981. *On Becoming Human: A Model of the Transition from Ape to Human and the Reconstruction of Early Human Social Life.* Cambridge and New York: Cambridge University Press.

Taylor, Paul. 1986. *Respect for Nature: A Theory of Environmental Ethics.* Princeton, N.J.: Princeton University Press.

Thomas, Keith. 1984. *Man and the Natural World: Changing Attitudes in England 1500-1800.* New York: Penguin.

Tinbergen, Niko. 1951. *The Study of Instinct.* Oxford: Oxford University Press.

Von Rad, Gerhard. 1961, 1972. *Genesis: A Commentary.* Philadelphia: The Westminster Press.

Walker, Alice. 1983. *In Search of Our Mothers' Gardens: Womanist Prose.* San Diego: Harcourt Brace Jovanovich.

———. 1988. "Am I Blue." In *Living By the Word: Selected Writings: 1973-1987.* San Diego: Harcourt Brace Jovanovich.

Warren, Karen J. 1990. "The Power and the Promise of Ecological Feminism." *Environmental Ethics* 12 (Summer): 125-46.

Westermann, Claus. 1982. *Elements of Old Testament Theology.* Trans. Douglas W. Stott. Atlanta: John Knox Press.

Wilson, Edward O. 1984. *Biophilia.* Cambridge, Mass.: Harvard University Press.

Wilson, Edward O., and Frances M. Peter, eds. 1988. *Biodiversity.* National Academy Press.

Wolgast, Elizabeth. 1987. *The Grammar of Justice.* Ithaca, N.Y.: Cornell University Press.

Wolterstorff, Nicholas. 1987. "Why Animals Don't Speak." *Faith and Philosophy* 4(4) (October): 463-85.

World Resources Institute. 1990. *World Resources 1990-91.* New York: Oxford University Press.

2613681R00144

Printed in Great Britain
by Amazon.co.uk, Ltd.,
Marston Gate.